Sarah Maria Burnham

**Pleasant Memories of Foreign Travel**

Sarah Maria Burnham

**Pleasant Memories of Foreign Travel**

ISBN/EAN: 9783337207274

Printed in Europe, USA, Canada, Australia, Japan

Cover: Foto ©Andreas Hilbeck / pixelio.de

More available books at **www.hansebooks.com**

# PLEASANT MEMORIES

OF

# FOREIGN TRAVEL

BY S. M. BURNHAM

AUTHOR OF

"THE HISTORY AND USES OF LIMESTONES AND MARBLES,"
"PRECIOUS STONES IN NATURE, ART AND LITERATURE,"
"THE STRUGGLES OF THE NATIONS."

Illustrated

BOSTON:
BRADLEE WHIDDEN
1896

# INTRODUCTION.

The rapid transit across the ocean at the present time has doubtless greatly increased the number of travellers to foreign lands. Some tourists make an annual trip of only a few weeks. There may be advantages in such a plan, especially for those who find it difficult to be absent from home and business for a prolonged visit, while, on the other hand, time and a careful study of the interesting objects and places to be seen, in order to derive the greatest pleasure and benefit, especially in visiting the celebrated art collections, is essential.

Most of the large cities of Europe attained their full growth ages ago, hence they appear to-day much the same as in past centuries, with the exception of having expanded their limits by absorbing adjacent territory. Towns and cities in America are often the growth of a few years, but it is not so in the Old World, where time was needed for their development. There antiquity is venerated; here it is frequently regarded with indifference. Mistakes and faults are common to both hemispheres; but frequent communication between the two will in time correct many of these errors, and bring the nations into a more familiar acquaintance with one another.

It requires weeks and months to explore and study the rich treasures of art found in the museums of any one great city, for which a special preparation is needed. One should be familiar with the history of the country or city to be visited, and should know what objects of interest are to be seen. He should understand the history of the fine arts, including architecture, and where the works of the great masters are to be found.

There are many books published on foreign travel, and

another added to the list may seem needless; but no two persons visit precisely the same places, or are interested in the same objects. Persons travel from different motives: some for pleasure and change, some from curiosity, while others are impelled by the desire of acquiring knowledge and to gratify a taste for works of art. Excursion parties are desirable for those whose time is limited; but the rapidity with which they move renders it impossible for those travelling by that method to gain any definite knowledge of what they see, especially in the vast museums of art.

The writer visited all the places described, and made the art collections a special study, so that the descriptions given are the result of personal observations. The year spent abroad was an eventful one in the history of some of the countries visited, which afforded an opportunity of witnessing scenes that will never occur again.

The incidents here described are from a daily journal kept during the visit made in **1877** and **1878**.

# CONTENTS.

### CHAPTER I.
#### *From Boston to Liverpool.*

The Voyage. The Mail Steamer China. The Passengers. Incidents of the Voyage. Cabin Steward. How the Time was Spent. Sabbath at Sea. Officers and Sailors. Reflections. The Custom House. Arrival at Liverpool. St. George's Hall. New Sights. Visit to Chester. A Roman Camp. Duke of Westminster. Walls of Chester. The Switzerland of Great Britain. Chester Cathedral. The Abbey. Church of St. John's. Racecourse. The Rows. Palace of the Stanleys. God's Providence House. Bishop Lloyd's House. Pemberton's Parlor. Grosvenor's Bridge. Eaton Hall. Estates of the Duke of Westminster. Birkenhead. Journey to Scotland. The Lake Region of England. Its Geological Formation. Building Stone. The Home of Mrs. Hemans. Grasmere. Rydal Mount. Rydal Water. Ambleside. Graves of Wordsworth and Coleridge. Homes of Arnold and Harriet Martineau. Keswick. Sounding the Horn. The Mighty Helvellyn. Southey's Home . . . . . . . . . . 1-12

### CHAPTER II.
#### *Scotland.*

Journey to Glasgow. Carlisle. Mary Queen of Scots. Journey to Edinburgh. Loch Lomond. The Trossachs. Sterling. Dumbarton Castle. William Wallace. A Legend. Vale of Leven. Smollett. Rob Roy's Rock. Scottish Lakes. Loch Katrine. Helen McGregor. Interesting Palaces. Nature of the Trossachs. Highland Animals. Fitz James. Roderick Dhu. Callender. Snowdown. Bannochburn. Walter Scott. Monuments of Distinguished Scotchmen. Museums and Art Galleries. The Castle. Carlton Hill. St. Andrew's Square. Roslin Castle. Apprentices' Pillar.

A Tragical Story. Hawthornden. Scenery on the Esk. Drummond. Sword of Bruce. Knox. An Interesting Family. Holyrood Palace. Tombs of the Scottish Kings. Lord Darnley. Rizzio. Queen Mary. Royal Apartments. Private Dwellings. Portraits of Scottish Kings. Holyrood Castle. Mons Megs. Scottish Regalia. Arthur's Seat. Agreeable Surprises. Iron Church. Heart of Mid Lothian. Melrose Abbey. Abbotsford. A Valuable Guide. Sir Walter Leeds . . . . . . . . . 13–23

## CHAPTER III.

### From Edinburgh to London.

Sheffield. The English. Scenery. Vegetation. London. Westminster Abbey. Its History. St. Paul's. The Whispering Gallery. Westminster Palace or House of Parliament. House of Lords. The Woolsack. St. Stephen's Hall. Historical Events. A National Capitol. Zoölogical Gardens. National Gallery. Turner's Paintings. Kensington Museum. Raphael's Cartoons. Albert Memorial. Equipages of the Nobility. Parks of London. British Museum. The Portland Vase. The Crystal Palace. College for the Blind. Bank of England. The Royal Exchange. Statue of George Peabody. The Mansion House. The Lord Mayor. Temple Bar. Covent Garden Market. The Tabernacle. Mr. Spurgeon. The Royal Academy. Palace of Hampton Court. Cardinal Wolsey. Sloane's Museum. London Tower. Wax Works. Museum of Practical Geology. Kew Gardens. The Guildhall. St. James' Palace and Park. Temple Church. Inns of Court. Windsor Castle. Chapel of St. George. Greenwich. Dulwich. Downing Street. Dean Stanley. Journey to Paris. Dieppe. Admiral Duquesne. Rouen. Place de la Pucelle. Prince Arthur. Notre Dame . . . . . . . 24–47

## CHAPTER IV.

### Visit to France.

Scenes in Paris. The Louvre. Arc de Triomphe. Hotel de Dieu. Jardin des Plantes. Labyrinth. Museum of Geology. Museum of Comparative Anatomy. Place de la Concord. Obelisk of Luxor. The Guillotine. The Tuileries. The Gardens. Champ de Mars. Hôtel des Invalides. Tomb of Napoleon. Bois de Boulogne. The Madeleine. Cathedral

of Notre Dame. The Pantheon. Church of St. Germain.
St. Bartholomew. Père-le-Chaise. A Strange History.
Au Bon Marché. Magasin du Louvre. Palais Royal.
Cardinal Richlieu. Communists. Hotel du Luxemburg.
The Gardens. Rosa Bonheur. Statue of Marshal Ney.
Palace of the Louvre. Versailles. Places of Interest.
The Bourse. Place Vendome. Napoleon's Column. Hotel
de Cluny. Gobelin Tapestry. Porcelain Manufactory. Isle
de la Cité. Sainte Chapelle. Church of St. Eustache . 48-61

## CHAPTER V.

*Belgium.— Switzerland.*

Amiens. Brussels. Waterloo. A Veteran. The Belgians.
Antwerp. Cologne. The Cathedral. Church of St. Ursula.
Sail on the Rhine. Ruined Castles. Coblence. Erenbreightstein. Mayence. Heidelberg. Its Castle. Strasburg. The Cathedral. The Black Forest. Lake Constance.
City of Constance. The Cathedral. Schaffhausen. The
Falls. Westhausen. The Rhine. Zurich. Zwingli. Lucerne. The Righi. Mt. Pilatus. Uri. Engelberg. The
Cathedral. Lion of Lucerne. Glacial Gardens. Ascent
of Mt. Righi. Flueleu. Lake Lucerne. William Tell.
Vitznau. An Accident. Brienz. The Wetterhorn. Falls
of Griesbach. The Illumination. Lakes Hagel and Hexen.
The Edleweisse. Lake Brienz. Boenigen. Darlingen. Lake
Thun. Berne. The Aure. A Swiss Sunset. Geneva.
Hotel de Ville. The Alabama Commissioners. Lake
Geneva. The Rhone. The Russian Church. Chimneytops. Cathedral of St. Peter. The Arve. Les Bois de la
Bâtie. Prigny. Rothschilds. Chamounix. View of
Mt. Blanc. Les Aiguilles. Montanvert. Mer de Glace.
Glacier des Bois. Moving Glaciers. Mauvais Pas. A
Dangerous Descent. Peculiar Rocks. Martigny. Tête
Noire. Col de Forclax. Swiss Peasants. Leuk. Brieg . 62-80

## CHAPTER VI.

*Switzerland to Italy.*

Stresa. Lake Maggiore. The Simplon. Napoleon. Brenner
Pass. Galleries and Tunnels. Cascades. Houses of
Refuge. The Hospice. Haltwasser Glacier. Avalanches.
Gallery of Algarby. Ravine of Gondo. The Diveria. San
Marco. Custom House. Domo d' Ossola. Gold and Marble

iv                    CONTENTS.

Mines. Monté Rosa. Bernina Pass. Hotel Milano.
Sunny Italy. Borromean Islands. Sail on Lake Maggiore.
Laverno. Verese. Lake Lugano. The Grande Hotel.
Swiss Mountains. Porto. Custom House. Managgio.
Lake Como. Colico. Town of Como. Hotel d'Italia.
Cathedral. Statue of Volta. From Como to Milan. Monza.
The Cathedral. The Iron Crown. Corso Victor Emmanuel. Milan Cathedral. St. Dionysius. St. Carlo Borromeo. Theâtre de la Scala. San Carlos. Leonardo da Vinci. The Brera. Amphitheatre de l'Arena. Arc de la Paix. The Last Supper. Churches. Arcades. Royal Palace. Certosa. Parria. Monastery. From Italy to Germany. Return to Como. Bellagio. Lombardy. European Towns . . . . . . . . . .    81-89

CHAPTER VII.
*From Italy to Germany.*

Colico. Pass of the Splugen. Chiavenna. Babel. Via Malo. Chur. Rorschach. Lindau. Munich. The Glyptothek. Barberina Fawn. Schwanthaler. Wagner. Cornelius. Artists of Munich. Exhibition Building. The Propylæa. Royal Palace. Statues of Kings. The Niberlungen. Ludwig Strasse. Public Buildings. Siegesthor, or Gate of Victory. The New Pinakothek. Munich Gallery. The Theatines. The Royal Vaults. Charles VI. Ludwigskirche. The Last Judgment. Frauenkirche. St. Michael. Thorwaldsen. St. Gregory. The Old Pinakothek. Rubens. Antique Vases. Loggie, or Arcade. Glass Works. Bronze Works. American Subjects. Rogers. Maximilian Strasse. The Iser. The Maximileaneum. The Basilica. Crystal Palace. Botanical Gardens. Bavarian National Museum. Historical Gallery. Journey to Leipsic. Ratisbon. Fairs of Leipsic. Museum of Modern Works. De-la-Roche. Other Artists. Battle of Leipsic. Poniatowski. Journey to Berlin. The Swiss. Unter Den Linden. Brandenburg Gate. Monument to Victory. Thiergarten. Museums. Tapestries. Assyrian Sculpture. Gems. The Silver Treasure. Cabinet of Coins. Royal Palace. Elector Frederick. Going through a Palace. Felt Slippers. Throne Room. Portraits of Prussian Kings. White Saloon. Palace Chapel. A Ghost Story. Rathause. Mineral Collections. Churches. National Gallery. Biergarten. The Germans. National Bank. Jewish Syna-

gogue. Chateau of Monbijou. The Reichstag. Industrial
Museum. Lüneburg Collection. Wax Statuary. Kaiser
Gallery. Sans Souci. Potsdam. The New Palace. The
Lustgarten. Church of Peace. Works of Art. Frederick
the Great. The Park. The Clock. Orangery. The Grotto
Saloon. Voltair's Room. Lessons Taught. Paris of the
North. Price of a Statue. Ancient Art. Roman Wall.
Zoölogical Gardens. Journey to Dresden. Churches.
Royal Vaults. The Zwinger. Museum. Johanneum
Museum. Porcelains. Royal Manufactory. Historical
Museum. Armor. Paintings. Green Vaults. Chimney
and Silver Rooms. Hall of Precious Things. A Cherry-
Stone. Crown Jewels. Polish Regalia. Minerals. Casts. 90–115

## CHAPTER VIII.

### *Prague and Vienna.*

The Switzerland of Saxony. The Elbe. Battle of Dresden.
Towns on the Elbe. Prague. Hradschin Platz. Cathedral.
Kings' Monuments. St. John Nepomuc. His Silver Shrine.
Fortifications. The Moldau. Imperial Palace. Count
Thun. Palace of Wallestein and other Palaces. Great
Battles of History. Museum. Jewish Synagogue. The
Bridges. Journey to Vienna. Brünn. Baron Trenck.
Silvio Pellico. A Fossil Forest. The Burg at Vienna.
Imperial Jewels. Various Collections. Museum of Art and
Industry. The Belvedere. Prince Eugene of Savoy. Paint-
ings. Minerals. Amusing Blunder. Imperial Stables.
Impertinent Guide. Royal Palace. Churches. Monument
in Grabben Strasse. The Votive Church. Americans.
The Schönbrunn. The Gloriette. The Capuchins. Impe-
rial Vaults. Picture Gallery. Ambras Collection. Church
of St. Augustino. Monuments. Statue of Francis I. Austrian Soldiers. The Arsenal. The Prata. Vienna a Beautiful City . . . . . . . . . . 116–131

## CHAPTER IX.

### *Second Visit to Italy.*

From Vienna to Trieste. Semmering Pass. Tunnels and
Galleries. The Scenery. Gratz. The Citadel. Castle of
Wildon. Tycho Brahe. The Drau. Cave of Adelsburg.
Julian Alps. The Adriatic. Bay of Trieste. Railway over
the Semmering. Trieste. Venice. Grand Canal. Gon-

## CONTENTS.

dolas. Custom House. Square of St. Mark. Campanile. San Marco. Ducal Palace. The Pigeons. Royal Palace. Churches. Funeral Procession. San Zaccaria. Paintings. S. M. Formosa. Works of Art. St. Salvatore. St. Giovanni. Crisostomo. Art Treasures. Santi Apostolo. S. Felice. S. M. dell Orto. A Sail to the Ledo. Glorious Sunset. Queen of the Adriatic. S. M. Gloriosa dei Frosinone. Monument of Titian. Monument of Canova. A Monastery. S. Rococo. Scuola di S. Rococo. Paintings. Wood Carving. St. Pantaleone. Church of the Jesuits. S. S. Giovanni e Paolo. Tombs of the Doges. The Valier. Academy of Fine Arts. The Old Masters. Opinion of Ruskin. Palace Giovanelli. The Doge's Palace. Secret Tragedies. La Loggia. Porta della Carta. Silvio Pellico. Scarla dei Giganti. Hall of the Great Council. Tintoretto's Paradise. Voting Hall. Library of St. Mark's. Museum. Sala della Bussola. The Three Inquisitors. Bocca di Leone. Council of Ten. The Carcerie or Prison. Ponte dei Sospere. Ascent of the Campanile. The Grand Canal. A Visit to Padua. An Ancient City. Its Wars. University. Schools of Painting. Basilica of S. Antonio. Monument of Petrarch. Statues. Cathedral. Municipio. Bologna. Este. Rovego. Leaning Towers. Terrara. Story of Tasso. Alphonso of Este. Savonarola. Monti Euganei. Noted Buildings. Prince Henry. A Tragedy. S. Petronio. Monuments of the Bacciocchi. Paintings. St. Domenico. Madonna di S. Luca. Campo Santo. Via di Saragozza. Monte della Guardia. St. Luca. Fine Views. Tradition. Monuments of the Murats of Mezzofanti, Galiani, and Others. Leaning Towers of Bologna. The University. Female Professors. A Celebrated Linguist. College Students. Academy of Fine Arts. Picture Gallery. Bologna School of Art. Raphael's St. Cecilia. City of Arcades. Churches. Monasteries. St. Stefano. Piazza Victor Emanuele . . . . . . 132–150

## CHAPTER X.

*Florence, Perugia, Terni.*

Journey to Florence. Crossing the Apennines. Numerous Tunnels. Pistoja. Prato. Monteferrato. Verde di Prato. Arrival at Florence. The Cathedral. Campanile. Baptistery. Bronze Doors. Picture Gallery. Ascending the Dome. Extensive Views. Pitti Palace. Uffizi Palace. Its

Art Collections. Paintings. Statuary. Gems. Perugia. San Giovanni. Arezzio. Macenas. Birthplaces of Eminent Men. Cortona. Lake Trassemene. Perugia. S. Lorenzo Cathedral. Chamber of Commerce. Palace Constabile. Raphael's Madonna. Arco di Augusto. University. Umbrian Painters. St. Severo. The Curiosity of the Perugians. Terni and the Falls. A Persistent Guide. Picturesque Scenery. Papigno. Velino and Neva Rivers. Cascate delle Marmore. Petrefactions. Inundations. From Terni to Rome. The "Eternal City." Plans for the Future . . . . . . . . . 151–159

## CHAPTER XI.

*Rome.*

Colosseum. St. Peter's Church. Castle of St. Angelo. The Pantheon. Narrow Streets. Churches. Monuments of Leo X. and Clement VII. The Christ of M. Angelo. Monastery. Galileo's Retraction. Library. Via St. Ignazio. Piazza Navona. Fountains. St. Agnes. Piazza del Popolo. The Pincio. Albion Hills. Along the Tiber. A December Rose. S. M. del Popolo. Grave of Emperor Nero. A Tradition. Luther in Rome. Corsini Palace. Gallery of Paintings. The Old Masters. Corsini Vase. Christina, Queen of Sweden. Engravings. Gardens. S. M. dell' Anima. S. M. delle Pace. Raphael's Sybils. St. Andrea della Valle. Strozzi Chapel. Barberini Chapel. SS. Luca e Martino. Marmatine Prison. Capitoline Museum. Statue of a River God. Pasquino. S. M. Campitelli. Image of the Virgin. St. Ignazio. Arch of Constantine. Arch of Titus. Basilica of Constantine. Temple of Venus and Roma. The Ruins of Rome. Colosseum. SS. Cosma e Domiano. Palace of the Conservatori. Ruins of the Palatine. Busts of Distinguished Persons. Bronzes, Paintings, and other Art Collections. S. M. Maggiore. Tradition. Tombs of the Popes. Sistine Chapel. Borghese Chapel. S. Praxedis. S. Paolo. Gifts to this Church. Costly Churches. The Poor Classes. Baths of Diocletian. S. Bernardo. S. M. Degli. Barbarini Palace. Statue of Thorwaldsen. Beatrice Cenci. The Fornarina. G. Rene's Aurora. Rospigliosi Palace. The Casino. The Andromeda. Domenichino. Rubens. Sabbath in Europe. Wonders of Rome. The Vatican. Museum. The Close of the Year . . . 160–169

## CHAPTER XII.

*Rome, Continued.*

S. Pietro in Vincoli. The Moses of M. Angelo. Reflections. S. Lorenzo in Lucina. The Crucifixion. SS. Trinita di Monte. Piazza di Spagna. Borghese Palace. Its Paintings. Colonna Palace. Its Art Treasures. S. John Lateran. Ascent to the Top of St. Peter's. Palaces of the Cæsars. Villas and Palaces. Church of the Capuchins. Sobieski. Ghastly Sights. St. Pietro in Montorio. The Tempietto. Acquia Paolo. Trastevere. Ancient Romans. The Janiculus. Italians. Roman Streets. Vatican Museum. Doria Palace. St. Carlo al Corso. Piazza di Pietra. Custom House. Temple of Antoninus Pius. Death of the King. Mausoleum of Augustus. Nuovo Braccio. Its Art Collections. Battle of Constantine and Maxentius. Quirinal Palace. Attractions of Rome. Access to the Vatican Museum Difficult. King Victor Emmanuel. St. Croce in Gerusalemme. The Amphitheatre. St. Giovanni in Laterano. Palace of the Popes. Works of Art. Trajan's Forum and Column. Triumphal Arches. Funeral Ceremonies of the King. A Magnificent Procession. Italian Nobles. Soldiers. Banners. Foreign Ambassadors. Their Decorations. American Minister. Spectators. Italian Courtesy. Impatience of Tourists. A Festival. St. Trinita de Pelleguina. Hospital. The Crucifixion. S. M. in Monticello. The Cenci Palace. Count Cenci. The Pincio. Gardens of Lucullus. Villa Borghese. Piazza del Popolo. Obelisk from Heliopolis. The Casino and its Works of Art. Paulina Borghese. Classical Scenes. St. Andrea della Fratti. Statue by Harriet Hosmer. Monuments. Academy of San Luca. Its Presidents. Works of Art. Via Bonella. Ancient Gateway. Forums of Cæsar and Augustus. Baths of Caracalla. Their Influence. The Cælian Hill. St. Stefano Rotondo. Palace Spada alla Regola. Statue of Pompey. Portraits. Farnese Palace. Arch of Janus. The Cloaca Maxima. The Aventine. S. M. in Casmedin. The Bocca della Verita. Opus Alexandrinum. Temple. S. M. del Sole. House of Crescentius, or Casa di Rienzi. The Campagna. Appian Way. Casale Rotondo. Gate of St. Sebastian. Queen of Roads. Ruins. Aqueduct of Claudius. Alban Hills. Frascati. Catacombs of St. Calixtus. Explorations. Sixtus II. St.

CONTENTS. ix

Cecilia. Asylum for Christians. Danger of being Lost.
Church of St. Sebastian. Tradition. Circus Maximus.
Tomb of Cecilia Metella. Villa Medici. The Belvedere.
French Academy of Arts. Visits to the Vatican Museum.
Church of St. Onofrio. The Poet Tasso. His Monument.
Mementos of the Poet. Works of Raphael. Artists. Villa
Albani. Porta Salara. Prince Torlonia. Napoleon I.
Vatican Mosaics. Villa Ludovisi. St. Clemente. Prior
Mullooly. Interesting Discoveries. Obelisk of Thebes.
Ascending the Colosseum. Church of St. Marco. Monument of J. Bonaparte. Museum Kircheriano. A Remarkable Casket. "Permissos." The Sacristan. German
Tourists. Œcumenical Council. Works of the Masters.
Manufacture of Mosaics. Vatican Library. No Volumes
Seen. Art Treasures. Pius IX. Church of the Gesù.
Castle of St. Angelo. Hadrian's Tomb. Covered Passage.
Dungeon of Beatrice Cenci. Under the Palatine Hill.
Palaces of the Cæsars. The Guard. Studio of Edmonia
Lewis. Death of Pius IX. Artists' Studios. Modern
Painters. Ancient Masters. Rogers, the American Sculptor. Miss Hosmer. Reviews. The Pope lying in State.
Vast Multitudes. Thieves. Church of S. M. Maggiore.
The Confessio. Final Resting-place of Pius IX. . . 170-192

CHAPTER XIII.

*Journey to Naples.*

Mt. Vesuvius. The Museum. Streets of Naples. Villa Nazionale. The Riviera. "Rotten Row" of Naples. The
Mediterranean. Visit to Capri. Sorrento. The Blue Grotto.
Villages near the Volcano. Scenery about Naples. The
Sabbath. Chapel of San Severo. Works of Art. Royal
Palace. Palace of Capodimonte. Art Treasures. Visit to
Vesuvius. Cabmen. Beggars. The Poor Classes. Life
on the Street. Fields of Lava. Fantastic Rocks. Utter
Desolation. The Observatory. The Hermitage. An Accident. Cathedral of Naples. Chapel of St. Januarius.
Crown of the Saint. Treasures. Churches. Excursion to
Pompeii. Institution of Fine Arts. Paintings. Church
of the Jesuits. St. Severino. St. Martino. Castle of St.
Elmo. The Certosa. Collections. Different Nationalities.
A Modern Babel. Vegetation in March. Visit to Pozzuoli
and Baia. The Grotto. Posilipo. Puteoli. Tomb of

Virgil. Lake Agnano. Grotto del Cane. Grotto dell Ammoniaca. Baths of S. Germano. The White Mountains. Edible Earth. Trachyte. Thermal Mineral Baths. Views and Guides. The Solfatara. Sulphurous Fumes. Echoes. Eruption. Puzzalano. Strange Phenomena. Ruins in Pozzuoli. A Remarkable Temple. Mt. Nuovo. Lake Avernus. Grotto della Sibilla. Baths of Nero. Lake Lucinus. Ruins. Heathen Temples. Baia. Ancient Palaces. Grotto of Sijanus. Pausily Pon. The Museum. Pompeiian Collection. Views from Naples. Volcanic Tufa. Frisio. Naples a Paradise for Artists. Count Gigliano. Autographs. A Curiosity. A Linguistic Family. An American Singer. Snow on the Mountains. Uncomfortable Houses. Another Visit to the Museum. Mosaic Pavements. Botanical Gardens. The Reclusoria. Via Cavour. Other Streets. Portici. Resina. Herculaneum. Explorations. Effects of a Storm. Caserta. Amusing Incident. Officials. Palace at Caserta. Avenue. Statues . . . . . 193–207

## CHAPTER XIV.

### *Return to Rome and Other Cities.*

Storm. Hotel Milano. Guests. Visit to the Churches. S. M. in Ara Cœli. S. M. Liberatrice. Roman Forum. S. M. in Transtevere. St. Cecilia. St. Prasede. Sacred Relics. Museums. Custodians. St. John Lateran. Court of the Monastery. Works of Art. Scala Santa. The Oldest Obelisk. Other Antiquities. Villa Doria Pamfili. S. M. della Valle. St. Pietro in Vincoli. The Moses. S. M. del Anima. Monuments. St. Luigi di Francesi. St. Marco. A Scotch Family. St. Peter's and the Vatican. Sermon by an Irish Priest. Tarpeian Rock. The Capitol. Journey to Sienna and Chiusi. Views in Sienna. Institution of Fine Arts. St. Catherine. Siennese Artists. Gloomy Saints. Church of St. Giovanni. A Baptism. The Duomo. The Pulpit of Pisano. Stained Glass. Library. Pavement of Graffito. Palazzo Publico. Tower del Mangia. The Del Campo. Fountain Gaga. Location and Houses of Sienna. Pisa. Sinalunga. Garibaldi. Empoli. Duomo of Pisa. Ascent of the Tower. The Lungano. Genoa. The Scenery. Thatched Cottages. Marble Quarries. Buildings. Churches. Palace. Monument to Columbus. Palazzo Ducale. Palace of Pallavicini. Art Gallery. The Terazzo di Marmo.

Business Part of the City. The Ponte Carignano. Situation of Genoa. Numerous Palaces. Commercial Pursuits. Villa Pallavicini. Grotto of Stalactites. The Acquasola. Villa Negro. The Buildings of Genoa. Art Collections. Turin. Tunnels. Places of Interest. Novi. Marengo. Asti. Cathedral of Turin. Tombs of the Dukes of Savoy. Maria Adelaid. Monastery of Capuchins. Grand Views. The Superga. Peculiarities of Turin. Jewish Synagogue. Palace and Royal Armory. Monument of Cavour. A Sermon in Italian. Cathedral. Academy of Art. Egyptian Museum. Italy and Its People . . . . . 208–221

## CHAPTER XV.

### From Turin to Paris. — Second Visit.

The Journey. Grand Scenery. Modane. San Ambrogia. Abbey St. Michele della Chiusi. Petrefactions. Mt. Cenis. The Tunnel. Col de Fréjus. Customs at Modane. Change of Carriages. Stone Quarries. Travelling in France. Rain Storm. Our "Pension." The Paris Exposition. A Grand Procession. Distinguished Persons. Fireworks. Au Bon Marché. Magasin du Louvre. Churches. Notre Dame. Sainte Chapelle. The Madeleine. A Tragical Event. St. Germain l'Auxerrais. Notre Dame de Lorette. Grounds of the Exposition. Versailles. Its Fountains. Palaces of France. Church of the Sorbonne. Visit to the Exposition. Churches of St. Etienne du Mont. St. Geneviéve. St. Germaine des Prés. Tomb of the Kings. Massacre of Prisoners. Fine Arts at the Exposition. Cluny. St. Sulpice. Marbles. L'Ecole des Mines. Collection of the Prince of Wales. Park Monceau. Bibliothèque Nationale. Its Numerous Collections. The Marble Workers. Church of St. Clotilde. Hôtel de Ville. Church of St. Gervais. Isle and Church of St. Louis. Hotel Lambert. Trocadéro at the Exposition. Museum of the Louvre. Last Visit to the Exposition. Danish Landscapes . . . . 222–230

## CHAPTER XVI.

### From Paris to Boston.

Route to England. Crossing the Channel. The Steamers. A Delightful Region. Stop in London. Visiting New Scenes, and revisiting those seen Before. St. Paul's. Wellington's Monument. British Museum. Ancient Remains. Library. Mineral Collections. London Weather. St. James' Park. " Trooping the Colors." Queen's Birthday. Princes and Nobles. National Gallery. Turner's Paintings. Landseer. Westminster Abbey. Royal Architectural Museum. Museum of Practical Geology. Crown Prince and Princess of Germany. Custodian's Reply. Information of the Masses. Eminent Preachers. Dean Stanley. Spurgeon. Parker. From London to Liverpool. England a Garden. Its Scenery. Manufactures. St. George's Hall, Liverpool. Picture Gallery. Museum. Paintings. The Last Moments of Charles II. Stuffed Birds. Classification for Objects at the Museum. The Steamer Marathon. A Review of the Past Year. Lessons learned. Remarks about the English, Germans, French, Swiss, Italians. Arrival at Queenstown. Time spent on Board. Subjects for Observation. The Passengers. A Sailor's Life. The "Banks." A Dense Fog. Vigilance of the Captain. Sailors' Entertainments. The Marathon Suddenly stops. Passengers Anxious. Buoys the Cause. Placed by the Submarine Telegraph Co. A Pilot taken on Board. Cape Cod. Custom House and Quarantine Officers. Landing in Boston. Meeting Friends. Lessons taught by Travel. A Preparation Necessary . . . . . . 231–240

# PLEASANT MEMORIES OF FOREIGN TRAVEL.

## CHAPTER I.

*From Boston to Liverpool, Chester, and the Lake Region.*

THE passion for travel is strong with most of the human family, but with Americans it is irresistible; therefore to gratify this propensity, after having visited most of our own states and cities, we decided to make a journey across the ocean and see our transatlantic cousins in their native homes.

Having made due preparation for a prolonged absence, we embarked, June 16, on board the Royal Mail Steamer China, of the Cunard Line, for Liverpool.

In these days of rapid transit, what is gained in time is small compensation, except to business men, for the pleasure and quiet rest of a longer voyage, provided one escapes the much dreaded attack of sea-sickness. There were on board, besides many steerage passengers, between seventy and eighty persons occupying staterooms; these passengers comprised several nationalities. We were fortunate in securing two rooms all to ourselves. These were directly opposite those of Sir C. Y. and Lady, very quiet neighbors, but completely environed by stately reserve, so that for ten days we passed and repassed one another without a sign of recognition, which they would not probably have given for an earl's coronet.

Four regular meals, besides a late supper for those who wished it, were served on board the steamer, so that no one was in immediate danger of starvation. While at dinner on the first day of the voyage, a number of the passengers suddenly left the table, an act which on land would have been regarded as a violation of the rules of good breeding; at tea only one lady was present.

Life at sea is so monotonous, dreamy, and indolent that the passengers avail themselves of every opportunity to meet their fellow-travellers, and this can be enjoyed at table and on deck. The second day of the voyage was Sunday, a beautiful day, but how strange the serene stillness about us! Not a church bell was heard, nor the sound of a carriage or pedestrian; not a living creature to be seen or heard, except on board our ship. We were so enveloped by fog that we seemed to be sailing in a very small circle; but towards evening we were favored with a magnificent sight—a glorious sunset, while, to the delight of all the passengers, a sail was discovered on the verge of the distant horizon.

By the second day of our voyage we had become tolerably familiar with the swell of the sea and the rocking of the vessel, so that to one comfortably bundled into a ship chair, watching the efforts of inexperienced voyagers in their attempts to promenade the deck, it was very amusing. They had the symptoms of one who had taken too much wine at dinner. However, a passenger soon acquires confidence and skill in maintaining his centre of gravity; and in spite of an occasional pirouette, and a plunge against the bulwarks, he soon acquires a genuine sailor gait. There was one indefatigable walker on board, so cautious that he managed his limbs as if they were glass, and in danger of breaking.

On the anniversary of the battle of Bunker Hill, we were presented, by an American gentleman, with a small national flag, which we fondly cherished and kept for protection, as no foreign stranger would have the impertinence to insult our government in the person of one of its citizens bearing its flag.

We were more fortunate than most of our fellow-passengers, in escaping the usual penalty of a sea voyage, which excited the surprise of our cabin steward, who could hardly be persuaded it was our first experience on the ocean. *Apropos* of this official, he was a stalwart Englishman, very capable, faithful, and obliging, and who seemed much above his calling, though wholly unconscious of the fact. He served in the capacity of cabin and table steward; and if he was a type of an English waiter, we thought it would be fortunate to be served by such.

After the convalescents made their appearance, there was more animation on board, and one after another, the vacant seats at table were filled, while the deck, at certain hours, afforded a social and agreeable scene. Couples paired for evening promenades, notwithstanding there were long rows of mummies arranged along the deck, too indolent or too timid to venture on a pedestrian exercise, which, when one becomes accustomed to it, is not only healthful, but also enjoyable.

The luxurious sea chairs are valued as household gods; and who could refuse the tempting pleasure of reclining in such a cradle, rocked by the great ship, half dreaming, half awake, with nothing to do but gaze at the sky and the ocean, bills all paid, luggage carefully stowed away, nothing to care for, nothing to fear unless it be that of arriving too soon at the end of the voyage, when dreams end and all sorts of annoyances peculiar to travel begin, such as impositions, extortions, beggars, fees, and the like.

The weather at sea is much cooler than on land, even in the same latitude, so that we needed an abundant supply of wraps when on deck. We had selected June for our voyage, because it was considered less liable to storms than the other months of the year; and in this respect we were not disappointed, though on the third day after leaving home there were signs of such an event, when the sky became overcast and the sun went down in a cloud. As grand as a storm must be on the ocean, we felt that pleasant weather and smooth sailing were more to be preferred. However, the steamer rolled and tossed unpleasantly, giving us a hint what she could do in a storm. The weather prognostics did not altogether fail, since the next morning was foggy, windy, and somewhat rainy, causing the "invalids" to relapse and the deck to be vacated, though we persevered in maintaining our post of observation.

Life at sea would be unbearable if one could not be on deck; at its best, it is very monotonous, after the novelty has worn off. We saw very few sails, for this line of steamers has a route of its own as well defined as a highway on land. This is an advantage by avoiding collisions, but would it not be inconvenient in case of accidents? Little groups of passengers were scattered about as if at a loss for amusement. When one is shut out from the great busy world, he must depend upon his own resources for entertainment, and lonely, indeed, is that poor traveller who has none. A book, especially a guide-book, serves the purpose, not only of diversion, but also of instruction, when one is weary of gazing at the sky, the water, or the same people seen every day, though on the whole our time passed very pleasantly, since there had been little to disturb the *dolce far niente* life on board an ocean steamer. The sensation to us was very peculiar; perhaps others have experienced the same. We seemed to be sailing in a deep, circular basin, with its broad rim surrounding us, though we were never able to reach its border.

One evening the sailors entertained the passengers with music, songs, and acrobatic feats, for which a collection was taken, and on Sunday religious services were held in the dining-saloon, when the Rev. Mr. B. officiated. As our genial company would soon separate, never to meet collectively again, a particular description of some of the party may not be uninteresting. There were four Cubans, who kept by themselves and spoke only Spanish, one Pole, who could converse in English, a French professor, an American professor, an archbishop, four clergymen, an English baronet and lady, several students, business men, women and children, including many nationalities. The Rev. Mr. B. was the jolliest man on board, with a face like a full moon, and a genuine Scotch accent; Mr. F., a true Yankee in manners and nasal peculiarities; Mrs. W., a few days' bride, formerly a widow, with a young son of inquisitive, mischievous ways, who had unlimited indulgence, as the bride and bridegroom were wholly absorbed with each other; an English couple who had been to America to spend their honeymoon; and an Englishman who was very interesting in conversation. The captain was very quiet and reserved, and the surgeon was a tall Irishman, who was evidently very much fascinated by a certain young lady with whom he sought every opportunity to promenade. A number of ladies kept their staterooms, and seldom appeared on deck. All the arrangements on board were quiet, neat, and orderly. The officers and sailors showed excellent training, and the stewards were capable and obliging; in short, there was nothing wanting for the comfort and entertainment of the passengers, so that the end of the voyage was not an object to be desired.

As the steamer neared Queenstown, where many of the passengers were to land, there was some eager curiosity to catch the first glimpse of terra firma. Here a pilot came on board with the first tidings from America, when the steamer proceeded to Liverpool, the end of our voyage. What a change from ship to shore! On the vessel no one was a foreigner; the ocean is the birthright of all nations, and equally the home of every one. Not so when one steps on shore. Here in Europe are different customs, manners, languages, and laws; different races and social life; indeed, everything is new, strange and peculiar. One is set adrift on an unknown ocean to encounter whatever may chance to be his destiny, with no one to feel the slightest interest in his welfare; he is to be engulfed in the great sea of humanity which is seething with conflicting passions struggling for the mastery. After some delay we landed and went through the ordeal at the Custom House, which was quite superficial, the only objection being the rough and careless manner in which the porters handled our baggage, or luggage as it is called abroad, throwing heavy trunks from their shoulders onto the floor without the least concern whether they were broken or not.

It being settled that we had no contraband goods, our luggage was transferred to a van, while our little party, that is, Mr. and Mrs. P. and the writer, took a cab for the Adelphi, considered the best hotel in Liverpool. The arrangements were comfortable, but not elegant; everything seemed English, or, in other words, staid, orderly, and slow. The waiters, in their black coats and white cravats, looked as solemn as clergymen at a funeral, and they were as stiff as they were grave. Mr. P. ordered a dinner of roast beef, but it could not be ready for nearly an hour; therefore as we were anxious to begin sight-seeing, we took a lunch and started out. We first went to St. George's Hall, an elegant building of dark sandstone of the Grecian style of architecture. Then taking a public conveyance, we rode several miles into the suburbs of the town. Here we had our first view of English country seats, quite like what our imagination had pictured. An American soon perceives how different everything is from his native land: the buildings, both in town and country, are unlike those of his own; the quaintness of many houses arrests his attention, especially the peculiar chimney tops of pottery, arranged in different styles, some grouped in a row, while others stand solitary; another peculiarity is the tiled roof.

While stopping at Liverpool we visited Chester, a quaint old town, fifteen miles from there. It is on the site of the Roman camp, and is supposed to have received its name from Castra, meaning a camp. The walls of the town, still in excellent preservation, occupy the same lines drawn by the Imperial Roman generals. They were built by the conquerors, and restored by a daughter of Alfred the Great, in the beginning of the tenth century. Chester, being a walled town, has been considered an important place to hold, in all the wars and revolutions of the island, down to the Fenian raid. On arriving there, we made our headquarters at the Grosvenor Hotel, the name being derived from the family of the Duke of Westminster, whose estates are quite near, and whose eldest son bears the title of Earl of Grosvenor. Our first visit was to the wall of the town, which we ascended by steps, and upon which we walked as far as the Phœnix Tower, an old structure upon the broad wall where Charles I. watched the defeat of his army at Rowton Moor. During the civil war between the king and Parliament, Chester was one of the most loyal towns of all

PALACE OF THE STANLEYS

ST. JOHN'S CHURCH

PEMBERTON'S PARLOR

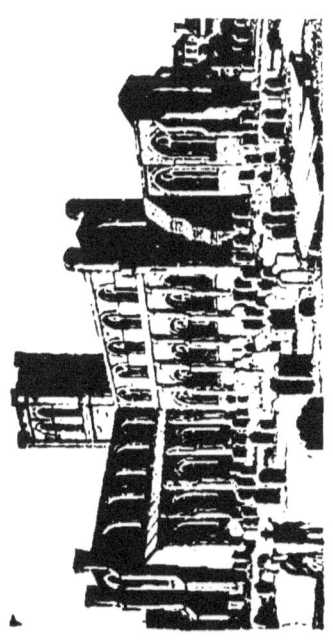

CHESTER CATHEDRAL

VIEWS IN CHESTER

England. One can walk entirely around the city on its walls, from which fine views of the surrounding country may be seen. This old town is on the River Dee, near the borders of Wales; and though we did not cross the boundary, yet we could view the "Switzerland of Great Britain" from the Phœnix Tower.

The Chester Cathedral is very ancient, having been founded in 1093 by Hugh Lupus, nephew of William the Conqueror. It was constructed of red sandstone, the prevailing rock in this part of England. As it was some centuries before it was completed, it represents the styles of different periods, as the Norman and the Late Decorated Gothic. The exterior of the building is grand and imposing. The west front is very beautiful, with its elegant windows, elaborate tracery, ornamental mouldings, spandrils, embattled parapets, and other decorations peculiar to the fascinating Gothic style of architecture. The interior does not equal the exterior in attractive beauty, some portions being quite destitute of ornament, though others are highly embellished. The choir, separated from the nave by a Gothic screen of stone very elaborately sculptured, is the most interesting part of the interior, with its pavement of black and white marble, beautifully carved stalls, canopies, pinnacles, pendants, and the Bishop's Throne. The Cathedral is enriched by elegant stained glass windows. During our visit to this venerable church, we had the opportunity of attending a choral service, the singing being mainly by boys. The ruined abbey, near the old cloisters, with their little enclosure of greensward, carried the imagination back for many centuries, when monks lived and died here, and their steps left traces in the worn pavements. The Cathedral, though very ancient, is not the oldest church in the city, for just outside the walls, St. John's, founded in 689 A. D., claims this honor. At the east end are the ruins of chapels recently exhumed, containing some beautiful relics of Gothic ornaments, windows, bosses, etc., the whole overgrown with moss and ivy.

Near Chester is the famous Rood-eye racecourse. Having seen a racecourse, one can easily understand why it should be called "the turf," for the ground is covered with a soft, green turf or sward that appears as harmless to fall upon as a bed of feathers. Another peculiar feature of Chester is what receives the name of the "Rows," found in the old Roman streets of the town. They consist of two terraces of shops, one above another, occupying the front, and reached by steps at certain distances apart.

Some of the other notable buildings are the "Palace of the Stanleys," with three gables joined, presenting the appearance of three houses with plain, heavy, projecting eaves and numerous small windows. The lower story resembles underground rooms, as if they might be fruit cellars or beer saloons. "God's Providence" is a building so called from the circumstance that its inmates were spared during a deadly plague; the house is decorated with ornamental panels. Bishop Lloyd's residence is another of the quaint buildings found here, while "Pemberton's Parlor" was an old tower on the walls, of historical interest. The oddity and quaintness of many of the houses, some having peculiar ornaments on their exterior, render Chester a place of interest to the traveller. Grosvenor's Bridge, over the Dee, a modern structure, is remarkable for its single arch of two hundred feet in length, forty feet in height, and forty-eight in thickness.

Leaving Chester, our party drove to Eaton Hall, the English country seat of the Duke of Westminster. His grounds embrace ninety-six square miles, while in addition to this estate he owns one in Ireland and another in Wales, and is the proprietor of entire villages. Every house in Aldford, except one, whose owner refuses to part with it for any sum, is owned by this nobleman. One can hardly form a correct idea from any verbal description of the variety, extent, and beauty of an English peer's hereditary estate. Deer, sheep, cattle, and horses are scattered over the grounds, not promiscuously, but in separate pastures; while noble trees, charming driveways, green fields, and grazing cattle constitute interesting features in the scene. Nor is this all, for fruits and flowers in great variety are seen on every hand, while greenhouses and hothouses are

CHARLES I. TOWER.

WATER GATE STREET.

GOD'S PROVIDENCE HOUSE.

BISHOP LLOYD'S HOUSE.

VIEWS IN CHESTER.

scattered about, filled with rare and beautiful flowers and delicious fruits, both native and exotic. Eaton Hall, the residence of the proprietor, was under repairs and not open to visitors. It is a magnificent pile four hundred and sixty feet long, of light-colored sandstone and Gothic in style, with numerous towers, parapets, turrets, windows, etc., and, it is said, a sumptuous interior, the marble floor of the entrance hall alone costing sixteen hundred guineas, or between eleven and twelve thousand dollars. It constitutes a fitting ornament to the magnificent park it adorns.

After our delightful excursion to Chester and its environs, we returned to Liverpool by water, which took us past Birkenhead, where the Alabama was built, which we Americans have cause to remember with no amiable feelings towards Great Britain. We left Liverpool June 28 for the "lake region" on our way to Scotland. As we journeyed north, the scenery became more diversified, and we feasted our eyes on hills and mountains, an agreeable change from the lowlands we had left. The first part of our route lay along the "Sands," as the region is styled, by the side of Morecambe Bay, a branch of the Irish Sea. We passed some charming small towns, comprising Grange, a picturesque little place situated partly on the side of a hill and partly in a valley. The declivities grew more rugged and steep as we advanced into the "lake region," reminding one of the hilly sections of New Hampshire, excepting those of the White Mountains; there is nothing in England to compare with them for grandeur. Arriving at the foot of Lake Windermere, we embarked in a trim little steamer for the head of the lake; and as we sailed towards the north, the scenery became more grand, resembling somewhat that on the Hudson as one approaches the Highlands. Windermere is eleven miles long, but only one mile wide, so in appearance it is only a medium sized river. The hills and mountains here afford a peculiar geological formation. The prevailing rock is slate, which in many localities is broken into blocks disposed in regular layers, as if arranged by the hand of art. All the buildings in this region were constructed of this dark slate, while those of Liverpool and Chester were of sandstone, showing that the predominant rocks of the different localities are of distinct species. The dark stone houses, barns, walls, and every other kind of structure impart a sombre aspect to the landscape, though when embowered in the rich green shrubbery and covered with numerous creeping plants, which concealed their rough surfaces, the effect was pleasing. The loveliness of the "lake region" of England has not been exaggerated by the poets, and the tourist will be well repaid for a journey thither. Near the head of Lake Windermere we passed Dove's Nest, the residence of Mrs. Hemans; and on arriving at Waterhead, the end of our voyage, we went to a very comfortable, very English hotel, where we passed the night; but as it was some time before the close of day, we engaged a carriage and drove to Grasmere, Grasmere Lake, Rydal Mount, Rydal Water, a lake in miniature, and Ambleside, places memorable in the literature of England. Wordsworth and his family lie buried in the churchyard of the little village of Grasmere, under the yew tree; and near the poet's grave is that of Hartley Coleridge, who died in 1851, a year after Wordsworth. We entered the little ancient church adjoining, said to be eight or nine hundred years old, a statement we could believe from the extreme rudeness of its construction. Near the pulpit was the square pew bearing the name Rydal Mount, and on the wall was a tablet with the likeness of the poet in marble relief. We entered and sat down on the same seat he occupied so many years; for Wordsworth was a constant attendant at religious worship, though his home was a good distance from the church. Leaving Grasmere, the last resting-place of the bard, we went to Rydal Mount, his home while living; but we could see the exterior only, as the house had passed into the hands of those who declined to gratify the curiosity of strangers, by admitting them to the interior. The house is very modest and quite small for so distinguished an occupant as its former master; but like so many English country homes, it was enveloped in shrubbery and surrounded by trees. Opposite the cottage is quite a large grove of beeches, in which rooks were flying about with considerable noise. The place is very appropriately named Rydal Mount, since it is situated on the declivity of a hill of considerable size. A little distance off, there is a high rock, ascended by steps cut into the cliff, where Wordsworth was accustomed to compose his poems.

Not far from Rydal Mount was the home of Coleridge; and at some distance from the road is Fox How, the home of Arnold. Ambleside, the residence of Harriet Martineau, at the foot of Wansfel, a mountain a little more than fifteen hundred feet in height, is quite peculiar; the streets, which can hardly be called such, are laid out without any regularity, and the buildings seem to have been scattered at random. As we came to the cottage of Miss Martineau, one of our party alighted to enter, and was admitted to the room where she died. After returning to our hotel, we were booked for outside seats on the stage for Keswick, but alas for our comfort! as the morning was rainy. There was no help for us; and as we had secured our seats to enjoy the prospect, we were compelled to keep them. Keswick was seventeen miles away, so we had an opportunity of knowing what an English rainy day was like. Our landlady, with genuine hospitality, furnished us with waterproofs, to be returned by the stage, as ours were packed away in our luggage; so in spite of the rain we had some compensation for our premature choice of seats. We had the pleasure of witnessing an old English custom, that of sounding a horn on the arrival and departure of the stage. This horn was a formidable instrument, being as long as a musket, and no one but an expert could produce the peculiar sound of which it was capable.

The scenery between Ambleside and Keswick is beautifully picturesque, with hills and mountains on each side, and charming valleys, richly cultivated, lying between, while here and there a little town reposes in their quiet bosoms. We passed a good distance along the base of the " Mighty Helvellyn," three thousand feet high, on whose side is " Striden Edge round the Red Tarn bending, and Catchedicam its left verge defending," as Scott says. After several hours we reached Keswick, situated on the Derwentwater, where the scenery is more wild and rugged than at Windermere. This little sheet of water is studded with islands. One of them, appearing and disappearing at intervals, is a floating island. About a mile from the village is Greta Hall, the home of the poet Southey, who was buried in the yard of the ancient parish church. The whole of this region, including that about Grasmere and Windermere, is memorable in the literature of England. Every mountain, hill, valley, lake, stream, and almost every crag has a history, whose quaint names have become a part of the language of the country. The landscape is picturesque rather than grand; the mountains are not lofty. Helvellyn and Skiddaw, a trifle more than three thousand feet, are among the highest, while the lakes are not wider than our medium sized rivers. It is a peculiarity of this country that the traveller has everything in a nutshell; for as soon as he leaves one charming view, another quickly follows like those of a panorama. There is an advantage in this arrangement if his time is limited, but there is also a disadvantage, since so many different prospects following in rapid succession are confusing, making it difficult to retain any vivid impression of them.

## CHAPTER II.

*A Visit to Scotland.*

WE stopped at Keswick only a few hours, then started for Glasgow by rail, through the ancient town of Carlisle, famous for its share in the "border wars," and for the imprisonment of Mary Queen of Scots in a castle built by William Rufus. We arrived at Glasgow very late in the evening; but without the aid of gas or electricity we could read with ease the signs on the buildings, suggesting the thought that we were approaching the north pole. We gave only a short time to this business city; and bidding farewell to our travelling companions, Mr. and Mrs. P., whom we found very agreeable, we left for Edinburgh by way of Loch Lomond, the Trossachs, and Sterling. There was on board the train a picnic company going to the lake, composed of Scotch belonging to the laboring classes, who were very social, but decorous and respectful. They sang several pieces of sacred music, accompanied by a few violins; and when the train came in sight of Dunbarton Castle, associated with the history of William Wallace, they sang the well-known address of that chieftain to his followers. The castle in which he was confined, after having been betrayed by Monteith, is built on a rock in the Leven, five hundred and sixty feet high. The following legend is connected with the foundation of this stronghold: St. Patrick, a native of this region, having been assailed by Satan or his subordinates, was compelled to flee to Ireland in a boat. His enemies, exasperated that their victim should escape, seized a hugh bowlder from the neighboring hills, and hurled it after him, but it fell short of the mark, and dropped at the mouth of the Leven, where it remains to this day. The Vale of Leven has been rendered immortal by Smollet, the author of "Roderick Random," in the ode beginning "On Leven's banks while free to rove."

Early in the morning the weather bade fair for a pleasant day; but as soon as we embarked at Balloch, the wind and rain disturbed our quiet sail to the end of our voyage. Loch Lomond, celebrated for its thirty-two islands and its historical and poetical associations, has been considered the most beautiful of all the Scotch lakes. In its neighborhood are the ruins of several old castles which belonged to ancient families prominent in Scotch history. We passed many places and objects of peculiar interest, including a rock rising thirty feet from the water, called Rob Roy's Rock, where that chieftain used to lower his captives by a rope into the lake, then draw them out, repeating the experiment until they agreed to pay the required ransom. Indeed, the shores of Loch Lomond constantly remind one of that redoubtable outlaw. Here is Rob Roy's Prison; farther on, Rob Roy's Cave, etc.

The scenery of the lake region of Scotland differs from that of England in being more wild and grand. Leaving the steamer at Inversnaid, we took the stage to Loch Katrine, a distance of five miles, passing two houses of historical interest: one, the residence of Rob Roy, the other, the birthplace of Helen McGregor. Loch Katrine, famous in the tale of the "Lady of the Lake," the most interesting of Scott's poems, is the most romantic of all the lakes in this region. The captain of our little steamer was perfectly familiar with the poem, and repeated portions, pointing out the interesting localities, as the Silver Sand, where Ellen Douglas met Fitz James; Ellen's Isle, the abode of the heroine and her outlawed father; the old oak, where she received her visitor; the Goblin's Cave, etc.

The views on Loch Katrine are exceedingly picturesque, with Ben Venue on the right, Ben An on the left, and several minor elevations on both sides. Ellen's Isle, so named for the heroine, in the southern extremity of the lake, and covered with trees, contains a rocky cavern which appears as if it might have afforded a safe hiding-place for a fugitive. On the right bank of the lake is the Goblin's Cave; and eight hundred feet above is the glen called the Pass of the Cattle, through which the animals seized during a Lowland foray were driven to the Trossachs for shelter. The landing-place at the Trossachs coincided with the romantic scenery of this region. A rustic, winding colonnade decked with moss and vines, led up from the pier to the stage waiting for its passengers, when we gave our parting look at the classic spot and took our seats for a ride through the pass. Our company comprised a party of Americans from Philadelphia; and though it was raining, we were disposed to make the best of our conditions and have a good time.

The Trossachs were not exactly what we expected, — deep, narrow ravines with precipitous mountains on either side, forming a natural wall, — but mere valleys winding between the hills, sometimes narrow, and in other places wide, with an occasional sheet of water, cultivated fields, and a few scattered dwellings. A castle-like hotel, with its grounds and inviting walks, induced us to alight for dinner and spend some time rambling about the premises, to gather some of Burns' "wee tippet daisies," often called gowans by the natives. The mountains and valleys are covered with heather in places, though this is not the time for blossoms. This shrub is of a dark epidote green, contrasting harmoniously with the lighter shades of green seen in the rest of the vegetation. Highland cattle with shaggy hair and Highland sheep with long wool, just as Landseer has represented them, were grazing in the pastures; and to complete the picture, here were the Highland dogs. In going through the Trossachs we passed several places rendered memorable by Sir Walter Scott, as the Brig of Turk, where Fitz James discovered he had left his followers behind; the place where, at the whistle of Roderick Dhu, a host of armed men sprang up, to the astonishment of Fitz James; the muster-field of Clan Alpine, the Fiery Cross followers; and the ford to which Roderick Dhu conducted the king, all places of interest in Scotch history.

Our journey by stage ended at Callender, a pretty modern looking town, with some fine buildings and gardens. Here we exchanged our stage for the railway train, en route for Sterling, passing through many places of historical interest, as is the case of almost the whole of Scotland. The old town of Sterling, situated on the Forth, with its venerable castle, formerly called Snowdown, frowning from its rocky eminence, has been the scene of memorable events, while in the city and vicinity are localities bearing names found in Scotch history, poetry, and romance. From Sterling to Edinburgh, we pass Bannockburn, the field of Bruce's victory, and Linlithgow, the birthplace of Mary Queen of Scots and the place where the Regent Murray was assassinated. It gives the foreign traveller a peculiar sensation to hear these classic names announced by the conductor or guard at railway stations; it seems an almost ridiculous descent from the romantic and the heroic to the dull prose of ordinary life.

One of the agreeable incidents of travel is the pleasant acquaintances sometimes formed. This was our good fortune during the journey to Edinburgh, as well as in other places, where we met a very agreeable Scotch lady with an interesting family of children; and being strangers, we found her advice very serviceable. She bade her manly son, perhaps twelve years of age, to secure us a carriage, which relieved us from considerable embarrassment, as it was quite late in the evening, and we were soon on our way to the Waverly House, on Prince's Street, near Scott's Monument; and here, July 1, we found a resting-place in the celebrated and picturesque capital of Scotland. The city, comprising the Old and the New Towns, is built upon several hills, the material of which the houses are constructed being a light-colored sandstone, but deepened into a dark gray from the effects of the climate. The two sections of the town are separated by a deep ravine spanned by bridges, while the narrow valley is appropriated to public gardens tastefully laid out, affording agreeable promenades, and through it the principal railways pass. Prince's Street, in the New Town, is very fine, containing some of the best buildings and the leading hotels. Here are some of the most celebrated monuments, notably that of Scott, an elegant

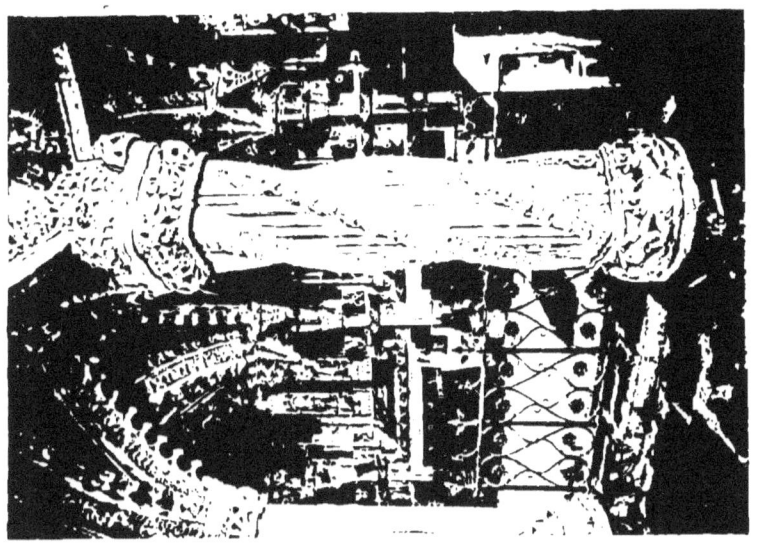

APPRENTICE'S PILLAR, ROSLIN CASTLE.

BURNS' STATUE, GLASGOW.

Gothic column two hundred feet in height. Under the principal arch are the statues of Sir Walter and his dog Maida, in light-gray Carrara marble. Five figures representing some of the novelist's characters occupy niches above; namely, Prince Charles Edward, Meg Merriles, the Last Minstrel, Lady of the Lake, and Heriot. The architect of this beautiful monument, George M. Kemp, was self-taught, having been a stonemason, but he died before the work was completed. Near this monument there are several statues of eminent Scotchmen, including those of Wilson, Christopher North, and Allen Ramsay. On Prince's Street are the Royal Institution for the Encouragement of the Fine Arts; a gallery of statues with the casts in Elgin marbles; the Scottish Antiquarian Museum; the National Gallery, of the Ionic order of architecture, containing paintings both ancient and modern; and the Museum of Antiquities, built after the Doric order.

From our hotel we look across the ravine to the Old Town; and the most conspicuous object is the castle, perched on its high rock; and in another direction is Carlton Hill, affording excellent views of the city. This eminence is adorned with several monuments, including those of Dugald Stewart, Professor Playfair, and Robert Burns; but the most conspicuous is that of Lord Nelson, who has been styled the "naval divinity of Great Britain." There is an unfinished National Monument in imitation of the Parthenon, in honor of the fallen heroes of the Peninsular War. Edinburgh honors her eminent men by these memorials, an example which our own country might imitate with credit.

St. Andrews Square, in the New Town, contains some fine buildings and several statues. The Douglas Hotel, not remarkable in appearance, is the resort of the royal family and other important persons during their visits to this city. A fluted column one hundred and thirty-six feet high, supporting the statue of Viscount Melville, fourteen feet in height, occupies the centre of the square.

A party of four persons made a visit to Roslin Castle, seven miles from Edinburgh; and after paying a fee of one shilling, we were admitted to the interior. Like many other ancient buildings, it was in a state of partial decay. The castle was built by William St. Clair of Roslin, Prince of Orkney, in 1446, and contains the remains of the earls and countesses of Roslin. The chapel is small, of the Gothic style, decorated with a profusion of sculptured ornaments, both in the interior and on the exterior. It contains the monument called the "Apprentice's Pillar," connected with a tragical story like the following, briefly told: An apprentice had carved a column so beautiful as to excite the envy of his master; and to remove so formidable a rival, he assassinated his pupil whom he could not equal. This barbarous act only served to perpetuate the fame of the apprentice and the perfidy of his master.

We went from the chapel to the castle, a short distance off; and as we first entered the ruins, nothing but broken walls and heaps of stones were to be seen; but passing by these, our guide conducted us down a flight of steps to the rear, and led us through several dark, low, winding passages into a number of gloomy, prison-like rooms cut in the solid rock, with but one narrow window, admitting only sufficient light to show the rough stone walls. One of these rooms was the kitchen of the castle, and the others were used by the retainers of the lords of Roslin. The rooms of the tower had small round holes, through which the besieged could send their missiles when beset by foes outside. Judging from the interior arrangements, the domestic life of the highest classes must have been very rude and simple in those days.

Roslin Castle was built at the same time and by the same nobleman as the chapel, and was a place of great strength, with moat and drawbridge. It suffered during the wars with England, and in 1303 it became the scene of three successive victories of the Scotch over the English.

Leaving the castle, we followed the Esk, in its windings between precipitous walls of sandstone, to Hawthornden, about two miles distant. The path was narrow, sometimes on the side of a cliff just above the river, with towering crags over our heads. The Esk here is a small stream no larger than a good-sized brook, but its banks are lined with trees and shrubs, and the rocks on its borders are worn into a great variety of shapes, some rising like walls and towers, while others are excavated like caverns and grottos. In places the narrow path lies along dizzy heights where one would not care to meet a foe. Between Roslin and Hawthornden, the scenery along the Esk is the wildest and grandest we have yet seen in this country, and reminds us of views in America. After crossing the bridge over the Esk, for which we paid a shilling apiece, — everything is a shilling a sight; we expected to be charged a shilling for looking at the moon, — we entered the grounds of Sir James Drummond, of Hawthornden House, where the poet Drummond, contemporary with Ben Jonson, lived. On the banks of the river was what was called Bruce's Cave, which seemed like the ruins of a castle or some stronghold. We passed through a dark low passage into a room where were kept the sword of Bruce, a rusty weapon so heavy that it would need a mighty Hercules to wield it, and the writing-desk of John Knox, a simple, rude pine desk carved in school-boy fashion, proving that if the stern reformer did use it he was much like other boys.

Having seen the curiosities of the Drummond estate, with its lofty precipice and caverns cut in freestone rock, which tradition assigns to the Pictish monarchs, faint and weary, we came to the railway station, where we found a place for refreshments, a snug little house occupied by a Scotch woman and her son, the gate tender. As her little parlor was already occupied by guests, we were entertained in the kitchen, where the domestic arrangements reminded one of descriptions given by story tellers. — the tea kettle on the hob, the rows of plates on the shelves of the open cupboard, the heavy wood chairs, the little bed in the curtained recess, all so quaint and tidy. The good wife, who had lost her husband, was seventy-six years old and the mother of fifteen children, yet appeared fresh and young for one of her age. Her son, the gate tender, was quite an artist, though having had no training. His mother, proud of her boy, took great pleasure in showing us his paintings, which were very creditable. To complete the day's sight-seeing, after returning to Edinburgh, we visited Holyrood Palace.

It is situated at the foot of Cannongate, a street once famous in the history of Edinburgh, but now occupied by the poorer classes. This quadrangular pile is two hundred and thirty feet in length; and with its battlements, round towers, and conical domes, it makes a grand appearance. The Abbey Church or Royal Chapel is now in ruins, but these give evidence of its former architectural beauty. It contains the tombs of Scotland's kings, whose portraits line a hall in the palace. We were shown Lord Darnley's room, and those where the unfortunate Rizzio was murdered and through which his body was dragged, also the private stairs up which the assassins were conducted by Darnley, and what purported to be blood stains on the floor. There were several portraits of Mary and one of Darnley, who is represented as being tall, but we could not see anything about it very captivating. The queen's portraits in this palace are disappointing; and if they are faithful, she was not as beautiful as represented by her biographers. Her sad fate had, undoubtedly, much to do with her charms.

In one room was a bed which had been occupied by the queen, and in another, one that had been used by Charles I. The royal apartments were dark and gloomy, with very low doorways and narrow stairs. Though some of the rooms were highly decorated, others were without ornament or only partially covered with faded tapestry. "Departed glory" is written upon all these once beautiful but now faded and decayed objects. It is depressing to see the elaborate carving and fine ornamental decorations of palaces, chapels, and churches gradually crumbling to dust.

Though the public buildings were so rich, elegant, and highly decorated, yet the private dwellings of the highest classes, even, were such that no respectable person of the present day would think of occupying. In the Gallery of Kings there are one hundred and six portraits, representing the

DUNROBIN CASTLE, FROM THE GARDEN.

THE CHANCEL, MELROSE ABBEY.

Scottish sovereigns from earliest times, painted from fancy, pictures, or old coins.

Leaving Holyrood Palace, we visited the castle, situated on a high rocky mount, a large building occupying a slate rock, which on one side rises very abruptly three hundred and eighty-three feet. Having passed the outer barriers, we came to a palisade with a ditch spanned by a drawbridge, and defended by two gates. The castle was guarded by Highland soldiers, who were going through their military exercises. On the highest platform of the castle stands Mons Meg, a large gun made at Mons, in Brittany, 1486. From the Esplanade fine views were enjoyed. The royal apartments occupied the eastern side of the fortress. The Crown Room contains the Scottish Regalia, consisting of crown, sceptre, sword, and other valuable treasures, such as the Golden Collar, presented by Queen Elizabeth to James VI., with the George and Dragon, supposed to be the most magnificent one of the kind existing, and the crown of Robert Bruce. In Mary's drawing-room are two portraits of the queen, one being taken at the age of eighteen, when she was Dauphiness of France, the most beautiful one we had seen. Arthur's Seat is a crested hill, overlooking the town, but we did not attempt the difficult feat of reaching it.

In walking through Edinburgh one is constantly meeting with agreeable surprises. There are so many hills in and around the city, so many windings, so many ascents and descents, flights of stone steps which, like Jacob's ladder, reach to heaven, so many narrow passage-ways (closes, as they are called here) between lofty stone buildings, that they seem the realization of wild dreams. Those on the verge of precipices have a grand and almost threatening aspect, lest they tumble down the steep acclivity. Edinburgh is built on hills, steep crags, tablelands, and in valleys. The Old Town is very quaint and picturesque; some of the buildings are from seven to ten stories high, while the narrow passages or streets remind one of the winding paths between the walls of a fortification. Indeed, many

of these old buildings look like fortresses. The New
Town is quite different, the streets being wider, the houses
lower and finer. Another feature of Edinburgh is the series
of hills rising on several sides, the most conspicuous being
Arthur's Seat, with a road passing around, giving the upper
part the appearance of a crown, and another called the Salis-
bury Crag. On the other side of the River Clyde is the harbor,
with its shipping.

The Scotch express gratitude and reverence for their distinguished men by erecting to their memory suitable monuments, which both adorn their cities and teach the lessons of
patriotism to future generations. There are many public
buildings in Edinburgh, including its celebrated University;
but perhaps no one is more interesting, on account of its
antiquity, than the old Iron Church, whose tower, in the form
of a crown, looms up very conspicuously. St. Giles is another
ancient church. We visited the spot designated the Heart of
Mid-Lothian, rendered memorable by the great novelist, but
now it is recognized only by a stone in the pavement, marking
the place where it stood.

July 4 we bade adieu to Edinburgh, and started for London
via Melrose. The day was fine, and the scenery we passed
quietly beautiful. We crossed the Esk and Gala Water,
celebrated by the poet Burns, and, at a distance on the left,
the Hills of Lammermoor. Melrose Abbey! How often had
we seen the venerable ruins represented by the hand of art;
but here it stood in its romantic, declining beauty, just as we
had pictured it in our imagination, with its exquisite Gothic
windows, its crumbling buttresses, its moss-covered walls, the
headstones on the grass lawn in front, and surrounded by the
Eildon hills, on which the Romans had an encampment half
a mile in circumference. The abbey was founded by David I.
in 1136, but was several times destroyed or partially destroyed
during the numerous wars of Scotland, and was as often
restored or rebuilt. Its remains prove that the building was a
fine specimen of the Gothic style of architecture. While lin-
gering about the ruins we met two passengers from the China,

and planned an excursion to Abbotsford, about three miles distant on the Tweed. We could make only a hurried visit to the house of the famous novelist, though the grounds presented an attractive feature, with their trees and agreeable walks. The house was built by Sir Walter, as is well known, of stone gathered from all parts of the country, and one block was from the old Tolbooth at Edinburgh. Though the building defies every style of architecture, yet its composition is pleasing and picturesque.

Abbotsford is a museum in itself, containing some valuable relics from almost every part of the globe. The very formal and very polite guide went through his catechism with great minuteness and fidelity, but he had the lesson so thoroughly that it was difficult to follow his rapid utterances. It was Sir Walter in every sentence, so that his name and title were about all we could retain; however, a few ideas were brought away. The novelist's study contained a large writing-desk, a small one made from the wood of the Spanish Armada, and a chair made from one used by William Wallace. In the library there were several chairs elegantly carved; while the books, furniture, pictures, and everything in the room were precisely as he left them when he died, and the same was true of all the other apartments occupied by Sir Walter, as our guide affirmed. One room was appropriated to arms and armor, most of which had belonged to eminent persons of different periods, and under a glass case were the last garments worn by the novelist, while windows of stained glass bore the escutcheons of his own and the royal family of Scotland.

With regret we left these classic scenes for Leeds, England, a very old town, and the chief seat of the woollen manufactures.

## CHAPTER III.

*From Edinburgh to London.*

Our route to London lay through the centre of England, though we did not pass any places of special interest until we came to Sheffield, a busy town enveloped in the smoke of a thousand chimneys. During our journey we had for travelling companions a very social Englishman who had been in America, and came home fascinated with the country and the people, and an English lady disposed to be quite communicative. Thus far we had found the natives of Great Britain more inclined to be social than we expected. They are reserved at first, but after further acquaintance they seem more accessible and cordial. There is much to be admired in the orderly, quiet, and dignified bearing of the English. They are calm and self-possessed, a trait very noticeable in all whom we met.

The natural scenery of the southern part of Scotland and the northern regions of England is much the same: quiet, beautiful, and exceedingly fresh at this season of the year. The land is under the highest state of cultivation, with not a foot running to waste. Trees, shrubs, and hedgerows divide the fields into plots, which diversify the landscape, though there is an absence of grand views. Sometimes the prospect is varied by ledges of building stone, almost the only material used in construction. We had not seen a wooden house since landing in Great Britain.

The towns and villages have a very ancient and weather-stained appearance, which forms a striking contrast to the freshness of the verdant landscape. In the western part of England almost every house and stone wall is more or less concealed with running plants, which impart an indescribable charm to rural life. The ivy is seen clinging to the walls wherever it can fasten its tendrils, while mosses with soft green and brown colors cover the trees and cottages. Here are seen the yew, holly, hawthorn, heath, furz, and broom, about which we had read, and the daisy, not the showy flower so called, but the "wee, purple, tippet flower" of Burns. The feathered songsters comprise the lapwing, bulfinch, skylark, nightingale, and others. English life and English scenes have been so vividly and faithfully delineated by native poets and romancers that one may gain almost an accurate knowledge of the country from their writings.

Bidding farewell to green fields, beautiful flowers, charming lakes, and picturesque hills and vales, we finally reached the great, busy city of London, a world of itself, and stopped at the hotel of the Golden Cross, situated on the Strand. The first place to be visited was, of course, Westminster Abbey, but we took a walk around Trafalgar Square before entering this historical building. Westminster Abbey, originally a Benedictine monastery, occupies the site of a church existing in the time of Offa, King of Mercia, in the eighth century. A new one was erected by Edward the Confessor, 1065, but only a very small part of his church can be identified with that now existing. The oldest portions, the choir and transepts, were built by Henry III., though additions have been made at different times. The length of the abbey is 416 feet; the transepts, 203 feet; the choir, 155 feet; from the pavement to the roof, nearly 102 feet; and the towers, 225 feet. In the north transept are the monuments of several distinguished persons, comprising Pitt, Fox, Grattan, Canning, Lord Chatham, Sir Robert Peel, William Wilberforce, and others. The south transept contains the Poets' Corner, where are monuments and tablets to many of England's celebrated poets and writers from Chaucer, 1400 A. D., to the present time, nearly five centuries. Americans as well as Englishmen should feel an interest in this hallowed spot, for here are names as familiar and as highly cherished in one country as in the other — names that have enriched and ennobled the common language of both.

The abbey has a place in English hearts from its connection with the political institutions of the country, for it is here that the sovereigns from Edward the Confessor to Queen Victoria have been crowned, in the centre of the choir under the tower, and here also more than twenty of them lie buried. Back of the high altar is the chapel of Edward the Confessor, or, as it is called, the Chapel of the Kings. The centre is occupied by the Shrine of Edward, originally ornamented with rich mosaic work, small remnants of which still remain, and it is said with slabs of porphyry brought from Rome, but which vandal hands have carried off. Around this shrine are the tombs of nine kings and queens, including those of Henry III., Edward I., and Eleanor, his queen, Edward III. and Philippa, his queen, Richard II. and his consort, and Henry V. Here are also the two coronation chairs. The oldest, one used for crowning the monarchs of Great Britain, contains the "Stone of Scone," formerly used in Ireland, and then in Scotland, upon which the candidate was placed when crowned. It was brought from Scotland by Edward I. It is a piece of rough, gray sandstone fastened to the under side of the coronation chair. The other chair, much like the first, was made for the use of Mary, the wife of William I., as in the joint-coronation two chairs would be needed. Six chapels surround Edward's shrine. The one called St. Edmund's contains twenty monuments of distinguished persons. Henry VII. and his queen lie buried in a chapel entered by twelve steps, and ornamented with various devices, comprising the crown and the roses of York and Lancaster; on the right of the chapel is a monument of Mary Queen of Scots, whose remains were brought from Peterborough Cathedral and buried here; and on the opposite side is the tomb of her rival, Queen Elizabeth. Henry VII.'s Chapel was the place where the Knights of the Bath, an order which ranks next to the Order of the Garter, were installed; and here are their banners and stalls, while back of their seats are brass plates with the names and armorial bearings of the members, which comprise some royal names. The tomb of Henry VII. is a Gothic structure of black marble decorated with gilt figures in high relief. Indeed, the entire chapel is covered with a great variety of ornaments, which would require much study and time to describe. These royal tombs teach the lesson that death is no respecter of rank, pomp, station, or honor, and that the most powerful monarchs must share the common lot. " Passing away " is written upon everything earthly.

There are monuments in every part of this interesting building : some beautiful, others commonplace, showy, or unadorned. A little of American history is found here, where there is a monument to Major Andre; but the outrage perpetrated upon the figure of Washington in bas-relief, by depriving it of a head three times, is shocking to Americans and disgraceful to the English. The cloisters and chapter house form a part of the abbey ; the latter is an octagon with groined roof resting, apparently, on a tall column of Purbec marble, but really supported by external buttresses. It was built in 1250, by Henry III. The first House of Commons met here, and occupied it for that purpose three hundred years. The building has recently been restored, and now presents something of its primitive beauty. What conflicting emotions are excited by a first visit to this grand old historical church : it saddens and it fascinates ; it fills the mind with admiration for the magnificence and beauty of its architecture, with awe for its majestic proportions, and with sadness for the ephemeral nature of human greatness. The cloisters call up the figures of the Benedictine monks who paced up and down these arcades during their secluded and monotonous lives.

Westminster and St. Paul's! The contrast between the two buildings is very wide : the styles are entirely different, the impression they make upon the visitor is different. St. Paul's belongs to the present, Westminster to the past. The former is grand and imposing, with its dome, its massive arches, columns, and pilasters; but it has less variety, less fascinating beauty, less graceful ornamentation than the latter. The great size of St. Paul's — five hundred and fifty feet in length and three hundred and seventy in height — and its beautiful and well-proportioned dome render it a conspicuous and noble structure. The style of architecture is Grecian. The entire building, begun in 1675, was the work of one architect, Sir Christopher Wren; therefore there is a unity in design not always seen in older churches. The material used is Portland stone, naturally of a light color; but the smoke of London has deepened the tint in places to a very dark hue, which gives it a shaded appearance. The choir is very rich in wood carving; and the two organs, one on each side, are similar in ornament, while the pulpit is of different kinds of marble. Compared with the abbey, the interior of St. Paul's is almost without ornament. The paintings in the dome represent events in the life of St. Paul. The church contains a number of monuments and statues of eminent Englishmen; as John Howard, Doctor Johnson, Sir Joshua Reynolds, Bishop Heber, Duke of Wellington, Lords Nelson and Cornwallis, Sir John Moore, Collingwood, Sir William Jones, and others. This church contains the tomb of Benjamin West, an American artist. "The Whispering Gallery," reached by a flight of two hundred and sixty steps, is a peculiarity of this church. The softest whisper uttered at one side of the gallery is distinctly heard on the opposite side, by placing the ear against the wall.

The next important place we visited was Westminster Palace, or the House of Parliament, a building which extends nine hundred and forty feet along the left bank of the Thames, and covers nearly eight acres of ground. It is constructed of different kinds of stone and iron, in the style called Perpendicular Gothic, and contains eleven hundred apartments. The Victoria Tower is three hundred and forty feet in height, and the Clock Tower is three hundred and twenty feet; the dial of the clock is thirty feet in diameter. A tower in the centre rises like the spire of a church. This immense building is best seen from the river or from Westminster Bridge. It is open to the public on Saturdays, when tickets of admission are given at the building. Ascending the royal staircase, we pass

CORONATION CHAIR.

HIGH ALTAR, WESTMINSTER ABBEY.

through the Norman Porch into the Queen's Robing-room, an apartment highly decorated by carving and frescos, the subjects being scenes taken from the life of King Arthur; and a chair of state, richly ornamented, occupies one end of the room. From this apartment we passed into the gallery, one hundred and ten feet in length, where the public are allowed to view the royal procession on the way from the Robing-room to the House of Peers, where the Queen opens and prorogues Parliament. The gallery contains the gilt statues of some of the English sovereigns and a few paintings. Passing into the Prince's Chamber, we see a statue of the Queen in marble, with that of Justice on one side, and Clemency on the other, while the walls are decorated with bas-reliefs and portraits of the Tudor family. From the Prince's Chamber we enter the House of Lords, a splendid room, with the throne dazzling in gold and rich colors at one end, and the seat of the Lord Chancellor, called "the wool sack," looking very much like a bed with only a cushion on it, not a very comfortable or dignified position. At the end of the room opposite the throne is the Bar, and on both sides of the chamber are the seats of the members, arranged in tiers one above another, while everything about the room is rich and gorgeous; the same is true of the Peers' Lobby. After visiting the Peers' Library, Robing-room, and Corridor, we came to Central Hall, a room sixty feet in diameter, with four doors, highly ornamented.

There is a striking contrast between the House of Lords and the House of Commons. The latter has no gilding, though the woodwork is richly carved. It is seventy-five by forty-five feet, and forty-one feet in height. The Speaker's chair is opposite the Bar, near which is the official position of the sergeant-at-arms. The ministerial seats for those who vote "Aye" on any motion put by the Chair are on the right of the Speaker in front, while the leaders of the Opposition are on the left. Behind the Bar are places occupied by the peers who may be present at the debates. The seats of the members form a double tier along each side of the House, and at the end opposite the Speaker is the gallery for the Diplomatic Corps, while the reporters occupy a gallery above the Speaker's chair. As an act of courtesy, though against parliamentary rules, a place has been assigned behind a screen for the accommodation of ladies who may wish to listen to the debates. The lobbies are arranged along the sides of the House; while refreshment rooms, smoking-rooms, committee rooms, and some others are connected with it for the convenience of the members.

St. Stephen's Hall occupies the site of St. Stephen's Chapel, belonging to the old Westminster Palace, and was used for the meeting of Parliament from the time of Henry IV., 1400 A. D., until it was burned, in 1834. Westminster Hall, now included in the new House of Parliament, forms a part of English history. It was first built by William Rufus, about 1097, and rebuilt in its present form about a century later by Richard II. For nearly seven hundred years the great Law Courts of England have been established here. Within its walls Charles I. and Sir Thomas More were condemned to death, and here the famous trial of Warren Hastings took place. The last great state occasion celebrated in Westminster Hall was the coronation feast of George IV. The present House of Parliament was begun in 1840 and finished in 1857, though occupied some time before its completion. It is a singular fact that, though Great Britain is a wealthy and powerful nation, she never had what could properly be called a capitol until the reign of the present sovereign; the different buildings used for the purpose were not originally designed for a national capitol.

Sunday, July 8, we attended service at Westminster Abbey, and heard a Boston clergyman, or as much of his sermon as possible. Preaching in the abbey seemed like addressing an audience in a forest. In the afternoon we went to St. Paul's, where the congregation was more concentrated, and the words of the speaker were not lost among the mazes of Gothic architecture. The next day we devoted a part of the time to the Zoological Gardens, in Regents Park, which comprise, it is said, the largest and most complete collection of living animals in the world, including, at the time of our visit, more than five hundred quadrupeds, one thousand birds, and one hundred reptiles. Many of the species have for the first time been seen alive in this collection. The viceroy of Egypt presented it with a pair of hippopotomi, the first brought into the kingdom; the collection of living snakes is the largest in Europe.

The Gardens belong to the Zoological Society of London, instituted in 1826, by Sir H. Davy and Sir Stamford Raffles, for the advancement of science.

In the afternoon we paid our first visit to the National Gallery, Trafalgar Square, founded in 1824, and now comprising nearly nine hundred pictures by native artists, early Italian and later Italian schools, Spanish, French, German, Flemish, and Dutch masters, Turner's pictures occupying several rooms. Since Ruskin has bestowed so high commendation upon this artist, we gave considerable attention to his productions, but confess we were unable to see all the beauties he ascribes to them. They are conspicuous for their warmth of color, but they have a sort of hazy appearance which renders objects somewhat indistinct. One seems to be looking at them through a thin mist, as sometimes seen in a New England summer evening. The artist closely imitates Claude in some of his paintings. In one room a Claude and a Turner hang side by side, and it is difficult to see any difference in style between them. Turner is said to have had three distinct periods as an artist: first, as a water colorist, when his paintings were conspicuous for finish and subdued colors; second, as an oil painter, when he is said to resemble Wilson; third, from 1802 to 1830, when his pictures are conspicuous for brilliancy of coloring and masterly execution. The majority of his works belong to the latter period, including two of his finest paintings, Childe Harold and The Fighting Téméraire.

Turner's pictures are numerous and represent varied scenes, a large number being classical. This artist was a native of London, born in 1775, and died in 1851. He was buried in the crypt of St. Paul's by the side of Sir Joshua Reynolds.

The National Gallery contains Landseer's paintings, his most striking being those of animals. One of his pictures represents the Duke of Wellington and a lady, afterwards the

Duchess of Wellington, both on horseback. C. R. Leslie, an American by birth, has some paintings in this gallery; while West, also an American and president of the Royal Academy, exhibited two hundred and forty-nine of his paintings in the course of fifty years, but only a few of his works are in the National Gallery. Among other noted artists represented in this collection are Sir David Wilkie, Sir Joshua Reynolds, Mulready, Copley (a native of Boston, Mass.), Gilbert Stuart (a native of the United States), and James and Edward Ward.

We next paid a visit to the Kensington Museum, established in 1852 by the late Prince Consort. It was intended for art and manufactures, and has an extensive and varied collection of paintings, sculpture, jewels, enamels, gems, carving, tapestries, etc. The exhibits embrace ancient, mediæval, and modern works of more than twenty thousand objects, acquired by purchase, gifts, and bequests. The Architectural Court contains original monuments or casts of many famous works of early times, while one room is appropriated to the mosaic portraits of distinguished artists. The Prince Consort Gallery contains some of the most costly specimens, while those of the Loan Collections are very extensive. The celebrated Raphael Cartoons, formerly at Hampton Court, are now in this museum. They were drawn with chalk on paper and colored in distemper, and the originals are now in the Vatican Museum. Each cartoon is twelve feet in height, and represents scenes from scripture; they were designed for tapestry for Leo X., 1513. Near the Kensington Museum is the Albert Memorial, a very showy monument with a profusion of gilt and colors, which, to our thinking, is in bad taste; but it is the most gorgeous and expensive in England. It seems to us that an elegant structure in white marble would have been more appropriate to the character of the lamented prince.

In this vicinity may be seen, from four in the afternoon until six, the stylish equipages of the nobility and aristocracy, as they take the fashionable drive to Hyde Park. A continuous line of splendid teams with liveried servants lends enchantment to the scene; and if one is posted in heraldry, he could tell to what distinguished family some of them belonged, by their coats of arms. The fine parks of London constitute one of the most pleasing and important features of this great metropolis, and contribute not only to the pleasure of the inhabitants, but also to their health.

Of all the London collections, the British Museum is the most interesting and comprehensive. It was established in 1753 by act of Parliament, in what was known as the Montagu House, but additions have since been made until the building covers a very large space. It ranks among the first in Europe, of its kind, for the number and variety of its collections. The Department of Antiquities comprises Anglo-Roman, Greco-Roman, Lycian, Assyrian, Egyptian, and some varieties of architecture and sculpture. Marbles from the city of Ianthus, colonized by the Greeks, were discovered by Sir Charles Fellows, and removed to England 1842-46. They comprise reliefs from the Harpy Tomb, which stood on the Acropolis, dating, probably, from 500 B. C. Ten seated figures, together with a lion and a sphinx, were brought from the Sacred Way, leading to the Temple of Apollo, at Branchidæ, and some specimens of the earliest Greek sculpture from 580 to 520 B. C. One room of the museum contains the relics of the Mausoleum at Halicanassus, erected to Mausolus, Prince of Caria, by his queen, Artemisia, 352 B. C. The tomb, considered one of the wonders of the world, was one hundred and forty feet high, and bore on the top a chariot group in white marble, while numerous statues of Parian adorned the monument. The Elgin Marbles, so called from Lord Elgin, seen in the British Museum, were taken from the Parthenon, at Athens, built 440 B. C., as a temple to Minerva, which contained the statue of the goddess, of gold and ivory, made by Phidias. Here are the Phigalian Marbles, brought from the Temple of Apollo, found near the ancient city of Phigalia, in Arcadia. Much older than any Greek marbles are the Assyrian remains, collected mostly by Mr. Layard, 1847-50, which comprise specimens from Nimroud, probably dating from 880 to 630 B. C., besides those from other localities, notably one from the palace of Sennacherib, in gypsum, 700 B. C., as shown by the inscriptions, and others in limestone, of a later date. The illustrations consist of battle scenes in the history of the warlike Assyrians. The Nimroud Collection, obtained from the great mound at this place, is really history written in stone. A seated figure of Shalmaneser in black basalt was discovered fifty miles from Nimroud, at a place on the Tigris.

The Egyptian antiquities of the Museum cover a period of nearly three thousand years. The earliest monuments were found at Memphis; others were from Abydos, but the largest number of specimens was from the city of Thebes. Most of the relics are inscribed with hieroglyphics, and illustrate subjects connected with the religious, civil, and domestic life of the Egyptians; some of these show an advanced state of civilization. The Room of Gems contains a valuable collection of engraved precious stones, mostly intaglios, but impressions in plaster have been taken, which render the beautiful work very conspicuous. A fine cameo with the head of the Emperor Augustus is considered the largest of the kind in existence. King, in his work on Gems, describes some of these beautiful specimens. The famous Portland Vase, found near Rome, constitutes one of the rare treasures of the collection. It was once broken into a hundred pieces by a madman, but the fragments were carefully collected and cemented together. The ground is deep blue and the figures opaque white, representing classical scenes. Parts of an ancient jar of alabaster, found on the site of the Mausoleum, is inscribed with the name of "Xerxes the Great King," in four different languages.

The Geological Department comprises a very extensive collection of minerals and rocks, with numerous and varied fossil remains, while the birds and marine shells afford interesting studies for the naturalist. It is not possible even to glance at all the rich treasures of the Museum in one visit; it must be seen many times to get a tolerable idea of their character. Being free to the public, it becomes a most important school of object teaching to all classes; and the same is true of some other institutions; as the Zoological Gardens, the National Gallery, etc.

July 12 we visited the Crystal Palace, an immense structure of glass, containing a great variety of articles for permanent exhibition. The apartments are fitted up in the styles of architecture employed by different nations at various periods. The most elaborate decoration was seen in the Saracenic; there was not a square inch that had not its beautiful tracery, giving it the appearance of very fine needlework. The building contains some good paintings. The grounds about the palace are laid out in parterres of flowers scattered over the lawns, diversified with trees and artificial basins of water.

The opening of the College for the Blind, near the Crystal Palace, was an interesting occasion. This institution was founded by an American who was himself blind, about five years before our visit, and has been attended by highly gratifying results. There are now between sixty and seventy pupils, including both sexes of different ages. A concert was given while we were there by the older pupils, at which some distinguished visitors were present, including the Princess Louise and her husband, the Marquis of Lorne, the Duke of Westminster, and several other notable persons. The princess opened the college. The intelligence and quickness of apprehension shown by the pupils were remarkable, and no one who witnessed the exercises could fail to see the blessings of such an institution.

The Bank of England, founded in 1694, is one of the famous public institutions of London. It employs nine hundred persons, whose aggregate salaries amount to two hundred and ten thousand pounds a year. Near the Bank is the Royal Exchange, a noble looking building bearing the inscription " The earth is the Lord's and the fulness thereof," suggested by the late Prince Consort. In the rear of the Exchange is the statue of George Peabody, the American philanthropist, who died in London, 1869. A friend gave us tickets to a recitation in the Mansion House, the residence of the lord mayor during his term of office, which is not generally open to the public. The reading, which was from " The Tempest," was given in what is called the " Egyptian Room," though there was nothing Egyptian about it. To reach the room, we passed through a long hall with statues, armorial bearings, chairs richly decorated, and various other objects of interest. The lord mayor gives a ball and a banquet, in this hall, to three or four hundred persons on Easter Monday. This official is an important personage, and has the precedence in the city of all the royal family; and when the sovereign dies, he occupies a seat in the Privy Council, and is the first one to sign the documents. His salary is eight thousand pounds per annum, while his expenses generally exceed that sum. His instalment, November 9, is attended by a great public show, and a dinner in the Guildhall.

Temple Bar, now removed, was another historical place. It was built as a gateway across the road separating Fleet Street from the Strand, and was where the heads of persons executed for criminal and political offences were formerly exposed. There is or was a custom of closing this gate on occasions of the entrance of the sovereign into the city, when a herald sounds a trumpet, another official knocks at the gate, and a parley ensues. The gate is then opened, and the lord mayor passes a sword to the king or queen, who graciously returns it to him.

Covent Garden Market is an interesting place on Saturday morning on account of the fine display of fruits and flowers, apparently from all parts of the kingdom. It is entertaining to see how a great city is fed; and judging from this extensive market, it is fair to conclude that the people of London are good livers, at least, those who have the means to gratify their appetites.

Sunday, July 15, we went to the Tabernacle and heard Mr. Spurgeon, the celebrated preacher. There was nothing remarkable about his appearance; indeed, he did not at first impress us as being superior to ordinary preachers. He was plain, earnest, and evidently sincere, without any attempts at oratorical display, yet he has a wonderful power to draw a large audience. The Tabernacle can seat four thousand four hundred persons, yet it was full. The building is peculiar, without architectural beauty, symmetry, or any other characteristic of a fine edifice. It is elliptical in form, with two rows of galleries passing entirely around it, with the pulpit at one side, elevated to the level of the lower gallery, so that the speaker is midway between the floor and the upper one. There was not a musical instrument in the church, the singing being performed by the whole congregation, suggesting the company of celestial choristers, whose harmonious voices sounded like "many waters." The interior seemed like an amphitheatre, with its sea of heads rising from the base and reaching to the top of the wall under the dome.

The Royal Academy, instituted in 1768, had recently been removed from Trafalgar Square to Burlington House, Piccadilly. Its object is to afford a school of design and an annual exhibition of the works of living artists, as well as the old masters. The members are under the supervision of the Queen, who alone confirms all appointments; they comprise forty-two academicians. The exhibitions occur twice a year: in May for modern works, and in winter for those of the old masters, when the art treasures of private individuals are loaned to the Academy. The works of sculptors are included among the exhibits. Sir Joshua Reynolds and Benjamin West have both held the office of president; Sir Francis Grant now occupies that position. At the time we visited the Academy, it contained one thousand five hundred and thirty-nine specimens, comprising oil paintings, water colors, architectural drawings, etchings, miniatures, and sculptures, some by artists well known in America.

The Palace of Hampton Court, built by Cardinal Wolsey, stands on the north bank of the Thames several miles from Charing Cross. It was considered very magnificent, and excited the envy of Henry VIII.; therefore the politic cardinal presented it to his Majesty, and received in return the Manor House. While Wolsey occupied the palace, he lived in greater opulence than any potentate, keeping eight hundred retainers in his household, and giving sumptuous entertainments, notably to the French embassadors sent to confirm the peace agreed to by Henry VIII., Francis I., and Charles V. Hampton Court Palace is memorable for its historical events, having been the birthplace of Edward VI., and where Queen Elizabeth held festivals, and where the queen of James I. died; and it was here Charles I. had collected valuable paintings, which were scattered during the Protectorate, when it was occupied by Cromwell. It became the favorite residence of William III., who improved it and laid out the gardens and parks as they are now seen. George II. and Queen Caroline were the last royal persons who resided at Hampton Court. The palace consists of three principal quadrangles.

We entered under a lofty arcade, crossed a court, and passed through a colonnade to the King's Grand Staircase, leading to the state apartments. Paintings representing scenes from Greek mythology adorn the staircase, and in the Guard Chamber the walls are covered with designs formed of different kinds of armor, such as muskets, halberds, pistols, swords, daggers, and other weapons, sufficient to arm one thousand men. These warlike ornaments are interspersed with portraits and other paintings. The State Rooms comprise the presence chamber, audience chamber, dancing-hall, bedroom, dressing-room, and waiting-room, with their walls covered by the paintings of the old masters; the Queen's rooms and those of the Prince of Wales are similarly decorated. There are nine hundred and thirty-two paintings distributed throughout the different parts of the building. A Gothic hall, one hundred and six feet in length and sixty feet in height, is rich in armorial devices and stained-glass windows, while the walls are hung with Arras tapestry, illustrating the history of Abraham. The walls of the Great Hall, called the Withdrawing Room, are also hung with tapestry, but so faded that it is difficult to decipher the designs. The park and gardens are three miles in extent, and afford charming places of resort for rest, walking, or riding. What is called the "Wilderness" consists of a dense thicket of trees, and the "Maze" is a labyrinth of shrubs arranged in the form of certain puzzles; so that one going into it must keep winding round to find the clue in order to get out, which is not easily done. The Home Park is agreeably varied by beds of flowers, clusters of trees, avenues, fountains, and grass-plots, with artificial streams of water on which ducks swim and lilies bloom.

Separated by a fence, are extensive grassy plains, with avenues of noble trees stretching away in the distance, where domestic animals are feeding. The private garden contains flowers and fruits, including a remarkable grapevine, planted in 1768, and so large that it requires a house seventy-two feet long and thirty feet wide for its shelter. The vine is one hundred and ten feet in length, and sometimes bears more than two thousand bunches of grapes.

Sloane's Museum contains antique specimens, mostly of small size; and though the rooms are very narrow, the articles are so well arranged that they are easily examined. They comprise architectural remains from different countries, and some paintings, notably The Rake's Progress, by Hogarth. Another object worthy of attention was an Egyptian sarcophagus, found by Belzoni, consisting of a single piece of alabaster or aragonite more than nine feet in length. A lighted lamp placed inside shines through slabs two and one-half inches in thickness, thus illustrating their great translucency. The original copy of the Gerusalemme Liberata, in the handwriting of Tasso, is an object of interest to the admirers of that poet. The collection was made by Sir John Sloane, an eccentric man, who bequeathed all his property and his son to his country, believing the government would provide for him. The Museum is opposite Lincoln's Inn Fields, a small private park or garden near the famous Inn's Court, which is surrounded by old, respectable looking buildings, occupied by the legal profession.

London Tower! What strange, sad associations are connected with this memorable structure! It was very difficult to get any vivid impression of the place on a first visit, when hurried through the different apartments by a guide, whose rapid descriptions led us to say to ourselves, "Woe unto you, ye blind guides!" A place so identified with the past and the theatre of so many tragic scenes should be visited leisurely to afford time for reflection. Westminster Abbey and London Tower are places where one wishes to be left to his own thoughts. Explanations, conversation, and even the presence of company distract the mind and disturb the feelings, like merriment at religious worship or a funeral. Our previous ideas of the Tower were quite different from the reality. Instead of one tower, there are nearly twenty in all, of different sizes, occupying a quadrangle surrounded by a moat several feet wide; the area within the walls is little more than twelve acres. The tower keep, or donjon, called the White Tower, in the centre of the triangle, was built by William the Conqueror; and near it is the Horse Armory, with figures of men, some on horses, others on foot, clad in the armor of their times, from Henry VII., 1422, to James II., 1685. Besides these mailed warriors, a large number of ancient warlike weapons are seen.

Queen Elizabeth's Armory, in the White Tower, contains various instruments of torture for heretics, some of them being taken from the wreck of the Spanish Armada; but the objects of the most tragical interest were the heading block, mask, and axe. Those now in the Tower were employed in the execution of persons engaged in the rebellion of 1745. An equestrian figure of Queen Elizabeth represents her, in royal robes, going to St. Paul's, to return thanks for the deliverance of England from the Spanish invasion. We visited the room or cell, ten feet by eight, in a wall without a window, where Sir Walter Raleigh was imprisoned for many years and where he wrote his history of the world. We stood by the stairs ascended by so many unfortunates with a tragical end—kings, queens, princes, nobles, the innocent and the guilty. Within the area is a stone with an inscription signifying that was the spot where Anne Boleyn was beheaded; and St. Peter's Chapel, within the walls, is the burial-place of most of those who perished by the axe. The Wakefield Tower contains the Crown Jewels, a collection of crowns and other symbols of royalty, adorned with

The Houses of Parliament.

Church at Grasmere.

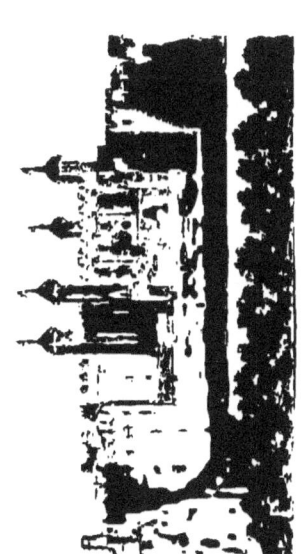

Tower of London.

St. Paul's Cathedral.

the most beautiful and costly gems. Victoria's crown is' the richest in the collection, and comprises 5 rubies, 17 sapphires, 11 emeralds, 277 pearls, and 2783 diamonds. The guides are selected as guardians of the Tower from veterans who have distinguished themselves in their country's service. Our guide through the Wakefield Tower was a Yeoman of the Guard, dressed in the uniform of that body, instituted by Henry VII.

The Waxworks of Madam Tussaud are remarkable; they are ingenious imitations or representations of persons, life size, and arranged in groups or singly in several different rooms. They include the present royal family — the queen, princes, and princesses with their consorts — and many prominent individuals of present and past ages, dressed in rich costumes in the styles of their times.

The Museum of Practical Geology, on Jermyn Street, is valuable for one interested in science, as here are collected specimens of the mineral products of Great Britain, comprising marbles of many varieties, granites, and many other rocks. This collection, considered as a branch of the one in the British Museum, forms one of the largest and best of its kind in Europe, if not in the world, and affords great facilities for the study of minerals. Nearly all the museums of art and science in London are either free to the public, or the terms of admission are so low as to exclude no one anxious to profit by them. The government places before the people the means of object teaching unsurpassed by those of any other country, but elementary instruction is essential to interest the masses in the study of nature's wonders. If the United States, with her graded schools, could supplement them by collections like those of Great Britain, we should have a most admirable system of public education.

July 20 we took a sail on the Thames to Kew Gardens, a few miles from the great crowded city. These botanical gardens contain two hundred and forty acres, appropriated to the culture of trees and flowers, tropical and native, in the grounds and in glass houses. The building for palms and other foreign trees is 362 feet in length, 100 in width, and 64 in height; and passing through it one seems to be in a tropical region, for here are growing cocoanuts, bananas, coffee, ginger, nutmeg, and clove trees, and the cycadeæ and upas of Java. The fern-houses contain six hundred species of ferns. The Victoria Lily, with its immense leaves, and the cinchora, yielding quinine, are rare specimens of the vegetable kingdom. In one of the buildings is seen an extensive collection of different kinds of wood brought from the various colonies of Great Britain, and highly polished. The arrangement of these delightful gardens is largely due, it is said, to Sir William Hooker.

The Guildhall, where public meetings and elections are held, was built in 1411, during the reign of Henry VI., but only a small portion of the old structure remains. The great wall is one hundred and fifty-three feet long. It is here that the new lord mayor, as before mentioned, gives a public dinner, attended with stately ceremonies, when her Majesty's ministers and the law officers of the Crown are guests. The bill of fare comprises nearly fifty courses. At one end of the hall is a dais called the "Hustings," from an old count of that name. The term "hustings" is also applied to the places where citizens vote. There are several statues in the hall, comprising those of the Pitts, father and son, Nelson, Wellington, and Lord Mayor Beckford, father of the author of "Vathek"; but the most conspicuous statues are those named Gog and Magog and sometimes by other terms. What these grotesque figures represent or what business they have here, no one knows. Contiguous to the Guildhall is the City Free Library, with forty thousand volumes and several different reading-rooms. It was built in 1872, and has a museum containing relics of Roman art found in and about London, left by the Romans. They are more extensive than was supposed, until recent discoveries.

In a second visit to St. Paul's we saw the crypt, containing the tombs of some of England's distinguished men. The sarcophagus of Wellington is made of porphyry, resting on a granite base. The crypt contains a chariot made of the guns captured by the duke in his wars, on which the hero, after his death, was conveyed from Chelsea Hospital to St. Paul's for interment, and some drapery used at his funeral hangs on the walls of the apartment. Less ostentatious tombs hold the remains of several distinguished artists; as Wren, Reynolds, West, Turner, and others. The great bell of St. Paul's never rings except at the death and funeral of a member of the royal family, a bishop of London, a dean of St. Paul's, or the lord mayor during his term of office. There was a public procession to this church in 1814, on the occasion of peace, and at the funeral of the Duke of Wellington, in 1852, and on the recovery of the Prince of Wales from a serious illness, when the Queen attended St. Paul's in state.

From St. Paul's to St. James' Park would be a good distance for any other city than London. The park has nothing specially attractive. The most notable object, perhaps, is the large artificial pond; being in or near the heart of the town, it is a convenient place of rendezvous for the poorer classes. Buckingham Palace, the residence of the royal family when in London, occupies a site on one side of the park. The palace is comparatively new, having been built in the reigns of George IV. and William IV., though it was not occupied by the royal family until the reign of Queen Victoria. It is said to contain valuable paintings, but it is not easily accessible to visitors. St. James' Palace, opposite the park, is a very ordinary, irregular structure, formerly the town residence of the English sovereigns from William III. to the present ruler. Charles I. spent his last night here before his execution, and walked through the park to his scaffold before Whitehall, the palace of the English rulers from Henry VIII. to William III.

In the Chapel Royal of St. James, the Queen and all the members of her family, to this date, have been married. The palace is guarded by the Brigade of Household Guards, who are changed every forenoon at a quarter before eleven.

Next to St. James' Palace is the Marlborough House, built by the great duke whose name it bears, and afterwards bought by the Crown for the Princess Charlotte and Prince Leopold, though the princess did not live to occupy it. Clarence House, the residence of the Duke and Duchess of Edinburgh, joins St. James' Palace; and near Kensington Gardens is Kensington Palace, the birthplace of Victoria.

July 22 being the Sabbath, we attended church at Holborn Viaduct, and heard the Rev. Dr. Parker, who always attracts a large congregation; and in the afternoon we went to the Temple Church, near Temple Bar, built by the Knights-Templars in 1185. This quaint building, interesting from its associations, is partly circular, according to the style of the Templars' churches. The interior is very beautiful, with its clustered columns of polished marble, stained-glass windows, and its frescoed, arched ceiling, while its tombs and effigies of armed Templars associate it with the past. A monument of white marble, erected to Selden, stands at the right of the altar; but the recumbent figures of the Knights, in their warlike shrouds, constitute the most impressive objects. The choir in the centre of the church was reserved for the Benchers and students during service, while the "Round" was the place where lawyers received their clients.

The famous Inns of Court comprise the Inner Temple, Middle Temple, Lincoln's Inn, and Gray's Inn. The first two are connected with the Temple Church; and near are the Temple Gardens, famous for the red and white roses, badges of York and Lancaster. Adjoining the church are the Cloisters, a place used for students' walks. The government of the Inns of Court is invested in Benchers, the most distinguished members of the English Bar, comprising three thousand and eighty barristers and twenty-eight sergeants-at-law.

The next day we made a pilgrimage to Windsor Castle, the favorite residence of the Queen, which is situated on the Thames a little more than twenty miles from London, overlooking an extensive region dotted with green fields, trees, and villages. The castle or palace, for it is both, covers a large tract of ground, and is in the form of a quadrangle, with towers, walls, ramparts, and other means of fortification. The present building was begun by William the Conqueror, though the site was previously occupied by the Saxon kings for a palace; therefore it has been the dwelling-place of English sovereigns for more than nine centuries. The Round Tower or Keep was the prison of James I. of Scotland, and in another tower King John of France, taken prisoner by the Black Prince, was confined. The Chapel of St. George, where the Knights of the Garter were installed, is very rich in beautiful Gothic work. Henry VIII., George III., Charles I., and some others of the royal family were buried in this chapel.

Some of the state apartments of Windsor Castle are quite plain, especially those of the earlier sovereigns; those occupied by later monarchs are more elegant in finish and decorations. The paintings comprise the portraits of royal persons and some landscapes, and the walls are covered with tapestry. The Guard Room contains a silver shield ornamented with gold, presented to Henry VIII. by Francis I. on the Field of the Cloth of Gold. The Royal Stables were plain but substantial, though the Queen had taken many of the horses to Osborn. The Great Park, open to the public, contains about four thousands acres, affording beautiful and diversified scenery.

During the next two days we repeated our visit to Kensington Museum, Hyde Park, Gray's Inn Court, Soho Square, the Crystal Palace, and some other places of interest, and on the 27th took a sail on the Thames for Greenwich, where there is a Hospital for Seamen, occupying the site of the old palace which was the birthplace of Henry VIII. and his daughters, Mary and Elizabeth. Several buildings are appropriated to the use of the hospital, where are seen portraits, busts, and statues of England's naval commanders. Connected with the hospital is the Royal Naval School. The ancient royal park, of one hundred and seventy-four acres, contains the famous Greenwich Observatory, located on a hill which commands a fine view of London. The Ship Hotel, near the boat landing, has been distinguished, from time immemorial, for its dinners of the fish called "whitebait." From Greenwich we went to Dulwich, a beautiful rural town, the seat of a college for actors, established by James I. in 1619, which contains a gallery of paintings by the old masters. The new college, built 1866–70, is capable of receiving seven hundred students at once.

Our next visit was to Downing Street, well known in diplomatic circles; and under the direction of a guide, we entered the government building where the foreign secretary transacts his business. This edifice is very large, in the form of a quadrangle, and surrounded by a good-sized court. The staircase leading to the apartments where state balls and parties are held is an example of architectural work, made of different colored marbles. The floor is mosaic and the ceiling is frescoed. The ball, reception, and dining-rooms are all elegantly decorated, and the furniture of the first is scarlet and gold. The English government is liberal in the magnificence of its public buildings.

On the last Sabbath of our present visit to London, we attended services at the Abbey, conducted by the eloquent and popular Dean Stanley; but the crowd of hearers rendered it impossible to get near the speaker, so that we heard only a part of his discourse. The next day we left London for Paris, and, arriving at Newhaven, embarked for Dieppe; but the steamer did not sail until the next morning, on account of low tide. Consequently we lost the first train to Paris; but our disappointment was an advantage in the end, as it gave us an opportunity of seeing some of the notable places on the route.

Dieppe, lying between the chalk cliffs, is one of the fishing-ports of France, and a summer watering-place. It was destroyed by the English in 1694, but was rebuilt; and though a very old town, its present buildings are comparatively modern. It contains the statue of Admiral Duquesne, a native of the city.

Our next stopping-place was Rouen, the ancient capital of Normandy, a town situated on the Seine; and from its extensive manufactures it has been compared to Manchester, England. It occupies an important place in French history. The Place de la Pucelle contains an insignificant statue of Jeanne d'Arc, erected on the spot where she was burned by the English, in 1431. Rouen contains a Museum of Antiquities, with Roman relics and historic painted glass, a Ceramic Museum, and the Palace of Justice. The building called Les Halles, forming a part of the Vieille Tour, is where Prince Arthur was murdered by order of King John. The Cathedral of Notre Dame has a grand Gothic façade with elaborate decorations, and a spire rising four hundred and eighty-two feet from the ground. The Tour de Beurre was so called, it is said, from having been built with money paid for indulgences to eat butter during Lent. The interior of the church is four hundred and thirty-five feet in length, and is in the early pointed style, with beautiful carving and old painted glass. Rollo, the first Duke of Normandy, was buried in the chapel at the end of the nave, and the heart of Richard Cœur-de-Lion and the remains of some other royal persons are entombed in the choir. Besides the cathedral, the Church of St. Owen, begun in 1318 and completed in 1853, the Church of St. Maclou, with its triple porch, and some of the other public buildings are interesting to the tourist.

After a brief visit to this ancient city, we resumed our journey to Paris, the Mecca of all travellers, where we arrived late at night, and, after some bickering with " cabby," drove to our place of rest, the Hotel Britannique, on the Avenue Victoria.

## CHAPTER IV.

*France. — Scenes in Paris.*

WE made our first visit to the Louvre August 1; a marvel in itself, containing invaluable treasures of art, which will require many days' study before a tolerable idea of them can be gained. Leaving the Art Gallery, we went to the Arc de Triumphe, at the end of the Champs-Élysées, begun by Napoleon I., 1806, in commemoration of the victories of the French, and finished in 1838, by Louis Philippe. It is Grecian in design, one hundred and sixty-one feet in height, and cost more than two million dollars. The arch contains a large number of reliefs, representing the different battles of the great conqueror, and the names of nearly four hundred of his generals. Some of the other notable places in Paris or its neighborhood are the following : —

The Hotel de Dieu, the oldest hospital in the city, said to have been founded by King Clovis, 465–511, is on both sides of the Seine, the different parts being connected by a bridge; but on account of the inconvenient and unhealthy location, preparations were going forward for its removal.

The Jardin des Plantes are not equal to the Gardens at Kew, though they contain large collections from the animal, vegetable, and mineral kingdoms. The latter is large and well selected, but the zoological department is surpassed by that of Regent's Park. During the bombardment of Paris, in 1871, considerable damage was done to the garden, and many of the animals were killed for food during the siege. The Labyrinth, so called, is a complicated series of winding paths leading to the summit of a mound, forming a kind of pavilion shaded by a cedar of Lebanon.

GRAND BOULEVARD, PARIS.

HOTEL DE VILLE, PARIS.

The Museum of Geology and Mineralogy contains the collection of Haüy, the founder of crystallography and scientific mineralogy, while the collection of fossil animals was the work of Cuvier. The library of the museum comprises about seventy thousand volumes. The Museum of Comparative Anatomy, also instituted by Cuvier, is said to be the largest of its kind in Europe, and is furnished with laboratories and lecture rooms, to which students are admitted almost free of charge; and during the summer fifteen hundred attend free lectures. There are sixteen professors, and some of the most eminent naturalists of France have been connected with this museum.

Returning to Paris by boat, we made another visit to the Louvre, thence to the Gardens of the Tuileries and the Place de la Concord, remarkable for its decorations and its associations with historical events. It is considered the "culminating point" in "the most splendid city of the world." The centre of the "place" is occupied by an equestrian statue of Louis XV., erected in 1763. Here twelve hundred persons, it is said, lost their lives during a panic, on the occasion of celebrating the marriage of the Dauphin and Marie Antoinette.

The Obelisk of Luxor, a monolith of red Egyptian granite or syenite, brought from the great Temple of Thebes, where it was erected by Rameses the Great, 1350 B. C., is a little more than seventy-four feet in height, and weighs five hundred thousand pounds; it cost four hundred thousand dollars to remove it to France. Near the spot occupied by this obelisk, the guillotine was erected for the execution of Louis XVI.; and here between one and two thousand persons, including members of the royal family and other distinguished individuals, perished in the same manner. The Place de la Concord is adorned by eight colossal statues representing different cities, and is furnished with two fountains. During the Franco-German War this beautiful park was occupied by foreign troops, and subsequently was much injured during the civil war with the Communists.

The Palace of the Tuileries, begun in 1564, received additions from various sovereigns, but it was not completed until the reign of Louis Philippe. It was considered the finest specimen of the Renaissance style in France, but its historical interest far exceeds its architectural. Louis XVI., when brought a prisoner from Versailles, 1789, was confined here until his execution, in 1793; but it was not generally used as a royal abode until the time of Napoleon I. The Tuileries was a conspicuous figure in the great French Revolution, when it was assailed by the mob on several occasions. During one of these outbursts the Swiss Guards, two hundred National Guards, and one hundred domestics were massacred by the infuriated populace. When the National Convention was sitting in this palace, Bonaparte, with eight thousand troops, defended it, and cleared the streets of forty thousand assailants. The palace was sacked in the Revolution of July, 1830, and again in 1848, when the mob seized it after the flight of Louis Philippe, and in 1871 it was nearly ruined. It was captured and pillaged several times, and finally destroyed, with nothing left but parts of the walls. The Gardens of the Tuileries extend from the palace to the Place de la Concord, and, being supplied with grass-plots, flowers, water basins, statues, etc., constitute a favorite place of resort for Parisians.

The Champ de Mars, which we reached by boat, is a parade ground covering seven hundred and fifty thousand square yards. The earthen ramparts were raised by sixty thousand Parisians of both sexes in one week, to be in readiness for the Grande Fête de la Fédération, celebrated July, 1790. Prince Talleyrand, then Bishop of Autun, officiated, assisted by four hundred priests, at a temporary altar, in the presence of the king, National Assembly, and one hundred thousand spectators, when the sovereign swore fidelity to the Constitution. A Military School occupies a place in these grounds, which have been the theatre of imposing fêtes and parades, both peaceful and revolutionary.

The Hôtel des Invalides, founded by Louis XIV., as a home for aged, infirm, and wounded veterans, is near the Seine, not far from the Military School; and an esplanade, planted with trees, extends from the river to the hospital. The hotel, with its eighteen courts, occupies sixteen acres, and has a front six hundred feet in length. The church connected with it, considered one of the finest in Paris, has a nave two hundred and twenty feet long and seventy wide, with battle-flags suspended from the roof; three thousand of these were taken in the wars of Napoleon. His tomb, nineteen feet below the pavement, surrounded by a circular marble balustrade, is under the dome. The sarcophagus is said to be of polished granite from Russia, though it has been designated porphyry; marble staircases lead to the vault. Both Jerome and Joseph Bonaparte were buried in the Church of the Hôtel des Invalides.

To close the day's adventures, we went to the Bois de Boulogne, called the Hyde Park of Paris, though until 1852, when Napoleon III. improved and adorned it, and presented the park to the city, it was a kind of forest with walks and drives. It covers about two thousand five hundred acres, with numerous artificial ponds, or lakes, and waterfalls; the most remarkable being the Cascade de Longchamps, consisting of rock-work, with caverns and precipices, over which the water descends forty feet. A small Zoological Garden occupies a place in the park. The Bois de Boulogne embraces more variety than some of the English parks; but it has fewer large trees, many of them having been cut down by hostile armies. Having given some time to the public institutions and places, we resumed our study of the churches.

The celebrated Church of the Madeleine, built in imitation of a Grecian temple, was founded in 1764, but it was not completed until 1842. It is surrounded by porticos of fifty-two fluted columns, ninety-four feet in height. The south pediment has a representation in bas-relief of the Last Judgment, and on the bronze doors are pictured The Giving of the Commandments. The church, with its four domes, is decorated with colored marbles, and over the High Altar is a marble group of the Assumption of the Virgin, while paintings and statuary adorn the walls. Though the Madeleine is one of the most fashionable churches in Paris and cost half a million pounds, yet, in our humble opinion, it is open to criticism.

It is lighted from above, which to us seemed objectionable. The Cathedral of Notre Dame, on the Isle de la Cité, in the Seine, was begun 1160 ; but as is usual with the celebrated churches of Europe, it was not completed until centuries afterwards. During the Revolution, 1793, it was desecrated by the rabble and named the "Temple of Reason," where they celebrated the "Feast of the Goddess," personated by a printer's wife. The west front of the building has three lofty portals, ornamented with reliefs, representing the Last Judgment, the Life of the Virgin, and the Life of St. Anne ; and the niches at the side are filled with statues of angels, prophets, and saints, while a series of twenty-eight arches above are occupied by those of the kings of Judah. Two massive towers, two hundred and twenty-four feet in height, intended to be surmounted by stone spires, have been left incomplete. The small, slender spire, rising from the centre, appears insignificant on so grand a structure. The exterior is flanked on all sides by flying buttresses, but the small height of the piers and arches of the nave detracts from the grandeur of the interior. The length of the nave is three hundred and ninety feet, and the height of the central aisle is one hundred and five feet. Spacious vaulted galleries, the High Altar, consisting of a marble group representing the Descent from the Cross, various monuments, both ancient and modern, colored glass, the gilded railing about the choir, are all interesting objects. Some of the historical memorials have been removed or destroyed during the revolutions and civil wars that have so often visited Paris.

The Pantheon or Church of St. Geneviève, situated on the highest ground in Paris, is three hundred and forty feet in length and two hundred and sixty-seven in height to the top of the lantern, and of fine proportions, and is in the Italian style of architecture. The dome, resembling those of St. Paul's, London, and St. Peter's, Rome, though smaller, is very beautiful and graceful in design. The columns are Corinthian, and the pediment has a group of statuary in relief, representing France distributing rewards to her distinguished sons.

Voltaire, Rousseau, and many other Frenchmen are buried here. The ecclesiastical part of the building is hardly in keeping with other departments. The choir is inferior, and some of the stone-work is entirely bare of ornament, while there are but few paintings, though the interior of the dome, as well as the exterior, is elegant. This edifice has a romantic history — a church in 1762, a pantheon in 1792, a church in 1822, a pantheon in 1831, and a church for the third time in 1853. It was a place of refuge for the insurgents of 1849, and suffered during the bombardment by the Prussians in 1871.

The Church of St. Germain l'Auxerrois, opposite the grand colonnade of the Louvre, is a fine and interesting building associated with historical and tragical events. It was founded by one of the early kings, and was the Court Church, but no part of the original edifice remains; the present structure dates from the twelfth century. The bell, now in the Palais de Justice, gave the signal for the massacre on St. Bartholomew's Eve, August, 1572. The church was sacked by a mob in 1831, and restored by Louis Philippe in 1838. The Lady Chapel forms a complete church of itself, but the numerous monuments that once adorned this ancient building are nearly all demolished or removed.

The Cemetery of Père-la-Chaise, located within the fortifications of the city, contains two hundred and twelve acres, and has been used as a burying-ground since 1804. The street leading to it suggests melancholy thoughts, being mostly occupied by dealers in sepulchral monuments, wreaths, and other artificial decorations for tombs. The immortelles are appropriate, but the bead-work and black flowers seemed inappropriate and deficient in taste. The grounds of Père-la-Chaise are beyond the walls, and are hilly, with clusters of trees in some portions. There are about sixteen thousand monuments, constructed, apparently, of stone from the Paris Basin, crowded closely together, with little artistic beauty, except in a few instances. Nearly all the " memorials " about the graves consisted of immortelles and bead-work, more appropriate for a child's playhouse than for a tomb. The avenues are badly paved, and far from neat in appearance, while the method of interments are repulsive. One class of graves can be occupied only five years, another ten, but a third is held by absolute right and cannot be used for other bodies; the latter, it is said, is the system now in use. Several of Napoleon's marshals, persons of noble birth, distinguished authors and artists, including Molière, La Fontaine, Balzac, Arago, Rossini, De Musset, Cuvier, and others were buried in Père-la-Chaise. The Jewish Cemetery within the grounds contains the remains of Mlle. Rachel and of the Queen and Prince of Oude, while in the English department are several good monuments. Even the tombs of Paris have not been respected by the rude hand of violence. In the war of 1814 the Russians drove off the defenders of this sacred spot and bivouacked here, and in this place the Communists made their last stand, where three hundred of their associates fell among the tombs, and a large number were buried in one grave. One of the most interesting graves, to the readers of romance, is that of Heloise and Abelard, whose remains have been deposited here. A monument was being constructed to the devoted lovers, but no one was working on it when we were there. What a strange history does Paris afford: so full of horrors, so replete with gayety and tragedy. Evidences of these contrasts are afforded in almost every part of this remarkable city.

From the quietness of Père-la-Chaise, we went to Au Bon Marché, one of the largest stores in Paris, situated on the Rue de Bac. The building is supplied with a library, a small gallery of paintings, and other attractions. Its rival, the Magasin du Louvre, is on the other side of the Seine. Both stores are immense, and seem like a city of shops with almost every kind of merchandise.

In the evening we went to see a fine display of jewelry by gaslight, at the Palais Royal, which stands on the site of the palace occupied by Cardinal Richlieu, which, after his death reverted to the Crown. The building was the scene of the disgraceful carousals of the regent and his daughter, and was nearly consumed by fire, but rebuilt in 1781. This historical building has been conspicuous in the revolutions of France: it was plundered in 1848, when the magnificent library of Louis Philippe was destroyed, and again in 1871, by the Communists.

The palace called the Hotel du Luxembourg was begun by Marie de Medici in 1615, who left it to the regent, the Duke of Orleans. It passed into different hands, and was used for various purposes, and was the place of meeting for the Chamber of Peers until the fall of the Second Empire. Since the destruction of the Hotel de Ville, it has been used as the Prefecture de la Seine. The state departments were not open to the public, but a part of the palace is employed as a gallery for the works of living French artists, corresponding to the Royal Academy of London, and is open to visitors. In this respect the Royal Academy has an advantage over the gallery of the Louvre, which admits no work of art until the artist has been dead at least ten years.

Some of the paintings were fine, others were mediocre. We had expected to see more of the productions of Rosa Bonheur in Paris, having found a number of them in other places; there was one of her paintings, called "Ploughing with Oxen," which occupied a place in one room of the gallery. The Gardens of the Luxembourg, with their trees, vines, vases, fountains, and statues, are a favorite place of resort for the citizens of Paris. At the rear of the gardens is the statue of Marshal Ney, marking the place where he was shot by the Allies in 1815. The Communists in 1871 made attempts to destroy the palace, but were prevented by the soldiers, who killed many of the insurgents.

The Palace of the Louvre is one of the largest and most beautiful in Paris or, probably, in France. The present structure occupies the site of an early feudal fortress built by Philip Augustus in 1200 A. D., and reconstructed, in part, during the reign of Francis I.; but it remained for Napoleon III. to complete it in its grand and beautiful form. Napoleon I. constituted it a Museum of Art. The Communists attempted to burn it, but only the Library of Art was destroyed, the greater portion of the other valuable treasures having been sent to the arsenal of Brest for safety. The collection of the Louvre is the largest in Europe, and has been pronounced the finest on the whole, though in Italian art it falls below those of Florence and the Vatican; in Dutch art, to those of the Hague, Amstersdam, and Antwerp; in Spanish, to those of Madrid; in Roman antiquities, to those of the Capitol and Naples, and in Greek sculpture, to the British Museum. Many visits to the Museum of the Louvre are necessary to gain only a general idea of what it contains, since it presents the whole history of art. We began to feel the need of a change after a succession of daily visits to different parts of the city, therefore planned an excursion to Versailles, about a dozen miles from Paris.

The celebrated city of Versailles, long the residence of the French Court, was once a barren region of sand, until Louis XIII. built a mansion as a resort for those pursuing the chase. Louis XIV. erected a magnificent palace on this spot, to prove what art could do against nature, and the visitor to this splendid royal domain can see how well he succeeded. The work of construction was begun in 1661, but it is not known what fabulous sums were lavished upon the enterprise, which suggests the thought that here was an incipient cause of the bloody Revolution a little later. The unfortunate Louis XVI. and Marie Antoinette were taken from this place by an excited mob, in 1789, and later suffered death by the guillotine. It was not much used by the royal princes after this event, until Louis Philippe restored it, and made it a museum for works illustrating the history of France. In front of the palace is the Place d'Armes, from which radiate three broad avenues; while between two extensive wings is the Cour Royal, and beyond this, the Cour Marbre, which has been the theatre of important events. The king's chamber, on the second floor opposite this court, was furnished with a balcony, from which his death was announced and his successor proclaimed. The clock was stopped at the moment of his decease, and remained silent for an indefinite time. King

NAPOLEON'S TOMB.

COLONNADE OF THE LOUVRE.

William of Prussia was proclaimed Emperor of Germany, in front of this palace, December 18, 1870, during the Franco-German War.

The Palace of Versailles is so extensive, being 1,362 feet in length, that between two and three hours are required to walk through the rooms, without stopping to examine carefully the objects it contains. The Chapel, 105 feet long and 79 in height, is the place where royal marriages have been solemnized. A ball was given at this palace in 1855, at which Queen Victoria and 4,000 other persons were present. The galleries and halls are almost numberless, and are adorned with paintings and statues; but of all these magnificent apartments, the Grand Gallery of Louis XIV., called the Galerie des Glaces, is the most splendid. It is 239 feet long, with 17 windows opening upon the garden, while on the walls, profusely decorated with gilt and paintings, are mirrors corresponding to the windows.

The Galerie de Constantine, embracing a suite of seven rooms, contains some of the best paintings, mostly battle scenes, in modern French history. The Attic du Nord is filled with historical portraits, including those of some eminent persons belonging to other countries. The Salon d'Hercule contains one of the largest paintings known on a ceiling; it was by L. Moyne. This hall, once a part of the chapel, was used by court preachers, including Bossuet, Massillon, and Bourdalous. The Salon d'Apollon, or Salle du Trone, was used for the reception of foreign embassadors, and contained the silver throne, afterwards sold to raise funds. Among the battle scenes in the Galerie des Batailles, a hall 392 feet in length, is a painting representing the battle of Yorktown, executed by Conder. The rooms with paintings, statues, and busts of the eminent men of France are too numerous to specify. The palace may be said to contain the pictorial history of France from an early period to the present time.

The gardens and park are as interesting as the palace of which they are adjuncts; but what is most remarkable is that the site was once a sandy waste, and that the trees had all been cut down, and the park had been replanted as late as 1775. Avenues, fountains, rock-work, trees, grass-plots, and flowers constitute a part of this delightful place. A Grand Canal, one mile in length, in the form of a Greek cross, occupies the grounds opposite the palace, while the Grand and Petit Trianons are in another part. It is a magnificent sight, when all the fountains are playing together, which does not often occur. The small fountains begin to play about four o'clock, P. M., and the large fountain, or Basin de Neptune, about five o'clock, when one can hardly imagine a more fairy-like scene. Our visit to Versailles was a memorable one, and we returned to Paris highly pleased and instructed by the day's excursion.

The Bourse is said to be one of the best examples of classical architecture in Paris. It is 212 feet long, 126 wide, and 57 in height, and is surrounded by a colonnade of 66 Corinthian columns. The corners are occupied by four statues representing Commerce, Commercial Law, Industry, and Agriculture. During business hours ladies are not admitted.

The Place Vendome is conspicuous in French history. The statue of Louis XIV., which originally occupied the centre, was destroyed in the first Revolution, and in its place Napoleon erected a column in imitation of Trajan's Column, at Rome, to commemorate his campaigns in 1805. The stone shaft was encased in metal obtained from cannon taken in battle, and covered with figures about 8 feet in height, that of Napoleon crowning the monument; the height to the top of the statue was 155 feet. After Paris was occupied by the Allied armies, the mob overthrew the statue, when it was melted down. Louis Philippe replaced the figure of the first emperor, but the Communists in 1871 pulled down the column. In 1874 it was replaced, and in 1875 the statue was restored; but what may be the future destiny of this monument, is uncertain, since the Parisian mobs seem to have an hereditary *penchant* to overthrow the structures of their own beautiful city.

The Hotel de Cluny, including the old Roman Palais des Thermes or Baths, is a very interesting place to the antiquary, where remains of the Baths are still to be seen. It is supposed the Emperor Constantine built a palace on the site, about 300 A. D., where Julian was proclaimed emperor. The Roman palace became subsequently the possession of the Abbey of Cluny; and the present hotel, erected by one of the abbots, was rented to the royal family, who occasionally resided here. It became the property of the nation at the Revolution, and is now used for a Museum of Ancient, Mediæval, and Modern Art; comprising objects in glass, enamel, pottery, carving, gems, jewelry, costumes, etc., arranged in a large number of apartments. Among these curiosities is a set of chessmen cut out of rock crystal.

The Manufactory for Gobelin Tapestry was established in 1450 by John Gobelin, but since 1662 it has belonged to the state.

Many of the rich tapestries found in the different palaces of Europe were manufactured at these works, where from twenty to thirty looms are employed in copying into these beautiful fabrics the best productions of the old masters and modern painters. The warp is hung vertically; while in the manufacture of carpets the workman stands in front of his work, with his copy above his head, for tapestry, his place is back of it, with his pattern behind him. The labor is all done with a needle, and some pieces require from five to ten years to finish them, at a cost of six thousand pounds. We saw only a few artists at work upon these tapestries, and it is said the whole number employed is comparatively small, usually from forty to fifty. The manufactory was burned by the Communists in 1871, when tapestries valued at one million francs were lost; only fifteen pieces were saved. On the same day about twenty Dominicans were murdered near this establishment.

The town of St. Cloud suffered in the Franco-German War, and the Palace of St. Cloud is in ruins, having been destroyed by French shells from Mt. Valérien in 1870. It was the favorite resort of some of the sovereigns of France, and it was here that Henry III. was assassinated. The park comprises about one thousand acres, and in front of the palace are two artificial cascades, one of them forming a large cataract. The garden was named Trocadero from a battle won in Spain. The walk through the Park of St. Cloud to Sèvres is charming.

The Porcelain Manufactory, a government institution, was established at Sèvres in 1770, by Louis XV. At first translucent porcelain was made, but since the discovery of kaolin, opaque ware has been manufactured. The Sèvres ware is remarkable for the beautiful manner in which it is painted. The exhibition of pottery at this manufactory is magnificent. Vases of every conceivable pattern and color, plates, cups, dishes of various kinds, busts, statues and pictures, besides numerous ornamental and useful objects, adorn the rooms of the establishment. We were admitted to the work-rooms and witnessed the process of making these various articles; and the ease and skill with which the artist could transform the plastic clay into so many different forms, with so little apparent effort, was surprising.

The Isle de la Cité, in the Seine, is an interesting locality, since it constituted the principal part of mediæval Paris, and is at present the site of many famous buildings, including the Palais de Justice, Notre Dame, Hotel Dieu, and others, besides constituting the legal quarter of the city. It is supposed that a Roman palace or castle once occupied the site of the Palais de Justice, which was the residence of the royal family until the close of the reign of Charles V., when it was used for a parliament building, courts of justice, and a prison. Nearly all the original structure was destroyed by fire. This palace has a tragical history, for here were held many of the trials of the Revolution, when the unfortunate victims of the guillotine were conducted from the Conciergerie, or prison, to be tried, including Queen Marie Antoinette, Madame Elizabeth, and many other distinguished persons. In September, 1792, an infuriated mob massacred 238 of the prisoners.

The Magasin du Louvre, on the north side of the Seine, corresponds, in some features, to Au Bon Marché, on the south side. Both are immense stores and seem to monopolize a large share of the trade in Paris, if we are to judge from their numerous patrons.

THE PANTHEON, PARIS.

L'ARC DE TRIOMPHE, PARIS.

Sainte Chapelle, considered one of the best specimens of Gothic architecture in France, is especially distinguished for its magnificent colored glass windows. This little architectural gem is enclosed in the courtyard of the Palais de Justice. Its slender, graceful spire is seen shooting up over the sombre pile surrounding it; and when the work of destruction, during the lawless reign of the Communists, was going on around it, this building was spared as if by a miracle. The design of Sainte Chapelle, founded in 1242 and completed five years after, was for a depository of sacred relics, which, tradition claims, included thorns from the Saviour's crown, a fragment of the true cross, and others. At the time of the Revolution, it was desecrated by being used as a clubroom, and then as a storehouse for grain, but it was restored by Louis Philippe and devoted to its original use. Divine service is performed in it only once a year, when the Courts of Law are opened, in November.

The chapel comprises two stories. The upper, which is gorgeously decorated, was intended for the members of the royal family, with its interior walls and roof covered with painting and gilding, while the columns of the nave support statues of the twelve Apostles. The windows are filled with scenes from Scripture and the martyrdom of the saints. The lower chapel was intended for the servants of the royal household, and contains several tombstones in the pavement.

The Church of St. Eustache is the second in size of those of Paris, Notre Dame being first. It is said to have the largest and wealthiest parish in the city. The interior is three hundred and thirty-seven feet in length and one hundred and nine in height. The building affords a study in the different styles of architecture, Grecian, Gothic, and Renaissance. The West façade is Doric below and Corinthian above, while the interior affords Doric, Ionic, Corinthian, and composite pilasters. The church contains numerous monuments, painted glass, and carved wood-work.

We made another visit to the Louvre collection, our last until our return after many months' wandering in other lands.

## CHAPTER V.

*From France to Belgium and Switzerland.*

AUGUST 13 we started for Amiens, and on our arrival went to the Hotel du Rhine; and after a short rest we found our way to the Cathedral, the object of our visit. It was founded in 1220, and is considered one of the finest in France, if not one of the noblest Gothic churches in Europe. The west front is entered by three very large, deeply recessed portals, with arches supported by statues instead of columns, while statuettes are employed for other architectural purposes. The building is 442 feet in length, with a spire ascending 422 feet from the ground. Its great height increases its grandeur, especially in the interior.

Amiens is a manufacturing town with a population of more than 60,000, but during our short visit the whole time was given to the Cathedral. Our next stopping-place was to be Brussels, where we did not arrive until late in the afternoon, on account of delays caused by taking the wrong train. The next day after our arrival was "The Fête of the Assumption," consequently a holiday for the Belgians. After visiting a church on Rue Neuve, we went to the Cathedral of St. Gudule, where there were imposing services in honor of the Virgin, with a display of episcopal banners, offerings, flowers, etc. Other places of interest in Brussels were the Park connected with the royal palace, the ducal palace, which contained a collection of paintings and statuary in plaster, the Hotel de Ville, with its spire rising 364 feet, and the Place des Martyrs, with a small monument erected to persons who had suffered on account of their religious principles. The exterior of the Hotel de Ville was quite ornate, and the interior contained some paintings of no special merit, gobelin tapestry, and a variety of other objects; but the Civic hall and ballroom were quite plain. We were detained some time at a church on account of a thunder-shower, the first we had witnessed since leaving America.

August 16 was a memorable day in the history of our travels, when we visited the famous battle-field of Waterloo. The distance from Brussels is about 12 miles, through a region of charming scenery. The field of one of the greatest conflicts of modern times is several minutes' walk from the railway station; and on our arrival we went to the Mound, in the centre of the battle-field, which is more than 100 feet in height, crowned by a monument with the figure of a lion on the top. The ascent to the Mound is made by steps on the outside, from which extensive views of the surrounding country are afforded. The land is perfectly level, covered with trees, grass, and fields of grain, with here and there a peasant's dwelling. A guide, who said he participated in the battle, manifested an old veteran's enthusiasm, and pointed out the positions of the different armies, he being in that of the Allies; the place where Napoleon entered the field, and that of his retreat after the conflict, and mentioned several incidents of that decisive event.

As the "Day of Waterloo" occurred in 1815, the guide must have been a very young soldier at the time. He said he was an accredited guide and had explained the battle to many distinguished visitors, including princes and sovereigns. On one side of the plain is the forest, so memorable in the great struggle; but it is impossible to imagine the fearful scenes of carnage that deluged these peaceful fields in human blood. Belgium is a level country, very populous and fertile, with vast forests and rich farms; but the scenery at Waterloo is rather monotonous. Besides the Monument and a small museum of relics, there is little to engage the attention of visitors; therefore after a few hours spent here, we returned to Brussels.

This city has a neat and agreeable appearance, and has been compared to Paris, but it must be Paris on a small scale. The buildings are constructed of a light-colored stone, similar to that used in the French capital; is not affected by the weather, and imparts a cheerful aspect to the streets, but there are not many elegant structures. Another visit to the Cathedral gives a better idea of its special features, notably the pulpit in fine carved wood. The church is situated on elevated ground, and is approached by flights of steps. The royal palace is plain in its exterior, the chief attraction being the park belonging to it.

Leaving Brussels, a few hours' ride brought us to Antwerp, an old city with narrow, crooked, and dirty streets, quaint buildings with pointed roofs and notched gables, looking like steps to the ridge-pole. The most interesting features of the city are the churches and the Museum of Art. The Cathedral is a grand pile, with a steeple reaching 403 feet and a chime of 99 bells. Its decorations are very rich; the choir, pulpit, confessionals, and screens are highly ornamented with carving, while some of the chapels are very gorgeous. The third centennial celebration of the birth of Rubens occurs on the 19th inst., and preparations are making for a great festival. Very rich banners are suspended in the Cathedral, which contains the masterpieces of the great painter. The Descent from the Cross is the chef d'œuvre of this prolific artist, and exhibits his excellences without his defects; for instance, grossness in delineating the human figure. The Church of St. Paul is in some respects peculiar. The statuary on the exterior represents scenes in the life of Christ; one group delineates souls in purgatory.

The Museum contains many good pictures, including some of the works of notable Flemish masters, some of large size, but the exquisite little Dutch landscapes were especially pleasing. Rubens, of course, graces the walls of the Museum. The streets of Antwerp are badly paved except in the newer part of the town, which renders walking uncomfortable.

August 18 we began our journey for Cologne through a level but fertile region, with noble trees scattered along the route. Our journey was uneventful until we came to Aix-la-Chapelle, where we met with some annoyances to which travellers are liable, especially if ignorant of the customs of the country. Our tickets were for the "train ordinaire," and we

AMIENS CATHEDRAL.

WATERLOO. (From an old Print.)

must wait for it or pay an additional sum to go on. As we did not know how long we might be detained, we chose the latter alternative. But a new difficulty arose: we were in German territory, and French money would not pass; so we had to begin our lesson in marks, pfennigs, and other outlandish money. There would be a jubilee among travellers if there was a universal currency.

After paying exorbitant fees to different porters, we resumed our journey and arrived in Cologne late in the afternoon, when we went to the Hotel du Dome, opposite the great Cathedral, to which we paid our first visit after a short rest. The impression it made on our minds was indescribable; it seemed the work of a divine hand, so beautiful, so grand did it appear, while the dim light and shadows lent a magical influence to the scene; the next day we attended services in the Cathedral. This wonderful building is constructed of light-colored stone, in Gothic style, and is conspicuous for its towers, turrets, buttresses, arches, and windows, with their decorations. It is five hundred and eleven feet in length and a hundred and forty-nine in breadth. The great height of the Cathedral, the beauty of its decorations, the splendid stained-glass windows, the great number of arches, rendered fairy-like by the soft tints of colored rays, the lofty clustered columns, crowned by carved capitols, the lengthened vistas from the nave and aisles, the high clerestory and triforium, all impress the visitors with solemn delight. It seems to us that a grand cathedral approaches nearer the works of the Creator than any other object made by man.

The Church of St. Ursula is an old dilapidated building, famous only for containing the bones of eleven thousand nuns murdered by the Huns. These relics are placed around the walls, forming a decoration not particularly agreeable. The Museum contains some fine specimens of stained glass and some good modern paintings, especially landscapes. The collections of other objects are quite ordinary.

Cologne, with a population of about a hundred and thirty-five thousand at the time of our visit, is not a very beautiful city, its chief attraction being the celebrated Cathedral, which holds a first rank among ecclesiastical buildings.

August 20 we embarked on board the steamboat for a sail on the Rhine. From Cologne to Bonn, the scenery is very monotonous, but above the latter place it is more variegated, and at the Drachinfelds the mountains are quite lofty; but not until we reached Coblence, did we find really grand views. The precipitous rocks were covered with a light soil adapted to the cultivation of the grape. One of the peculiar features of the Rhine is afforded by the terraces on the sides of the mountains in a series of tiers for the vines. These cultivated patches on the steep declivities present a novel sight, and suggest the idea of danger to the grape gatherers. Though there are steps placed at certain distances apart, leading to the terraces, yet the effort to reach the grapes on the brink must be attended with some risk.

We confess the Rhine was disappointing; it has no special attraction aside from its associations; the water, of a peculiar green tint, is muddy, therefore lacks the charm of a clear, pellucid stream. Its chief interest arises from its connection with historical events. Our own poet was correct when he called it the "castelled Rhine," on account of the great number of ruined castles on its banks. These remains form a link between the past and the present in human history, and reveal the state of civilization in early times.

Coblence is the largest town between Cologne and Mayence. The strong fortress of Erenbreightstein is called the Gibraltar of the Rhine, and it looked as if entitled to the proud distinction, for to our unmilitary eye it appeared perfectly impregnable. We regretted that it was so late in the day, when we passed "Bingen on the Rhine," that we could see but little of the town, which appeared to be delightfully situated on the hills that run parallel with the river.

Mayence, the end of our river excursion and where we passed the night, is not an interesting town. The Cathedral, which was undergoing repairs, was built of red sandstone in the Romanesque style, and its only attractive feature was the painted ceiling and the wood carving of the choir. The streets of the city are narrow; the market-place occupies an open square, where the women, in their quaint dresses, may be seen, having come from the country around with their produce and wares for sale. From Mayence we went to Heidelberg to see the remains of the famous castle; and arriving at the station, we engaged a carriage and drove to the ruins by a circuitous route. The castle occupied a high position on the side of a mountain covered with trees, different from most other hills on the Rhine.

This stronghold, built of red sandstone, was very large, and a considerable part, with the walls and apartments, is still preserved. The views from the castle are fine, overlooking the town and the deep ravine at the foot of the hill on which it was built. The winding paths, shady and cool, make it a charming spot, but our pleasure was marred by the hurried manner our guide conducted us over the ruins. We were shown the great "Tun" in the cellar which would hold three hundred thousand bottles of wine, besides another receptacle for liquor, nearly as large. Our guide told us that the "Court Fool" of one of the barons was accustomed to drink eighteen bottles of wine a day. We were shown the kitchen, which seemed like a cellar with a large chimney, where a whole ox was roasted at one time. The wine and the ox are pretty substantial proofs of the drinking and gastronomic habits of early times. Heidelberg offers many other attractions to the tourist, but our plans compelled us to forego the pleasure of seeing them, and after a few hours spent here we left for Strasburg. Our route lay through a level, uninteresting region, but it was not in a direct line, since the railway makes a large circuit nearly two thirds around the town, outside the fortifications, but the tall spire of the celebrated Cathedral served as a landmark. This building, the chief object of our visit to this place, is made of sandstone, and is memorable for the height of the spire, more than five hundred feet, and the highest in Europe, reaching to the clouds. One is inspired with a feeling of awe at the magnificence of the edifice. The carving of the principal entrance is remarkable for its delicate beauty.

Though the Cathedral was founded in 1015, yet at the time of our visit it was still unfinished, but has since been completed. The original design was for another tower and spire to correspond with the one finished; as it now appears, the building is wanting in symmetry, and might be compared to a veteran with one arm. The interior is less grand than the Cologne Cathedral; the columns are made of stone of two different colors, giving them a banded appearance. The most conspicuous features of the interior are the elegant carving of the pulpit and the remarkable astronomical clock. The Cathedral was considerably damaged in the Franco-German War, and during the bombardment the library of nearly two hundred thousand volumes was burned. Strasburg, formerly a "free city," was seized by Louis XIV., and remained in possession of the French until 1870, when it passed into the hands of the Germans. The walls and fortifications of this important military post prove that a severe struggle would be necessary to capture such a stronghold, if the besieged made a stubborn resistance.

After leaving Strasburg our journey was through the Black Forest, affording some of the grandest and most picturesque scenery we had thus far seen. We passed over and around mountains, with an occasional tunnel; and as we continued to ascend we could look down upon the road we had just passed over, sometimes on the right and then on the left, while along the whole distance fertile valleys and small villages were scattered, adding an agreeable variety to the landscape.

The country on the south slope of the mountains spreads out into plains reaching to Lake Constance, which affords beautiful scenery, though less grand than that of some of the other Swiss lakes. This lake is a lovely sheet of water, clear and of an emerald green, though it has been called blue — it may be sometimes, as blue is a more poetical color than green, and forms a better contrast to vegetation.

The city of Constance has an unenviable notoriety, as having been the place of the trial and martyrdom of John Huss and Jerome of Prague, about 1414 A. D. It is a quiet and rather

CATHEDRAL AT STRASBURG

GREAT CLOCK, STRASBURG CATHEDRAL

dull German town on the shore of the lake. As the day was rainy we did not take our intended sail on its waters, to visit the quaint town of Bregenze, saved by the heroism of a young maiden three hundred years ago; but when the storm ceased we took a walk through the town. The avenue bordering the lake forms a delightful promenade, with pretty houses and charming villas on the German side, and cultivated hills on the Swiss side. The Cathedral, begun in 1048, was rebuilt in the beginning of the sixteenth century. Its principal characteristics are the carved oak doors and the cloisters on the north side; while the brown stone of the building, with its soft tint, harmonizes with the green moss that covers it.

We left Constance, August 24, for Schaffhausen and Zurich by steamboat, and had a delightful sail, with the mountains in sight, while Stein Tower, crowning a lofty crag, stood like a sentinel over the surrounding country. The waters of the Rhine, as they issue from the lake, are a clear green, quite different from that farther below. The Falls of Schaffhausen, or more properly Westhausen, are the most noted in Switzerland. The river at this place is bordered by a high, precipitous bank, and forms a series of small cataracts, when it finally dashes over sharp rocks, and is broken into spray, rising in fine mist. In the middle of the cataract, two rocks ascend far above the foam, one of them being worn by the water until it forms two piers with an arch, like those of a bridge. The scenery about the falls is picturesque and sometimes grand, but Schaffhausen bears no comparison with Niagara. The encroachments of art on such grand scenes are unpleasantly obtrusive; for the mind, in its meditative moods, desires to hold intercourse with nature alone in her grand lessons.

Zurich is picturesquely situated on the declivity of lofty hills bordering Lake Zurich and the river Limmat; the upper part of the town commands a fine view of the surrounding mountains. Some of the more recent buildings are tasteful, and remind one of Brussels; but there are not many public edifices of special interest. The Post Office, of light-colored sandstone, is one of the finest. The Cathedral is an old building, very plain, the only ornaments being a painted glass window and a little carving on the capitals of the short, clumsy Norman columns. The only interest attached to this building arises from its being the place where the reformer Zwingli preached. The older part of the city has some quaint buildings and narrow streets.

The route from Zurich to Lucerne is through a delightful region, where we gained a full view of the lofty, snow-crowned Alps, so inspiring to the imagination, without the disappointment often attending the first sight of remarkable objects; they even exceeded our most sanguine expectations. Art has faithfully represented the grandeur of Alpine scenery, as well as art can represent nature; but when she has done her utmost, she falls very far below the reality. It is much easier to represent a mountain, a tree, a green meadow than a cascade, a flowing river, or the surging of an ocean billow, for the reason that sound and motion cannot be transferred to canvas, and these form a part of Swiss scenes. Lucerne is delightfully situated on the lake of the same name and the River Reuss, in an amphitheatre of lofty, snow-capped mountains and fertile foothills; it is considered one of the most charming towns, for its location, in Switzerland. The Righi, Mt. Pilatus, and the white tops of Uri and Engelberg are in sight. The walls and water towers of the town were built in 1385; the latter contain the archives of the city. The Cathedral, dating from 1506, contains a celebrated organ, a rival to that of Freiburg, which we had the good fortune to hear.

Near the Cathedral is the "Lion of Lucerne," the work of Thorwaldsen, completed in 1821, to commemorate the death of seven hundred and eighty-six Swiss soldiers who fell in defending the Tuileries in Paris August, 1792. The Lion, cut in high relief in a rock occupying its natural position, is twenty-eight feet in length, and is represented as reclining in a grotto, in a dying condition. This monument is one of the grandest and most impressive we have ever seen; it has the simplicity of nature, and is an appropriate tribute to the brave heroes who fell at the post of duty. What are called the "Glacial

HOTEL AND CASCADE OF THE GIESSBACH.

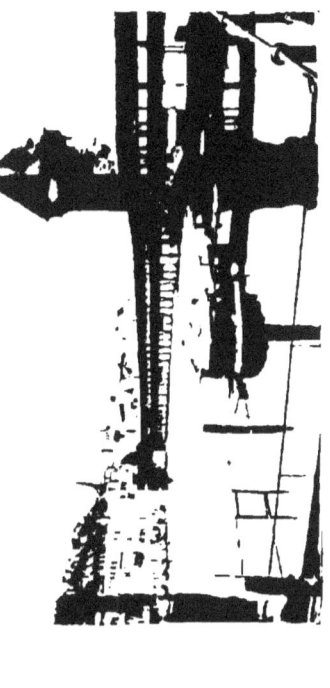

VIEW OF LUCERNE

ALTORF AND LAKE.

THE LION OF LUCERNE.

Gardens" consist of deep wells or holes made in the solid rock, by the action of glaciers, it is supposed. They are smooth and circular, and were probably caused by stones carried around by water. In some of these cavities were large rounded pebbles, which, like the pestle of a mortar, may have assisted in the work of excavation. The largest cavity is twenty-eight feet in diameter and thirty-three in depth. The sandstone rocks contain fossil shells and plants, while some of the bowlders are granite, which proves they were transported thither, since granite is not a native rock in this vicinity. The discovery of these pits was made in 1872, by workmen who were digging a cellar.

Monday, August 27, a memorable event occurred in our experience, the ascent of Mount Righi. The weather was all that could be desired for such an enterprise. The sail to Fluelen, at the end of Lake Lucerne, was in view of grand and picturesque scenery, mountains covered with snow, others with rocky walls and buttresses of great height, and others still were dotted to their summits with Swiss cottages and cultivated tracts of land. It seems incredible that the mountaineers can climb to these, apparently, inaccessible steeps, to gather their scanty crops. Lake Lucerne is famous in the poetry and romances of the country, as the scene of the adventures of William Tell. The Swiss, evidently, believe in the deeds of their hero, as his name is in some manner connected with different localities. If any person thinks Tell was a mythical character, let him come to Switzerland, when he will change his opinion; for traditions connected with events so near our own times, and possessing so much consistency, must have a foundation in historical facts. Scepticism is often more credulous than faith. On the summits of many Alpine mountains are to be seen small villages and isolated hotels, as if intended for the inhabitants of the air or the planetary worlds.

Returning from Fluelen, we landed at Vitznau for the train to the top of Righi, and after some delay started on our aerial journey. The road passes along the sides of the mountains, which are not very precipitous, except in a few places, and by cultivated fields extending to the summits. Magnificent prospects were open to our view until we reached the top, when a glorious vision burst upon us. Half way around the horizon, peak after peak, with their rocky and snow-covered crests of indefinite forms, reached to heaven, so that clouds and mountains were blended in outlines forming a panorama one might imagine to be a vision of the celestial world; indeed, it was difficult to believe the view was of earthly scenes. No pen or pencil could possibly represent the complete beauty and grandeur of the sight. On the other side of Righi, lying at its base, are beautiful valleys with their lovely lakes and green fields.

The Alps thus far are different from other mountains we have seen; their geological structure is different. The rocks, varied in appearance, sometimes assume the forms of walls and castles, while their soft tints afford a very agreeable effect, especially when they are suffused by the rays of the setting sun. Our day of exquisite enjoyment did not end without an accident to the engineer of the train, whose foot was crushed by the wheels; we were thankful it did not prove fatal.

Our journey from Lucerne to Brienz was made partly by steamboat and partly by the "diligence," through a region of grand and beautiful scenery, while the snow-clad Wetterhorn, with its triple peaks, was in sight most of the way. This was our first experience in crossing the Alps; and though this pass is less remarkable than most others, yet as we advanced, the views were grander, approaching the sublime.

Brienz is a small village on the shore of a lake which we crossed for the Falls of Griesbach, where we intended to spend the night in order to witness the illumination. Nothing could be more romantic than this place. The hotel is on the side of the mountain, some distance from its base, and opposite the Falls, which in the evening are illuminated by calcium lights, producing a magical effect. The spectacle lasts only a very short time, and the expense is defrayed by the travellers, whether they seek the entertainment or not. The next

morning we made an early visit to the Falls before the other guests were stirring, that we might be alone with nature in one of her grandest displays.

Lakes Hagel and Hexen are the source of these celebrated Falls, which descend from a great height, and are broken into fourteen distinct cascades, crossed by several foot-bridges, one of them occupying a place behind the cataract. The steep precipices over which the water falls must have been subjected to a great pressure, since the layers in some places are in a vertical position. The rocks are generally of a slaty structure, though there are large bowlders of greenish-colored granite or gneiss. The ascent is made by a zigzag path near the cascade. The mountain is covered with trees and the rocks with moss and wild plants. We made search for the Edelweisse, the little modest Alpine flower; but the natives take the precaution to gather them for sale to tourists. At the foot of the mountain lies Lake Brienz, with its opposite shore walled by the Alps. The hotel, romantically situated far above the lake, though large, is generally crowded with visitors at this season of the year.

August 29 we embarked for Boenigen, situated at the end of the lake, thence travelled by rail to Darlingen. The railway carriages are furnished with an upper story, where fine views are obtained of the surrounding country. At Darlingen we left the train for a sail on Lake Thun, said to be the deepest of all the Swiss lakes. The views everywhere are delightful, yet so varied that one never tires of them. At Thun, a town on the lake, we made another change from boat to train, and arrived at Berne, the capital of Switzerland. This city, on the River Aar, a winding stream, is surrounded by hills and terraces, with the Alps rising in numerous peaks in the distant horizon; and from one of these terraces we were favored with a magnificent view of a Swiss sunset, a sight not easily described nor soon forgotten. A soft haze suffused every object, while the effect of the sun's rays on the snow-covered mountains was glorious to behold. These Alpine heights do not seem to belong to earth, and it is difficult to feel they are a part of our planet. Their proper sphere is the clouds, as, to our narrow range of vision, they partake of the aerial nature of clouds, and might appropriately form the abode of beings superior to man. Beautiful, sublime, boundless, ethereal, they seem. What other material objects can inspire the mind with such awe and admiration? What scenes in nature can command such homage, or so elevate the feelings above the petty affairs of life, and direct them to the Author of the wonderful works of creation?

The old city of Berne is very quaint and distinguished for its peculiar roofs and chimneys, its arcades and dark shops, its numerous fountains, its odd clock, its Cathedral, with groups representing the Last Judgment carved on the door, and finally, the three bears maintained in state at the public expense. The Museum contains a very good collection of minerals and fossils mostly from the Alps; one specimen of smoky quartz weighed four hundred pounds. The Federal Palace, of light-colored sandstone in plain rustic work, though a large building, is in other respects quite in keeping with the little modest republic.

Leaving Berne for Geneva August 80, a very warm day, we landed at the Hotel du Lac, where we found letters from home; but the next day we went to a "Pension," or boarding-house, on Rue du Mont Blanc. Here we were in the city of Calvin, and soon to begin our sight-seeing. We first went to the Hotel de Ville, where the Alabama commissioners assembled. A marble tablet commemorating the event has been placed on the wall of the room where they held their deliberations. A peculiar feature of the hotel is a paved road like a winding carriage-way leading to the different stories instead of flights of steps. It might have been constructed for the convenience of the burgomasters who found it wearisome to climb a staircase.

Lake Geneva deserves all the encomium it has received from poet and tourist. "Clear, placid Leman" is a very appropriate epithet, since its waters are very clear, though they do not always appear blue. The Rhone, of a beryl-green hue, issues

GÖSCHENEN. THE ST. GOTHARD TUNNEL.

HOTEL OF THE ST. BERNARD

from its southern extremity on its swift course to the sea. The Botanical Gardens and the University are both places of interest; yet for want of time they received only a passing notice; but in our rambles we came to the Russian Church, a small building, with the peculiar-shaped domes of the Greek churches. This part of the city is comparatively new, and several buildings were in the process of construction. A stone of a delicate shade of green is much used, which produces a pleasing effect when employed with other colored stones, but it does not look so well when used alone. A whimsical effect is produced by the odd chimney tops, consisting of pipes, some erect, others inclining in all directions, while others have a cover raised a few inches from the pipe. More awkward contrivances for chimneys could hardly be invented. The streets of Geneva were never sprinkled when we were there, therefore the dust was very annoying, almost unendurable.

Sunday, September 2, we attended church at the Cathedral of St. Peter, where Calvin preached. It is a plain building, parts of which were constructed in the eleventh century. The service was more simple than that of the Roman church. The preacher seemed very fervent in his extempore prayer; but being in a foreign language, we could not understand it. We then went to the Russian church, which was decorated after the Byzantine style. There were no seats for the audience. Every one stood through the service except a few who were accommodated with temporary ones; but there was less ceremony than in the Catholic churches, though there is a similarity in their rituals, as the incense, the genuflections, etc. The priests' robes and the altar cloths are very rich.

Geneva has been the birthplace or the residence of many distinguished persons, and the scene of some of the great reforms and progressive movements of the world.

From the Rue du Mont Blanc we can see the monarch of the Alps, with his majestic head covered with snow, and it is well to have a view of it at some distance. We went to see the junction of the Arve and the Rhone, which are quite unlike in appearance. The waters of the former are clay color, due to the presence of sand, while those of the latter are blue or green; besides, the Rhone is a very swift river, while the Arve is slow. Hence the waters of the two streams flow side by side for a considerable distance without mingling, affording a novel sight. A foot-bridge spans the Arve which leads to a park called Les Bois de la Bâtie, affording excellent views of the city. Returning to town we came across a wood carving representing a plan of the Mt. Blanc range, Chamounix, and Martigny, places we intended to visit.

Prigny, on the shore of the lake, a few miles from Geneva, contains the park and mansion of Adolph Rothschild. It is built of light-colored stone, and is elegant in design and beautiful in its surroundings. The architectural ornaments are chaste and appropriate, while the flowers, trees, parks, and vases are beautiful and tasteful. The villa is on high ground, and commands a view of the lake and Mt. Blanc. The region between this place and Geneva affords charming villas and picturesque towns scattered along the shores of the lake, but the scenery is less grand than that on Lake Lucerne.

We left Geneva for Chamounix, travelling by diligence. The day was fine, and we took an early start, but were some annoyed about our seats, but after a little vexation we determined to enjoy as much of the scenery as we could. The exploit of getting into a diligence is considerable. We have to mount by a flight of steps, as the vehicle resembles a small house in height; our baggage is put into an apartment on the lower floor, while the passengers occupy the upper stories. We had six horses to draw our moving hotel. Our route along the delightful valley of the Chamounix, which in the first part of our course afforded views simply beautiful; but as we advanced, they became grand. The mountains on both sides of the valley rise to a great height, and are generally precipitous, with immense walls of rock. About noon we came in sight of Mt. Blanc, which we had seen at Geneva, a good distance off, but now it seemed very near. Before us was the grand Monarch, and what a sublime object! We never lost sight of it during our stay at this place, as we could see it from the balcony of our hotel.

CHAPEL OF WILLIAM TELL

MONT BLANC

The little village of Chamounix is enclosed by the loftiest mountains of the Alpine chain. We arrived in time to see the sun set or rather fall behind the vast ramparts of nature's works. The clouds, suffused with the warm tints of the descending sun, surrounded and partially enveloped the lofty peaks, so that they seemed like turrets and castles in the sky. The scene was constantly changing; the light-colored rocks of Les Aiguilles, shooting up to heaven, became luminous, while the snow on the mountain reflected a beautiful rose-tint, until the color gradually faded out, though the lofty peaks remained luminous long after the mountains on the opposite side of the valley were shrouded in darkness, and only presented their gloomy outlines. How insignificant the works of man compared with those of the Creator! These grand mountains are God's cathedrals, where bright-robed angels might celebrate his praise.

September 6 we ascended Mt. Montanvert, six thousand three hundred and three feet in height, on mules to the Mer de Glace, which required two hours. This glacier is twelve miles long, and from one to four wide, and fills the deepest gorges of the Mt. Blanc chain; the lower part of the glacier is called the Glacier des Bois. A hotel or pension for the entertainment of travellers, on the summit of Montanvert, was being constructed. Here we dismounted and left our mules in charge of our guide, for the purpose of exploring the glacier and other interesting objects in this region. The top of the mountain afforded magnificent views, while hundreds of feet below was a river of ice; and rising far above, were the Needles, or Les Aiguilles du Dru, 12,517 feet in height, Les Aiguilles du Moine, 11,214 feet, Les Aiguilles du Bochard, 8,766 feet, and Les Aiguilles Vert, 13,540 feet. The glacier is covered with snow mixed with sand, which, on a near view, imparts a gray tint to the ice, while deep crevices, through and under which the water rushes with a roar like a cataract, reminding one of the ocean billows. With some difficulty and danger, we descended the steep and rocky sides of the mountain to the Mer de Glace, where we could better examine this natural wonder. Towards the summit of the glacier, it had the appearance of a frozen waterfall, as described by Coleridge, while along its course were deep chasms into which one would not care to descend, and huge blocks of ice.

It has been proved that glaciers are constantly moving down the valley at the rate of a certain number of feet within a specified time. Our ascent from the glacier to the top of the precipice was far more laborious than the descent to the icy plain. Truly the poet said, "*Facilus descensus Averni, Sed revacare gradum, hic opus, hic labore est.*" However, after great toil we succeeded in climbing back, preferring this hardship to crossing the Mer de Glace and descending by the Mauvais Pas, and, after resting awhile, mounted our mules for the journey down the mountain. The path was circuitous and in some places quite steep; while the animals we rode, with mulish obstinacy, persisted in going so near the edge of the precipice, that we seemed to hang over it; but they were so well trained, and our guide was so careful, that our fears were quieted and we descended in safety. The only living creature we saw inhabiting this region was a little mouse that ran across our path.

The views were constantly changing, and grand beyond the power of description, while some were very peculiar, as where the water had cut deep furrows or paths on the side of the mountain several rods in width, branching off from the principal avenue, like the limbs from the trunk of a tree; other views opened to our sight: fields covered with vegetation and scattered dwellings of the mountaineers. The best view of Mt. Blanc was obtained in descending Montanvert. After our interesting experience, we visited a small collection of paintings representing Alpine scenery, and were deeply impressed with their fidelity to nature in those features which could be represented by art.

The rocks found in this region are mostly a coarse granite, of a greenish tint, mica schist, gneiss, slate, and limestone. The firs peculiar to the Alps grow wherever they can find soil, while the heather and some other shrubs are somewhat sparsely scattered about. The water flowing from the glaciers had generally a greenish color.

We left Chamounix for Martigny, by carriage, over Tête Noire; and during the first part of our route, the Mt. Blanc range, with its snow-crowned summits and sharp "Needles," were in sight, when, finally, we bade adieu to the grand Monarch, with his crowned head in the clouds, made luminous by the morning sun; and as we proceeded, new scenes opened to our view quite unlike those previously witnessed. The mountains along this pass rise in steep crags to a great height, and are nearly destitute of trees. The road lay between these gloomy precipices, sometimes overhanging deep ravines of several hundred feet. We stopped at a hotel on the brow of Tête Noire, 6,591 feet in height, where the sun is seen only two hours during any day; and here the wagons to and from Chamounix meet and pass one another, forming in all a large caravan. At this hotel are kept a large number of the famous St. Bernard dogs. Resting awhile, our party resumed the journey, some for Chamounix, others for Martigny. Our course for some time was descending, then it changed upward by the pass of the Col de Forclax, 4,997 feet. We had gone a considerable distance from the hotel at Tête Noire, when one of the company noticed a dog following our carriage, and inquired of the driver whether it was not a St. Bernard. The coachman had not observed the animal, and was much excited when told about it; and leaving his team, he attempted to drive him back. After much scolding and threatening with his whip, saying to the dog in French, "You must go back, it is necessary that you should go back," the disappointed creature left us to finish our journey without him. This incident showed how highly these dogs are valued by their masters.

The pass of the Col de la Forclax is steep and very winding, but finally we reached the summit, when we found the descent on the other side fearfully precipitous, with frequent and sudden curves. From here we had a view of the distant Monté Rosso chain, with its white tops. We found ourselves in the valley of the Rhone, surrounded by steep mountains, and soon came to the insignificant village of Martigny. The small farms and hamlets we have passed to-day are evidences of poverty, and it is difficult to understand how the inhabitants manage to obtain a living from the scanty vegetation everywhere apparent. No wonder beggars are numerous. Swiss women of the laboring classes work on the farms and bear the same burdens as the men. By this mode of life, they have lost the feminine softness of features, and are coarse and brown like the other sex, while the older women are bowed and shrivelled beyond most of those in other countries. The peasants of both sexes and all ages are accustomed to carry very heavy burdens on their backs, in large baskets fastened to their shoulders by straps. They climb the steep mountains with these loads, which is the usual mode of transporting everything over the Alps, even the heaviest materials.

Leaving Martigny, we travelled by rail to Leuk, thence by diligence to Brieg. All the villages in this region are small and uninteresting; the buildings have no architectural beauty; in fact, a large part of Swiss dwellings, outside the largest towns, are mere hovels and poor at that. In the villages the streets are winding and without sidewalks, and not unfrequently the houses stand directly on the pavement of the roads, while there is a want of tidiness and thrift everywhere. Our route lay between steep, rocky mountains, mostly destitute of vegetation on the north or Oberland side.

GLACIER AT MONTANVERT

LAKE OF THE FOUR CANTONS

## CHAPTER VI.

*From Switzerland to Italy.*

LEAVING Brieg for Stresa, Italy, situated on Lake Maggiore, we crossed the Simplon by diligence. This famous road was made by Napoleon I., 1800-1806, for a military passage to Italy, and is the second public road over the Alps, the first being the Brenner, used by the Romans. The Simplon is a macadamized road, while the pass is less steep than some others. The first part of the route presents no remarkable features for an Alpine region; but as we approached nearer the summit, the mountains became more rugged and steep, making galleries and tunnels necessary. Frequent cascades occur, and in one place the water falls over the tunnel or gallery, and dashes down a deep ravine; so that we passed *under* the cascade, while in another place it is precipitated over a precipice under the gallery, and the road passes directly *over* a waterfall. It is a fearful descent from the top of the mountain to the bottom of the ravine; and on both sides of the valley steep rocks rise to immense heights, in the form of bastions, buttresses, and walls so high that their summits were in the clouds, while numerous waterfalls descend from these immense elevations, and tumble into the river below. Only stunted trees and moss could grow in so rocky a soil. The highest point of the Simplon, is 6,595 feet. Frequent " Houses of Refuge" are scattered along the pass; and at the culminating point stands "The Hospice," established by Napoleon I. for the entertainment of travellers, but it remained unfinished until 1825, when it was purchased by the St. Bernard Hospice. The water of one of the cascades descends from the Haltwasser Glacier; and though the defile at this place has been fortified several times, yet the works have been repeatedly destroyed by avalanches, and some of their remains are still to be seen. As the road descends the Simplon, grand views are afforded of rugged mountains, with their glaciers and numerous little waterfalls, like threads of silver.

Beyond the gallery of Algaby, the ravine of Gondo begins, through which the Diveria, a noisy, rapid stream, flows. This ravine, one of the wildest and grandest in the Alps, becomes narrower and deeper, until its smooth and precipitous walls of mica slate completely overhang the road. The gallery of Gondo is 735 feet in length, and on either side the rocks ascend 2,000 feet; the hamlet of Gondo is the last Swiss village, before we enter Italy. At San Marco, the first Italian town, travellers are examined by the custom-house officials, which is a mere farce. As we descended to the lowlands the country was more fertile, and the buildings were better and of a different style from those in Switzerland; the method of training the grapevine was different, being on trellises. Leaving Domo d' Ossola, we passed the mountains from which the marble for Milan Cathedral was quarried, also a gold mine, said to be the oldest in Europe, and known to the ancient Romans; it is still worked. During our journey, we occasionally came in sight of Monté Rosso, with its four snow-clad peaks. Finally, the last pass of the Alps, called the Bernina, was made; and after a long day's ride, lasting from four o'clock A. M. to seven P. M., we arrived at the Hotel Milano, on the shore of Lake Maggiore. During the night there was a long and severe thunder-storm; but the next morning, September 10, was bright and beautiful, reminding us that we were in "sunny Italy." We had a fine view from our hotel of Lake Maggiore, with its charming islands, the Borromean, and of lovely villas. We embarked for a sail around an arm of the lake to Laverno, thence we journeyed by diligence to Verese. The landscape of this region was delightful, affording vineyards, fields of grain, and the mulberry and fig trees.

Verese is a delightful little town between Lake Maggiore and Lake Lugano, in a region dotted by charming villas and fertile fields. Here we stopped at the Grande Hotel, formerly a palace of some Italian noble, with extensive grounds containing a grotto, said to be natural, but appearing as if it had received some finishing touches from the hand of art. From the top of the hotel we were favored with magnificent views of the Simplon group of mountains, the Monté Rosso and Mont Blanc ranges. It was near sunset, and a more glorious scene can hardly be imagined. To the east, the lofty summits were made brilliant by the departing rays of the sun; while nearer, on the shores of the lake, the mountains were purple with the blossoms of the heather, which in the distance appear almost luminous. The scenery of the Alps is so varied, combining the grand and the beautiful, that one never tires of them; though there is a resemblance in some of the views, yet they are never monotonous. We left Verese at an early hour, by diligence, for Porto, on Lake Lugano, a small town at the foot of the lake, where we embarked on a steamboat for the town of Lugano, on the west side, where we were detained several hours, but found little to interest us. Though there were several hotels, we preferred to take our breakfast at a restaurant, the proprietor of which, a young Italian, as we supposed, spoke English well, and asked whether we were Americans, saying he was born at Saratoga, where he lived ten years, and then came to Italy. He seemed pleased to meet with persons from the United States, and said he had seen General Grant and other notable Americans.

The scenery of Lake Lugano, with its lofty mountains, surpasses in grandeur that of Lake Maggiore. We had a sail of two hours on this beautiful sheet of water, when we landed at a place where our luggage should have been examined by the custom officers; but we were not required even to unlock our valises; he only inquired whether we had any cigars, as if we had not been sufficiently annoyed by them in all our journey.

The traveller should be prepared for annoyances and delays he did not expect. After the pretended examination of our baggage we had the trouble of taking it back to the omnibus for Menaggio, situated on Lake Como, and here we were compelled to wait two hours on the wharf for the boat from Colico, which was to take us to Como, on the southern extremity of the lake, where we arrived late in the evening, and after many petty annoyances we found an asylum at the Hotel Italia, where we were glad to rest even in a room with a brick floor. The next morning we paid a visit to the Cathedral, one of the best, after that of Milan, in Northern Italy. It is principally of the Romanesque style, though parts of it are Gothic. The interior of the dome appeared nearly as high as that of St. Paul's, London; the ceiling is highly ornamented with colors and gold, while some of the chapels are very rich in beautiful marbles and gilt, and the choir and pulpit are decorated with wood carving. Though Como is a town of considerable size, the streets are narrow and crooked, and to follow them seems like threading the mazes of a labyrinth. It contains a statue of Volta, a celebrated Italian philanthropist, and a native of the city. The manufacture of silk is the leading industry of the place.

Our route from Como to Milan lay through the fertile plains of Lombardy and the town of Monza, whose Cathedral contains the iron crown used by the ancient kings of Lombardy, and was thought to have been formed of nails from the true cross; it is richly adorned with gold and precious stones.

Arriving at Milan we stopped at a hotel on the Corso Victor Emmanuel, near the Cathedral, which we visited after resting awhile. The remarkable beauty and grandeur of this church have not been exaggerated; indeed, it baffles all description; the first sight of it overwhelms the mind, for it does not seem to belong to earth. On a second visit we ascended to the top of the roof, which is a forest of turrets and spires, each being crowned with a statue and adorned with beautiful architectural ornaments. The Cathedral is built of light-colored marble, usually called white, but veined to some extent with delicate pink and blue. The building is nearly five hundred feet long and two hundred and fifty wide, and the height of the central spire is more than three hundred and fifty feet; there are one hundred and six turrets and four thousand five hundred statues. The double aisles each side of the nave have fifty-two columns, and the font of porphyry was formerly the sarcophagus of St. Dionysius, while the crypt contains the tomb of St. Carlo Borromeo. The architectural ornaments are peculiar to the Gothic style and very rich and elaborate. The Cathedral was begun in 1386 and finished by Napoleon I. Seen from the top it seems an object belonging to the heavens and a fit companion of the snow-crowned Alps, visible in the distance, — the latter a work of the Divine Mind, the former, of the human; yet so transcendent the genius that designed this wonderful structure, that we almost instinctively ascribe to the designer god-like powers. The numerous turrets, pinnacles, and statues on the elevated roof show as perfect workmanship as if they were intended for nearer inspection.

We met an English gentleman and lady with whom we had travelled from Como to Milan, and joined them for a tour about the city, which is surrounded by a wall with twelve gates. Our first object was the Teatro della Scala, considered the largest building of the kind in Europe, but it is only a trifle larger than San Carlos, in Naples; it will seat thirty thousand persons. The statue of Leonardo da Vinci occupies the piazza or square opposite the theatre. From the Scala we went to the Brera, a picture gallery which contains some of the works of the old masters, many of modern painters, and statuary; but our time was so limited that it was impossible to examine them carefully. Americans are somewhat notorious for "rushing," but we found our English cousins endowed with this trait, and concluded it must be an Anglo-Saxon quality. After a hasty visit to the gallery we engaged a carriage and drove to the Amphitheatre de l'Arena, which can be filled with water for nautical entertainments. It is furnished with stone seats arranged in tiers all round the arena, which can hold thirty thousand spectators. It was probably constructed by the Romans of ancient times.

The Arc de la Paix, begun by Napoleon I., to commemorate the completion of the Simplon road, which ends here, bears a close resemblance to the Arc de Triomphe in Paris. The one in Milan has six bronze horses attached to a chariot occupying the centre, and one on each corner, the whole forming a very beautiful gate. The celebrated fresco of Leonardo da Vinci's Last Supper is to be seen in the refectory of the monastery near the Church of Santa Maria della Grazie. The painting is on one end of a long hall, and is faded and otherwise injured by time and neglect, and before many years it will probably be in a much worse condition, if not entirely obliterated. It is sad to know that one of the great masterpieces of art is fast disappearing, though thousands of copies will transmit it to future generations. Perhaps there is no work of the old masters so often reproduced as the Last Supper. Near the Church of San Lorenzo, once a part of an ancient Roman palace, are sixteen Corinthian columns standing alone and supporting nothing, but which formerly must have constituted a part of some structure, perhaps a colonnade. The arcades, or walks covered with a glass roof, afford fine situations for shops or stores.

To one interested in church architecture, Milan offers some attractive studies. There are several churches, besides the splendid Cathedral, well worth visiting, comprising St. Ambrose, built of stone and brick combined; San Carlo, a basilica, very rich in decorations; and San Alessandro, which merits a particular description.

The exterior is not specially interesting, but the interior is highly decorated. The church is Romanesque in style, with numerous domes, arches, and columns. The ceiling and walls are adorned with frescos where they are not covered with ornamental marbles and paintings, while the high altar and pulpit are conspicuous for their antique marbles and gems, of beautiful and variegated colors; the same kind of ornaments are seen in the chapels. Silver candlesticks, a cross of gold and silver, pictures with marble frames, elegant wood carving and gilt, marble mosaic pavements, rich altar coverings and statues, all are profusely used in this highly decorated church. San Stefano is distinguished for its white and gold draperies. The numerous churches of Milan all differ from one another in their construction or decorations, thus affording a pleasing feature for the visitor.

TOMB OF CANOVA, GENOA.

MILAN CATHEDRAL.

We made another visit to the Duomo, and while there we had a view of the tomb of San Carlo Borromeo, which is before the high altar, and is exceedingly rich in gold and gems. The inner coffin is of crystal, therefore the remains of the saint, dressed in costly robes and jewels, can be seen by one visiting the crypt, for which five francs are demanded; but we were satisfied with a partial view afforded by the grating in the pavement, assisted by the light of the custodian's torch. The wood carving, metallic pulpits, with gilt ornaments, and the organs are all very rich. The capitals of the columns are peculiar; they are surmounted by statues arranged in niches, with canopies. The windows in the apse are very large, and the painted glass very beautiful.

The Arcades or Galleria Vittorio Emanuele are superior to any in Paris, and are claimed to be the best of the kind in Europe. The Royal Palace near the cathedral was built in the seventeenth century, and contains seven hundred rooms and several courts.

The celebrated Certosa near Pavia, which we visited, situated about seventeen miles from Milan, is one of the most remarkable monasteries of Europe for the richness and perfection of its designs. The façade of white marble is a marvel of beautiful sculpture, being covered with statues and relief, both high and low, executed by skilful workmanship; while in the interior, elegant and elaborate decorations are seen in every part, including carving in wood, ivory, and stone, variegated patterns of marble mosaics, exquisite designs in bronze, gold, and silver utensils, crosses, statues, frescos, bronze screens, and a profusion of gems, all combining to produce a magnificent display.

Nothing is superficial or tawdry, while perfect fidelity to thoroughness of execution is seen in every retired corner or dark space, equally with those more conspicuous. The attention is arrested by remarkably beautiful bronze screens, and the rare marbles employed for decoration in the chapels; even the ornaments of the ceiling are elaborate. The material used for sculpture in this monastery is a fine white marble, which enhances the impressive beauty of the interior. The mind is bewildered, on a first visit, by the splendor and profusion of the ornaments, and is amazed to witness the richness that must have equalled that of the Temple at Jerusalem.

Until recently no woman was allowed to enter any chapel belonging to the monastery, and could only view these sacred places from the outside of the screens; but now they are admitted to the same privileges as their brothers. A monk, with close-shaven head and white robes, conducted our party through all the apartments open to visitors, not only in the church but also in the monastery proper. We visited the refectory, cloisters, and a cell belonging to one of the monks, with its small garden adjoining. The buildings are surrounded by several acres of ground, enclosed on all sides by a high brick wall, which gave them the appearance of fortifications. The Certosa will remain in our memory "a thing of beauty forever." From all we had heard about it, we supposed it was remarkable for its beauty, grandeur, and architectural wealth, but our most sanguine expectations were more than realized. After spending nearly a day in viewing this miracle of art, we returned to Milan to resume our sight-seeing in this renowned city. In the evening we went to the Duomo, to view its exterior by the light of a bright full moon; but human language can give no adequate conception of its beauty and magnificence. It seemed as if it might have been the abode of the Infinite One, and inspired the soul with awe. The design and structure of this cathedral were the works of different architects and carried through several centuries; yet such is the harmony of the exterior, at least, that it seems to be the labor of only one mind. As we stood in the shadow of this sublime temple, we felt impressed as with a celestial vision; and it was with solemn thoughts that we bade adieu to this wonderful building, unsurpassed by any we had yet seen or expect to see.

As it was our purpose to visit some of the more northern countries of Europe before we advanced to the central and southern parts of Italy, we left Milan for Como, The Splugen and Germany, and here we parted reluctantly with our travelling companion, E. A., who returned to London, leaving

Arco Della Pace, Milan.

Certosa, Pavia.

us to pursue our journey alone, until we should meet some of our fellow-countrymen. The first part of our route was the same we had just passed over, therefore there was nothing specially new to attract our attention; and when we arrived at Como and found we must wait several hours for the boat to Bellagio, on the lake, we occupied the time in exploring the town more thoroughly than in our first short visit. Portions of the city are very quaint, with narrow streets and high buildings. Lombardy is flat and generally monotonous, but the region of the lakes affords some of the most beautiful views of Northern Italy. We left Como late in the afternoon and reached Bellagio, situated on a peninsula of the lake, a very beautiful and romantic spot which both nature and art have combined to render attractive to visitors. The principal hotels, among several others, are the Grand Hotel Bellagio and the Grand Hotel Bretagne. Both are large and surrounded by groves, gardens, and shady walks. The promontory on which the town is built rises abruptly to a considerable height, and on its summit there is a pension or boarding-house for visitors. The dwellings of the poorer classes are rude and the streets narrow, crooked, and dirty; while some are very steep, as they are on the side of a mountain. It is a peculiarity of most European towns to find wealth, elegance, and squalid poverty in close neighborhood.

The grounds about the principal hotels afford a great variety of beautiful and fragrant flowers, while views from the lake add to their attractions and offer an inducement to the tourist to prolong his visit. September 18 we left Bellagio for Colico, at the head of Lake Como. Small villages are scattered along the shore and on the mountain-sides, with here and there a pretty villa set as a jewel, on the sloping hill.

## CHAPTER VII.

*From Italy to Germany.*

BIDDING adieu to the enchanting Italian lakes, we prepared for the rugged scenery of the Alps. At Colico we exchanged the agreeable boat for the less comfortable quarters of a diligence, bound for the Splugen. It was so exceedingly dusty that, notwithstanding the oppressive heat, we were obliged to keep all the windows closed. The first part of the way afforded no features of special interest, but as we proceeded the scenery became wild and grand. The Pass of the Splugen is remarkable for its rocky and steep mountains. Nature in this region is seen in one of her most threatening attitudes, and no one but an eye-witness can form an adequate idea of her stern grandeur; frowning cliffs and yawning gulfs are everywhere impending, so that one feels in danger of being crushed or plunged to the bottom of a fearful abyss. Laughter and even conversation appeared out of place in the midst of so sublime scenery, and the traveller gazes with silent wonder and almost terror at the awful majesty that reigns in these solitudes. The narrow valleys are covered with rocks of various sizes which have fallen from their original places, while little patches of soil have here and there been made to yield a scanty harvest by the persistent struggles of the hardy mountaineers. Our progress to the summit of the pass was slow, so that we did not reach Splugen until midnight. The air was chilly; but the clear, full moon rendered the scenery so fascinating that we forgot our discomforts. Every object seemed to possess a weird, mysterious character; while the light-colored rocks, in striking contrast with the exceedingly dark vegetation, added a spectral appearance which strangely affected the imagination, if left to its unrestrained operation.

Chiavenna, the last Italian town we passed through, is situated in a region of wild grandeur. An old ruined castle is perched on an eminence near the inn at which we stopped, while high crags and rocky mountains encircled the few dilapidated buildings on the narrow and crooked streets. There was a babel at the poor, little hotel, where all the dialects of Christendom seemed to be represented. This public house, the most cheerless we had yet found in our travels, was not far from the summit, at an elevation of nine thousand feet, and afforded us poor accommodations for rest, as the arrival and departure of travellers at all hours and the noise of the porters made sleep impossible to any one except the "Seven Sleepers." The grandest, wildest, and most awe-inspiring scenery of the Splugen is found on the northern side; therefore had we passed it during the night, we should have lost an opportunity of studying nature in one of her most impressive lessons.

When we resumed our journey the next morning, September 19, the weather was very cold and the ground was covered with frost. Our route lay through the region called Via Mala, which surpassed anything we had yet seen in grandeur; we might say it was terrific. A deep, narrow ravine, enclosed by walls of rough stone several thousand feet in height, formed the bed of the Rhine, while between and around these precipices the road passes hundreds of feet from the bottom of the ravine. As we gazed in silent astonishment we felt certain that some tremendous convulsion of the earth's crust in past geological ages must have torn the rocks from their beds and rent them asunder, to form these natural walls. Passing the Via Mala, our journey to Chur was among scenes of a more quiet nature; here we exchanged the diligence for the railway. All the way from Chur to Rorschach, on Lake Constance, we were in sight of the distant Alps, whose bald and rocky heads reached to the clouds. The steamboat for Lindau, in Bavaria, did not leave for some time after our arrival; and as the town afforded no attractions we were compelled to amuse ourselves by watching the beautiful lake. At length we embarked and, but for the cold, the sail under the light of a clear, full moon would have been most enjoyable; however, under the circumstances, we were glad when we arrived at Lindau, where we bade adieu to the Swiss Alps, never to be forgotten as objects of some of nature's grandest works.

September 20 we left Lindau for Munich, a good day's journey through a comparatively level region. We had passed from some of the wildest and grandest scenes to quiet, cultivated fields, bounded by low ranges of distant mountains. Amid the terribly grand scenery of the Splugen Pass, the mental and moral faculties are toned up to their highest pitch; and one feels so small and insignificant, in the presence of such majesty, that he hardly dares to think, much less to speak. So when leaving this region for those of a different character, it was like passing from a grand heroic poem to the quiet pastoral, and a journey to Munich was a relaxation to the mind, especially, as among the six passengers in the same carriage scarcely a word was spoken. Such a thing could not have occurred in a company of voluble Frenchmen or Italians. Munich affords many places of interest to the stranger; therefore it was important to begin the task, or rather pleasure, of sightseeing soon after our arrival. Our first visit was to the Glyptothek, or museum of statuary, an elegant building of the Grecian Ionic order, well adapted to its purpose. It contains thirteen halls surrounding a central court, each one designated by the works it contains. The most interesting marbles consist of the original groups from the Temple of Minerva, at Ægina, found in 1811. They comprise two pediment groups. On one is the representation of ten Greeks and Trojans fighting for the body of Achilles; on the other are delineated the wars of Laomedon. The forms of these personages are perfect in grace and proportion, but their countenances have no expression, though they represent warriors engaged in deadly conflict. One is attempting to draw a dart from his side, with as much composure as a man would smoke a cigar; another is just ready to send a dart through his antagonist, but not a muscle of his face indicates an emotion; even the dying soldier

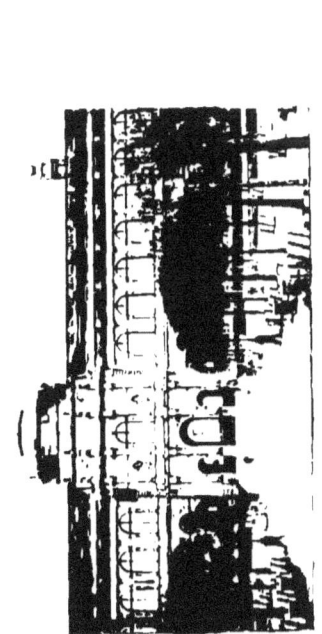

THE ZWINGER, DRESDEN.

RESIDENZ PLATZ, MUNICH.

PICTURE GALLERY, DRESDEN.

THE PROPYLÆA, MUNICH.

VIEWS IN GERMANY.

is perfectly calm. The Sleeping Satyr, or Barberina Faun, so well known to lovers of art, occupies the Hall of Bacchus. The bas-reliefs on the pediments over the doorways, by Schwanthaler, are exceedingly graceful.

The Museum contains six marble statues by Wagner, representing Pericles, Phidias, Vulcan, Hadrian, Daedalus, and Prometheus, besides the works of some other celebrated sculptors. The "Hall of the Gods" and some others are decorated by the frescos of Cornelius. The exhibition of statuary at Munich is smaller than that of London and Paris, but it has the advantage of possessing some valuable originals. Opposite the Glyptothek is the Exhibition Building, in the Grecian style, containing the paintings of modern artists of the Munich school. A few of these were especially notable, including Alpine views, one being a sunset. The moon was reflected on the lake among the mountains; and in the foreground was a woman standing alone upon a projecting rock, looking eagerly across the water, as if expecting some one, while not a dwelling was in sight, — nothing except the magnificent Alps were to be seen. The Propylæa, a fine gateway in imitation of the one at Athens, adorned with reliefs representing scenes in the Greek war of independence, stands between the Glyptothek and the Exhibition Building.

We paid our next visit to the Royal Palace. Strangers assemble in the Salon Hercules without any Hercules, and wait until 11 A. M. when a guide appears to conduct the party through a labyrinth of gaudily decorated rooms and halls. There was a large company, which continued to receive additions until the number exceeded one hundred, when the guard appeared and was followed by the visitors, as a shepherd by a flock of sheep. When he stopped we all stopped; when he moved forward, we did the same; he halted occasionally to give explanations in German about the paintings and other objects of interest, all of which was, of course, very instructive to us whose German vocabulary consisted of about a dozen words. It seemed to us there was a lack of taste in the decorations of the rooms; too much gilding, porcelain, marble, or something

of the sort. The royal bed was so bedecked with gilt that no
modern prince could have borne the weight; it needed a stout
old Barbarossa, accustomed to heavy armor, to lie safely under
such a covering. One cabinet was decorated with porcelain
vases, arranged on brackets covering the walls; another had
mural coverings of small pictures in gilt frames. In the
throne room there were twelve colossal gilt statues of the
kings of Bavaria, some of whom were very formidable looking
men. The frescos representing the Nibelungen by Schnorr,
were very fine and interesting to those versed in the great German epic. The only part of our guide's explanations we could
understand was the names of the heroes and heroines, being
some acquainted with them from a translation. The royal
chapel displayed magnificent marbles, but the gaudy decorations of the ceiling were not pleasing.

Leaving the palace, we walked through Ludwig Strasse, the
most noted street in Munich, where are a number of public
buildings, including the University, library, government buildings, palaces, and others. The Strasse is one hundred and fifty
feet wide and three fourths of a mile long, ending at the Siegesthor, or Gate of Victory, a kind of triumphal arch with a figure
representing Bavaria, in a chariot drawn by four lions, all in
bronze. The New Pinakothek is a gallery containing modern
paintings, and corresponds to the National Gallery of London;
the works, on the whole, are among the best we have yet seen.
The Munich Gallery has a high reputation; a large number of
the paintings are excellent. They have one marked feature:
the absence of nude figures, so conspicuous in Paris and some
other places. It will be necessary to make several examina-
tions before gaining a tolerable idea of this rich treasure of
art. Our next visit was made to some of the churches, including the Theatines, in which are the Royal Vaults where
the Emperor Charles VII. is buried.

The Ludwigskirche, with its two towers two hundred and
thirty-four feet in height, offers an imposing exterior, while its
roof is very peculiar, being covered with mosaic work of bright
variegated tiles, giving it the appearance of being carpeted.

The interior is quite plain compared with the Theatines, but it contains the Last Judgment, a fresco by Cornelius, sixty-six feet by forty. The Frauenkirche, or Church of Our Lady, is a cathedral built of brick, in 1468, and has towers three hundred and fifty-seven feet in height. The monument of the Emperor Louis, who died in 1347, made of dark marble and adorned with bronze figures, stands in the nave. The Church of St. Michael contains a monument by Thorwaldsen, erected to Eugene Beauharnais. These churches are in the Romanesque style of architecture. The latter has a high altar reaching to the top of the vaulting, and profusely decorated with gilt and other showy ornaments. There is a want of taste in such exhibitions, and one becomes weary of the display of gold, silver, jewels, wax images, shrines and drapery, all embellished with a profusion of decorations. In the Church of the Theatines, what is claimed to be the skeleton of St. Gregory, all covered with jewels, is exposed to the gaze of the multitude, in one of the chapels.

The Old Pinakothek contains more than one thousand four hundred paintings of the old masters, arranged chronologically, according to the schools; as German, French, Dutch, Italian, etc., with one saloon appropriated to Rubens. Among the paintings in this gallery are the Last Judgment, the Massacre of the Innocents, and the Lion Hunt. The Museum contains cabinets of engravings, drawings, and one thousand three hundred specimens of antique vases in terra cotta, including Etruscan, Greek, Sicilian, and Italian. On the south side of the Pinakothek is a Loggie or Arcade, with frescos by Cornelius representing the history of painting in the Middle Ages.

The glass-works of Munich have a celebrity, therefore they must be seen; but it was with some difficulty that we reached them. We engaged a coachman to take us to the establishment; but as the distance was considerable, he probably thought it a "smart" thing to leave his passengers at the small private shop of a glass-worker, not more than half way to the painted glass-works. He received his fee and drove off, congratulating himself, no doubt, on his good fortune, while we, on learning the facts, were much perplexed to find our way thither; but after making fruitless inquiries, a man, seeing our dilemma, very kindly offered to conduct us to the place; and though he went out of his way, he would receive no compensation for his services. We were greatly pleased with the beautiful specimens shown us, and learned the difference between stained glass and painted glass. The former is colored with the shading only painted on it, while the latter has all the figures painted. We next visited the bronze-works, and saw the plaster casts, some of them being of colossal size. There were a number of American subjects, among them the statues of Webster, Clay, Benton, Peabody, and others, and the casts of the bronze doors of the Capitol at Washington. One of the most interesting subjects was a winged goddess by Rogers intended for Hartford, said our guide. We were conducted into the forge; but as he spoke in German, we could not understand his explanations.

In the afternoon we took a walk through Maximilian Strasse, one of the fine streets of Munich, adorned with several statues, including that of Maximilian II., cut in dark stone. We crossed the rapid Iser, which has been appropriately called "swift flowing," and entered the Maximilianeum, an educational institution founded by the Emperor Max; a fine view of the city was obtained from the corridor. Some of the other interesting places visited were the Basilica, with sixty-six marble columns supporting arches covered with frescos, and a pulpit made of different kinds of wood; the Crystal Palace, and the Botanical Gardens. The Bavarian National Museum contains a large collection of various objects illustrating the progress of art and civilization, and the Bavarian Historical Gallery has a series of frescos representing the history of Bavaria.

September 25 we left Munich for Leipsic, a journey requiring the time from 7.30 A. M. to 8.30 P. M., a tedious day, since we saw but little that interested us, except the ancient town of Ratisbon or Regensburg, with its Cathedral. Our company comprised several German ladies, whose conversation,

MONUMENT OF MAXIMILIAN, MUNICH

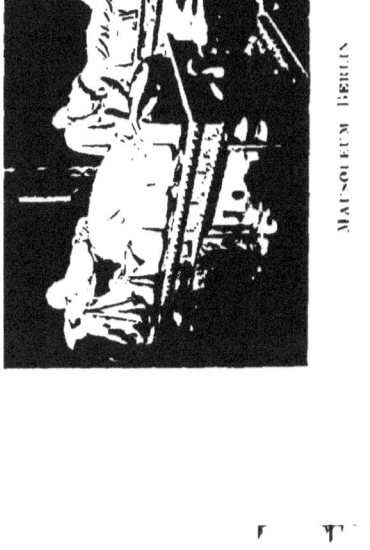

MAUSOLEUM BERLIN

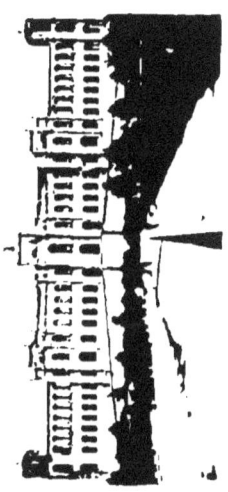

THE MAXIMILIANEUM, MUNICH

STATUE OF FREDERICK THE GREAT, BERLIN

no doubt, would have been instructive had we understood their language. The confusion of tongues might have had its advantages, but it is a misfortune to the modern traveller, who is not a polyglot. Leipsic, an ancient town, dating from the beginning of the eleventh century, is considered one of the most important commercial towns of Germany, and is distinguished for its book trade, its fairs, and university. We were fortunate to arrive in the city during one of these fairs, which have been held annually, and sometimes two or three times a year, since 1180. On such occasions a large number of strangers, including foreigners, as well as Germans, from thirty thousand to forty thousand, come to the city to attend these exhibitions. The public squares and portions of the broad streets are furnished with booths, where all kinds of merchandise are sold. They form a small town of themselves, being arranged like the streets of a city, thus affording easy access to these movable warehouses. Both men and women superintend the stalls, and offer their goods to customers. These fairs afford the traveller an excellent opportunity for studying the different ways and costumes of the peasants and villagers, and they are profitable to hotel-keepers, who charge one-half or one-third more than the usual rates, as long as they continue.

Wishing to purchase a book, after some inquiry, we found a place where they were for sale; and pending negotiations, during which the trader's German and our English became strangely blended, a gentleman stepped forward and politely offered his assistance; he proved to be one of our own countrymen and a student of the University of Leipsic. After arranging the bargain with the German, he conducted us to this institution of learning, and showed us some of the rooms used for lectures. They were exceedingly plain, and even rough looking, with deep carvings made in the desks, proving that the use of the jack-knife is not confined to Yankee boys. As it was vacation, the cabinets, much to our regret, were inaccessible to visitors; therefore we made a visit to the Museum, instituted in 1837, which contains mostly the works of modern artists. It has very little statuary, but some of the paintings are fine; one of Napoleon, at Fontainebleau, 1814, by Delaroche, is perhaps the best. Among the artists whose works are represented are Murillo, Sassoferrato, Zimmermann, Schrader, Lessing, and Overbeck. An extensive collection of engravings occupies nine rooms.

The streets and buildings of the more densely crowded parts of the town appear to be very ancient, carrying back the imagination to the early period of the city; but Leipsic lives in modern history as the scene of one of the most sanguinary and prolonged struggles on record. The battle fought October, 1813, between the French forces, numbering about one hundred and fifty thousand men, and the Allies, with three hundred thousand, lasted four days. During the conflict the Polish general, Poniatowski, was drowned in attempting to cross the Elster, which runs through the city.

September 27 we started early for Berlin; the weather was cold and disagreeable, and the region through which we journeyed, flat and uninteresting. In passing from Switzerland and Northern Italy to Germany, one perceives a great change in natural scenery: from grand and lofty mountains to level and monotonous tracts of land; but this is not all the difference perceptible to the tourist. He observes in the former countries mean, dilapidated dwellings, dirty, narrow streets, and numerous beggars, while in the latter there are indications of thrift; the people seem industrious and energetic, and we did not see any beggars among them.

The Swiss are from necessity industrious, for nothing less than constant diligence could gain a livelihood from their mountainous country, and it is surprising in what inhospitable regions their dwellings are found; sometimes clinging to the sides of steep acclivities or planted in some deep ravine, unvisited by the rays of the sun for the greater part of the year, as in the Splugen Pass; yet these hardy mountaineers live, by some means, among the rocks and glaciers of the Alps. Here men, women, and children are inured to hard labor; it is painful to see what burdens they carry on their backs, and what toils they endure, especially the women and children. One can excuse the persistence with which they solicit the traveller to purchase their wares.

We arrived in Berlin about one o'clock, and went to the Hotel de l'Europe, Tauben Strasse, a very favorable location for seeing the most interesting objects of the city. Having rested from our journey, we walked to the west end of the famous Unter den Linden (under the lindens) to the Brandenburg Gate. This street is one hundred and sixty-five feet wide and comprises five different streets or passage-ways, a broad driveway in the centre, and two narrow walks on each side separated by rows of linden trees. These trees are small but beautiful rather than majestic.

Beyond the Brandenburg Gate stands the Monument to Victory, one hundred and ninety-eight feet high, made of granite and bronze. It was inaugurated in 1873, to commemorate Prussian victories in the late wars, and the restoration of the German Empire. It is a very imposing memorial, even in Berlin, where monuments and statues are decidedly in vogue. Near the gate is a large and beautiful park called the Thiergarten. The Museums of Berlin are in the vicinity of the royal palaces. The Old Museum, two hundred and eighty-two feet in length and eighty-four in width, is in the Greek style, with eighteen Ionic columns; the central part is adorned with four groups in bronze, while statues and frescos decorate the vestibule, and eighteen ancient statues, the rotunda. The Museum contains also casts of ancient sculptures found on the site of the national shrine at Olympia, discovered in 1875, by explorations made at the expense of the German government. The upper walls of the rotunda are hung with tapestries woven at Arras, for Henry VIII., from designs by Raphael, copied from the tapestries of the Vatican, and similar to those at Dresden. These Berlin tapestries, after passing through the hands of different owners, were finally purchased by Frederick William IV. There were originally ten in number, but one is lost; they represent Scripture scenes.

The Assyrian sculptures of the rotunda obtained from the palaces of Calah and Nineveh, erected about 900 and 750 B. C., are of alabaster and represent battles, hunting scenes, etc. The antiquarian department contains many valuable engraved gems, comprising a cameo in agate representing the Apotheosis of Septimius Severus, and is one of the largest known, being nine inches by seven and one half; another cameo bears the representation of the Judgment of Paris. In the same room is kept the "Silver Treasure," found at Hildesheim, consisting of Roman works of the time of Augustus. The Cabinet of Coins includes ancient, mediæval, and modern specimens. There are more than fifty thousand antiques, while the mediæval and modern do not fall below in numbers.

The next day after our visit to the Museum we devoted to one of the numerous residences of the sovereigns,—the Royal Palace,—an immense edifice, five hundred and fifty-two feet long, three hundred and eighty-four wide, with six hundred apartments, but only a small number of these rooms are open to the public. The building was constructed by the Elector Frederick II., but improvements were made by several of his successors. The emperor, when in Berlin, occupies another palace, near this one, of smaller size.

The manner of going over a Royal Palace is attended with some formalities, like the following: Visitors, after paying the customary fee and receiving a ticket of admission, assemble in one of the vestibules and wait for the guide, who makes his appearance at 11 A. M. He then conducts the party up an inclined plane paved with brick, instead of ascending by flights of stairs. We then enter a long hall which contains nothing of much interest, where we halt, and the guide opens a box containing felt slippers and proceeds to supply each member of the party with a pair to be worn over the boots; they are all the same size and large enough for skates. We thought if these slippers represented the typical German foot, there was little to fear for the perpetuity of a nation with so broad foundations. The only way we could keep our slippers on our feet was to slide over the floor, which consisted of wood so highly

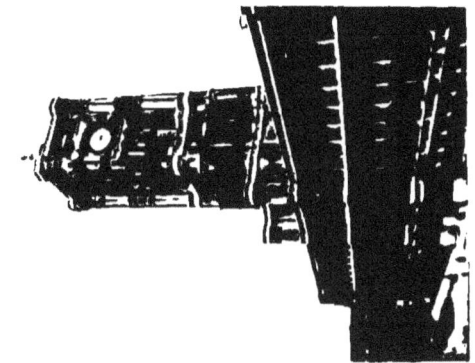
The Royal House

"UNTER DEN LINDEN."

The Bourse

The Passage

VIEWS IN BERLIN.

polished as to be smooth as glass. It was impossible to understand how the children in our party managed their pedal coverings.

After being properly shod we were conducted through a suite of richly decorated rooms, so overloaded with ornaments in gold, silver, and marble that but little definite idea could be retained of such ostentatious display, which may be necessary for royalty; but for ourselves we prefer the simplicity of Republican institutions. The Ritter-Saal or Throne Room abounds in articles made of the precious metals; the throne is of wrought silver. In this room there is a massive silver column, eight feet in height, presented to the emperor in 1867, by the army and navy officers, while another apartment contains pure white columns with silver bases and capitals. The Königo-Saal contains full-length portraits of the kings of Prussia, and the White Saloon holds the marble statues of the twelve Electors of Brandenburg, a statue of Victory, statues representing eight provinces of Prussia; while statues of Justinian, Constantine, Charlemagne and Rudolph II. occupy the staircase. The picture gallery of the palace includes paintings representing King William at the battle of Sadowa; the Coronation of the king in 1861, and King William presenting the crown prince with the Order of Merit, after the battle of Sadowa. The floors of the apartments are in designs of marquetry.

After completing the tour of the palace we cast off our slippers, to be gathered up by the guide, and ascended to the Palace Chapel, which was covered with frescoes; the altar was made of yellow and white alabaster, the reading desks of white Carrara marble, and a gilt crucifix was set with gems.

This palace has a ghost story connected with its history. It is said that the spectre of the White Lady haunts the palaces of Baireuth and Berlin, at certain times, as a forewarner of the death of one of the royal house; that this is the ghost of the Countess Agnes, who had committed a foul murder, that of her two children. The last time the spectre made its appearance at Berlin was in 1840, the same year in which Frederick William III. died.

The Rathaus is an imposing building of red brick, and forms a conspicuous object among others, of light-colored stone. It is in the Gothic style with some traces of the Italian, and has a tower two hundred and seventy-six feet high. The interior corresponds in architectural display to the exterior. The Fest-saal, with its coffered ceiling, carved oak doors, and beautiful marble columns, the Library, the Town Council Chamber, and the Magistrate's Saloon, are all richly and appropriately fitted up.

We had some difficulty in getting access to the mineral collection of the University. The custodian was at dinner, and did not wish to be disturbed, but finally opened the Museum, insisting on closing it after a short time. Consequently we were hurried through the numerous cabinets, greatly to our disappointment, since the collection is said to be the most extensive on the continent. It is certainly very large and contains remarkably fine specimens, notably a piece of amber from the region of the Baltic which was said to weigh fourteen pounds. There were some fine specimens of gems and a large variety of marbles, but we were not able to examine the rocks, fossils, and other geological collections. The columns of the Museum were made of a beautiful kind of marble, with a white ground sometimes shading into a soft yellow tint, intersected by veins of black. The churches of Berlin are far inferior to the other public buildings; some of them are constructed in a peculiar manner. The entrance is by a sort of "back door," through a long, dark vestibule separated from the nave by a row of short, clumsy columns, while the ceiling is vaulted; but there was little decoration compared with the churches we had seen, even in the Cathedral.

The National Gallery, containing the paintings of modern artists, is enclosed by an unfinished colonnade of Corinthian columns, and was originally intended to form the centre of an extensive building for all the art institutions of Berlin. It was opened in 1876, and contained at the time of our visit nearly four hundred paintings, several cartoons, and a few sculptures. Many of these paintings are highly finished, and show perfect fidelity to nature. The grand cartoons of Cornelius, occupying two large saloons, represent allegorical or mythological subjects. In one room, Grace, Peace, Poesy, Investigation, Humility, Enthusiasm, Strength, and Joy are symbolized, while the cartoons of this celebrated fresco painter illustrate the Christian Doctrine, pertaining to sin, death, and redemption, intended for the Campo Santo, in imitation of that at Pisa.

No one can understand German social life without visiting a biergarten; therefore being invited by a fellow-countryman, we ventured to enter one. The building was very large, and could accommodate at one time probably from twelve to fifteen hundred persons. We passed through a kind of arcade into a long hall with tables for six or eight persons each, filling all the space except narrow aisles for passage. As we entered, cigar smoke was so dense that at first thought we supposed the building was on fire. Germans are the most persistent smokers in the world; they smoke in all places, even at the table, without any regard to the guests. Parties of friends and acquaintances were assembled around the small table, taking their lunch of bread and ham. Often whole families, babies and all, visit these places of resort, while at the end of the hall is a music-stand, where a band plays for their entertainment. The people are very social, but the talking, music, and smoke rendered a prolonged visit undesirable, though the respectable classes of natives frequent the biergarten. The customs of nations offer an interesting study to the traveller, and it is necessary to be brought in contact with other people to avoid narrowness and intolerance. The Germans are an energetic, progressive, and intellectual people, but in some things they would be considered wanting in refinement of manners.

October 1 we started out in quest of adventures, like a knight-errant, and, fortunately, found new objects to be investigated; the first being the National Bank, a brick building of imposing appearance. We passed through a vestibule, ascended a flight of marble steps, and entered a kind of reception room of elegant finish, with walls of different kinds of marble, and spacious marble staircases on either side. Beyond, in the apse of the building, is a large room for bank business. Leaving this building we started for the Jewish Synagogue, and met on the way one of the guests of the hotel where we stopped, who joined us for the same purpose. Near the Synagogue is the garden of the Royal Chateau of Monbijou, erected for Queen Sophia Dorothea, consort of Frederick William I., but the grounds bore the appearance of neglect. The Jewish place of worship, built of different-colored brick, is 318 feet in length, in the interior, and 93 in width, finished in the Alhambra or Saracenic style, and has three domes, of which the highest is 165 feet. The building is entered by three elegant bronze doors, separated by columns of green granite. After passing through the smaller synagogue, we entered the beautiful inner temple, which will seat 10,000 people. On the ground floor are the seats for the men, while the women occupy the galleries. The ornaments, in the Moresque style, are very delicate and elaborate, and the colors are of subdued tints; there are no violent contrasts, nothing gaudy, the stained glass windows are simple and elegant in design. The apse, containing a structure with a dome, to hold the "Ark of the Covenant," is an interesting study of beautiful designs; and here the Sacred Scriptures, that is, the Old Testament, are kept. Gentile visitors are not permitted to enter the holy place. The entire structure affords, with its slender columns and peculiar capitals and arches, a study of the Moorish style of architecture. There are many Jews in Berlin, ten thousand, said our bright-eyed Hebrew maiden guide.

Our next visit was to the Reichstag, a building for the use of the lower branch of parliament, which was quite plain. The only thing especially interesting was the seat of Prince Bismarck when he was a member. Leaving the Reichstag, we engaged a carriage and drove to the Thiergarten, which begins just outside the Brandenburg Gate, and is about two miles in length and three fourths in width. The trees, though not large, are so close together that they form quite a dense

NATIONAL GALLERY.

THE MUSEUM

BRANDENBURG GATE

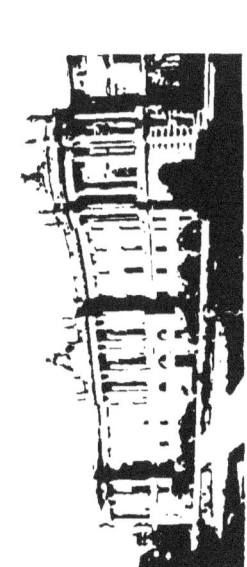

thicket, while carriage-drives cross it in every direction, with here and there a small opening, a statue, a plot of flowers, or a small lake. Following these paths, allured by their attractions, we sauntered on until we became weary, and were glad to find the gate by which we entered. The Industrial Museum contains a collection of antique and modern productions, from different countries, embracing plastic works, in wood, stone, etc., such as sculpture, wood carving, furniture inlaid with different woods and ivory; and in the department of ceramics were majolica and porcelains of different kinds, as Sèvres, Minton, Copeland, Berlin, Meissen, and Bohemian; glass of various kinds, woven fabrics, embroideries, tapestries, metal-work in gold, silver, bronze, and iron, enamels, mosaics, etc. One room contains the Lüneburg Collection of silver and silver-gilt plate purchased for 220,000 thalers. A brief summary gives some very rich and beautiful specimens of antique and modern art, rich furnitures, shrines, coffers, boxes, etc., while the exquisitely delicate engraving on glass was of modern workmanship.

The Panopticum, or Wax Statuary, was on exhibition in the Kaiser Gallery, a very beautiful arcade covered with glass, similar to the one at Milan, and containing shops and restaurants. The largest hall of statues is very rich in gilt ornaments, painted glass windows, and other decorations. The collection comprises a large number of wax statues, life size, of distinguished Prussians, including the emperor. Others represented persons and scenes that inspired disgust, and were very repulsive. The collection is larger and more varied than Madam Tussaud's of London, but in some rooms less pleasing. We did not see the "Chamber of Horrors," in the London Collection.

A visitor to Berlin should make a pilgrimage to Sans Souci, with which so many historical memories are associated. Potsdam, where it is located, is on an island in the River Havel, about seventeen miles from Berlin, and has a population of about forty-five thousand. Besides the Palace of Sans Souci, it contains the Royal Palace and the New Palace. The Old or

Royal Palace is near the Lustgarten, which is enclosed on one side by two rows of columns, and contains several bronze busts of celebrated generals, and many articles used by Frederick the Great, preserved in their original condition. At some distance from the palace is the Friedenskirche, or Church of Peace, built in the style of the early Christian basilica. The church occupies a quadrangle, with arcades containing some statuary. In the atrium, peculiar to basilicas, are groups of statues; on one side a Pieta by Rectschel, on the other Rauch's group of Moses supported by Aaron and Hur, while in the centre is the Risen Christ, by Thorwaldsen. Sixteen columns of black marble support galleries, while in front of the chancel are the tombs of Frederick IV., who died in 1861, and Queen Elizabeth, who died in 1873; and before these shrines there is an angel sculptured by Tenerani, of Rome. The altar is supported by four very beautiful columns of green jasper, highly polished, the gift of the Russian emperor. The walls of the apse consisted of variegated marble and the vaulting of mosaic-work, while the pulpit and reading-desk were of white Carrara marble.

The Palace of Sans Souci, built by Frederick the Great, as a place of retirement from the cares of state, is a one-story building standing on an eminence approached by a series of steps. The side of the hill is broken into terraces, covered with shrubs and flowers, and in front of the palace is a large fountain, with smaller ones on both sides.

The picture gallery connected with the palace is richly decorated with marble and gilding, and the walls are covered with paintings, but some of the best works have been transferred to the museums of Berlin. Many of the rooms of Sans Souci are precisely as Frederick left them; and the clock on the bureau, which suddenly stopped at the moment he breathed his last, twenty minutes past two o'clock, August 17, 1786, has never run since. One of the apartments called Voltaire's, because he once occupied it, is decorated in a peculiar manner. The walls and ceilings are covered with stucco, painted to represent fruits and flowers, looking very much like natural productions.

Groves, gardens, terraces, trees, shrubs, flowers, statues, and fountains diversify the scenery about Sans Souci. The grounds about the Orangery, a building nine hundred and ninety feet in length, are very delightful. Ceres and Flora and a copy of the Farnese Bull occupy places on the terrace, while the interior of the Orangery is decorated with paintings and statuary — some copies, others, original. The New Palace, built by Frederick the Great, is situated at the end of an avenue a little more than a mile from Sans Souci, apart from other buildings, except those occupied by soldiers. It was erected at the close of the Seven Years' War in 1763, and contains two hundred apartments. One room is so unique it deserves special notice. It is called the Grotto Saloon, and is inlaid with shells arranged in different patterns. A frieze running entirely around the room contains minerals and gems, affording a novel cabinet; a large chandelier made entirely of rock crystal hangs in one of the apartments. What is called the Marble Saloon is a hundred feet long. The costly splendor of palaces, interesting to the traveller, teaches the citizen of a republic this lesson: royal power and prestige are largely maintained by pomp and splendor, glittering equipage, magnificent palaces, the richness of royal surroundings, and a train of liveried dependents. Men are fascinated by such displays, and will cheerfully submit to be taxed to support them. After a day spent at Potsdam, a place long to be remembered, we returned to Berlin, to resume our sight-seeing in this fine city, which has been called by some one the "Paris of the North."

The next day being rainy induced us to make another visit to the Museum. Many of the statues and other sculptures in the Old Museum are copies of the antiques, though a good number are original. It has been said that one of the best works in the collection is the statue of a boy which was found in the Tiber, and purchased by Frederick the Great for ten thousand thalers, or about seventy-five hundred dollars. Art in the Roman period had declined, and one sees illustrations of the fact in the Roman Hall of the Museum. The Greeks made their statues ideal; the Romans copied more from nature, with too strict fidelity to truth. In their representations of distinguished men, they expressed the baser passions by which they were swayed, and consequently their countenances were sometimes very repulsive; while the Greeks, on the contrary, always sensitive to the beauty of form, made their heroes, however impelled by passion, preserve the graceful outlines of a calm and self-restrained expression. The parti-colored statues, are in our estimation, wanting in taste. There is no material so appropriate for sculpturing the human form as the pure, white marble; and though the Greeks, the unrivalled masters of the chisel, did sometimes employ other materials, as gold, ivory, and bronze, yet the best of their works that have been preserved are in marble.

We again examined some of the paintings of the earlier school, and find but little variety in the subject — generally Madonnas or some other Scripture character or event; but there is a devout, reverential spirit pervading these pictures, which appeals to the religious element in human nature, notwithstanding the grotesque that is sometimes apparent. Very few of the Madonnas yet seen — not all Italian works have to this time been examined — are satisfactory. It seems to us that the artists failed, generally, in their conceptions of the child Christ, as well as the Christ of riper years; but when they attempted to represent the Father, a purely spiritual Being, in the form of an earthly potentate, with the usual insignia of regal state, it seems presumptuous and repugnant to a feeling of reverence. Some of these sacred paintings are ludicrous from the peculiar association of ideas. For instance, while Mary and other personages are enraptured with the infant Redeemer, half a dozen cherubs in gay clothing and with pink, yellow, and green wings, like those of a parrot, are perched on the ridge-pole of a thatched cottage — one angel was actually crawling out of the window, like a burglar. In another instance, so little regard was paid to the symmetry of the human form, the figure of the Madonna was so tall that, when seated, she appeared like a person standing back of her own lap. The " Glory " with which the old masters were accustomed to represent the saints appeared, in these pictures, almost precisely like a gold plate at one side of their heads, but it was impossible to understand how it was held in that position. One sees the conventional red dress and blue mantle of the Madonnas of the different masters. The decided and bright colors, a want of softening by graduated tints, and the blending of inharmonious hues seemed to us too conspicuous to produce a pleasing effect.

The Zoological Gardens, just outside the Thiergarten, are worth a visit. The buildings for the animals are well adapted to their use, while some of them are really fine, especially the Elephants' House, a large structure of different colored bricks, arranged in mosaic-work, with domes, and an enclosure for the elephants to exercise in the open air. There were two of these animals; the male, a fine large specimen, had evidently been well trained in his manners, for he very politely bowed to the guests, especially when they gave him cakes and apples. He had, no doubt, been taught to dance, and seemed very fond of the pastime; while his female companion, in the opposite part of the hall, was equally fond of being fed; but if her visitors did not gratify her tastes, she would strike at them through the bars of her apartment. The lions and other animals were fine examples of their species; some of the birds were very rare and exceedingly beautiful; the collection of doves was especially so. The Berlin collection of animals is, in some respects, superior to those of London and Paris.

Berlin is a beautiful city; the streets are broad, the buildings fine, and some are elegant. For a city that contains one million or more inhabitants, there were two very noticeable features: the absence of foreigners and, apparently, of poverty. We have not visited a place where the citizens are so well dressed, taken as a whole, while there is an appearance of taste, neatness, and refinement about almost everything material. The soldiers are among the finest in appearance, and the best drilled in Europe, — if any fault is to be found with them, it is want of courtesy to private citizens,— and nearly all officials about railway stations, the police, etc., inspire one with confidence in their capacity, and respect for their manners; the attendants at hotels are polite and obliging. It is said the inhabitants of Berlin are proud of their city, and well they may be, since it has many attractions. Our visit was very pleasant, and it was with regret we left the German capital for other places.

Our journey to Dresden was through a level and monotonous region, with little of interest to engage the attention, except the kind and agreeable German lady, our travelling companion. After a ride of several hours, we reached Dresden at five o'clock in the afternoon, and went to Weber's Hotel, on the Ostra-Allee near the Zwinger. The next day we visited some of the churches of the city, as we were interested in church architecture. The Roman Catholic Court Church, built in 1737, in what is called the "baroque style," contains the royal vaults. The exterior, profusely decorated by statues, has sixty-four of these representing saints on the parapets and about the entrance; the altar-piece, delineating the Ascension, was the work of Raphael Mengo; this church is celebrated for its music. The Frauenkirche, or Church of Our Lady, has a lofty dome three hundred and ten feet in height, while the Kreuzkirche, the largest in Dresden, has a tower three hundred and forty-two feet high. A Gothic church near the Zwinger is very imposing, with its two towers and spires, its buttresses, and other appendages peculiar to this style; but the interior affords an instance of one of the peculiarities of the churches of this country (perhaps it is the only one of the kind), with galleries on one side and the pulpit on the other. The seats, consisting of wood benches, all face the pulpit; while at the end opposite the main entrance, the altar is placed, so that the hearers seem to be sitting sideways. The floor consisted of boards, without covering.

The Zwinger, begun in 1711, but not completed until more than a century after, is a peculiar structure, consisting of six pavilions connected by closed galleries of one story with gateways. The building surrounds a court three hundred and eighty-four by three hundred and fifty-one feet, in which are small fountains and plants, and a statue of Frederick Augustus in bronze. The entire edifice is highly ornamented with various kinds of decoration, like the "rococo," so much in vogue at one time; it has been called a fine illustration of the baroque style. The Museum of the famous Dresden Gallery occupies one side of the Zwinger.

On entering, the first object sought was the Sistine Madonna, the sole occupant of one of the rooms. It would be presumptuous to express an opinion of this famous picture by the prince of painters, as its reputation is established wherever art is known; but for us it would be far easier to study it were all the figures removed except the mother and child.

As our visits must be frequent to the Dresden Gallery, in the meantime we went to the Johanneum Museum, and the collection of porcelain, which comprises about fifteen thousand specimens of Chinese, Japanese, East Indian, Persian, French, and Dresden wares. The Chinese collection was very large and varied. The Saxon ware generally passes under the name of Dresden, which was not made here, but at Meissen, where the Royal Porcelain Manufactory, which employs six hundred workmen, is situated. It was founded in 1710, soon after the discovery of making porcelain, by Böttcher. Some of the specimens consisted of groups of statuary, while two others were rose trees growing in flower pots. The entire trees, stems, buds, and blossoms were of porcelain in the natural colors of the plant. Imitations of almost every object in nature, and some having no natural existence, are seen here.

One of the most remarkable specimens was the lace mantle covering a female bust; the imitation of the embroidery, its meshes and folds, was truly marvellous; Japanese, French, and Italian works were conspicuous.

The Historical Museum contains a very interesting collection of armor; weapons of different kinds, cabinets, mounted knights with horses richly caparisoned, costumes of princes, etc. Some of the swords, pistols, guns, and other weapons were richly decorated with jewels and inlaid with ivory, and other materials. Cups, drinking-horns ornamented with gold and silver, a goblet and sword which had belonged to Luther, a chessboard, with pieces containing the representation of the head of some warrior in relief, were among the numerous objects of curiosity. We entered a room where armored knights were mounted for the tournament, and two with lances in rest were ready for a tilt. Armor for the Saxon princes, and the princes themselves in gala suits, mounted on richly caparisoned horses, represented the customs of the past. The Pistol Chamber contained specimens of the firearms of the sixteenth and seventeenth centuries, including those of Charles XII., of Sweden, of Gustavus Adolphus, and Louis XIV., of France. Another saloon was a repository for weapons used in "The Thirty Years' War" and the batons of Pappenheim and Tilly. In the Saddle Room were displayed the figures of the horses belonging to the Saxon kings, with jewelled trappings, and jewelled shields, hemlets, and other armor. From these we learn something of the physical strength of the warriors of those times. It seems incredible that men could wear so heavy armor and carry such weapons at all, to say nothing of their wielding them in battle, when riding at full speed. The poles of their lances appeared to be at least fifteen feet in length. Little princes not more than ten years old were dressed in full armor, showing how early they were trained in these military exercises.

We made another visit to the Picture Gallery. Painting, like poetry, must be studied, in order to be appreciated. There are some pictures that fascinate us by their power over the imagination; we seem entranced when beholding them, and are oblivious to all things else, and live in a world of thought and feeling. In such a wilderness of paintings it is best to select a few for special study; for ourselves, beside the Sistine Madonna, before mentioned, we chose the Madonna of Holbein, Correggio's Adoration of the Shepherds, and his Mary Magdalene, the Marriage at Cana, and the Adoration of the Magi, by Paul Veronese, Ecce Homo, by Guido Rene, Tribute Money, by Titian, Landscapes by Poussin and Claude Lorrain. Besides those just mentioned, were the works by the Dutch School of painters, whose fidelity to nature is remarkable. Among these, are Teniers, Ruysdael, Wouvermans, Cuyp, Dürer, Rubens, Van Dyck, and Rembrandt, and of the Spanish painters, Velasquez and Murillo.

The Green Vaults in the Royal Palace contain untold treasures of jewels, plate, and costly works of art of different kinds Here are seen numerous works in bronze, ivory, and carving, many of them copies of ancient sculptures; some of the specimens are set in silver and ornamented with gems. The Chimney Room, so called from the wonderful chimney-piece occupying the centre, is embellished with reliefs in porcelain, various kinds of precious stones, and pearls. The specimens in amber were very striking, comprising a cabinet of oak covered with mosaics in this gem. The Silver Room comprises articles mostly in silver, and the Hall of Precious Things contains articles made of precious stones and rock crystal, and collections of cameos and gems. Here are seen the largest enamelled work known, thirty-four inches by eighteen, representing Mary Magdalene; a bust of Diana in Derbyshire spar; two hundred and fifty-four portraits engraved on gems; a ball of rock crystal twenty-two and one-half inches in circumference, and weighing fifteen pounds; the crystal goblet which had belonged to Martin Luther; a crystal drinking vessel ornamented with jewels valued at five thousand dollars; a beautiful ebony cabinet with columns and plates of rock crystal resembling the finest quality of glass, and the wonderful golden egg.

The Wood or Armory Room contains places in the walls for secreting the treasures of the Green Vaults in time of danger, while the panels are embossed with the escutcheons of old Saxon provinces. A marvel of workmanship was seen in a cherry-stone on which was cut the figure of eighty human heads, seen only through a powerful microscope, and was the work of a sculptor of Nürnberg. This room contains the sceptres, globes, and crowns richly ornamented with gems, that were used for the coronation of Augustus III. and his consort; though the precious stones had been removed and replaced by paste jewels.

The eighth and last room, painted in red and gold, comprised the most costly articles of all the collection,—the treasury of the Royal Saxon family. The crown jewels include diamonds without number, of various colors, as pink, yellow, and the celebrated green brilliant, besides colorless specimens, rubies, emeralds, sapphires, and other gems; they are sometimes called the Polish Regalia. The green diamond is the gem *par excellence* of these treasures and is remarkable for its rare color and peculiar splendor. Its weight is only forty and one-half carats, or one hundred and sixty grains, while the largest of the collection weighs one hundred and ninety-four and one-half grains. A fine ruby, weighing a little more than fifty-nine carats, a Bohemian garnet said to be the largest in Europe, an onyx in three colors, a rare specimen, six and two-thirds inches in length and four and one-fourth in width, claimed to be the largest known, belong to the Dresden collection. A group of one hundred and thirty-two figures in gold and enamel represented the celebration of the birth of an East Indian emperor, and the statue of an African was covered with gems, but the most grotesque objects were the models of two crocodiles completely covered with diamonds.

A large number of specimens in the Green Vaults, though exceedingly rich and exhibit great ingenuity in the workmanship, have no other value than to show what human skill and ingenuity can accomplish, but at the same time they afford proofs of misspent time and talents. They have no use or intrinsic beauty, and there is nothing noble in devoting years or perhaps a lifetime to making such baubles. There is an incongruity in the profuse employment of precious stones to ornament worthless objects, while it degrades the most beautiful things in nature to contemptible uses. Gems are intrinsically beautiful and most to be admired when seen alone or as ornaments to noble objects.

The Dresden Collection of Minerals includes a large number of native specimens; some of the agates were the largest we had ever seen, including one of variegated colors and nearly three feet in diameter; varieties of quartz, beautiful ruin, shell, and dendritic marbles, some of them very uncommon, and a peculiar specimen of transparent and iridescent zinc blend. In the gem department, which was inferior to that of the Green Vault, were copies of some of the famous diamonds of the world, notably a red Florentine and a blue diamond of one hundred and thirty-nine and one-half carats, which could not have been a copy of the "Hope" a much smaller gem. A study of rocks and minerals is very interesting as well as profitable to the naturalist, but one might think it otherwise without some previous knowledge of geology and mineralogy; and the same is true in examining works of art for which a preparation is important. The Collection of Casts seen in Dresden are copies of some of the most celebrated sculptures and are useful as studies.

We made several other visits to the Picture Gallery and at each visit discovered new features to be studied and new beauties to be admired. A wonderful art is painting, both in its influence and its delineations. It has a two-fold power, form and color, but there is a wide difference in pictures; some enchant us, some merely please us, while others make no lasting impression or repel us. There are some specimens of all these classes found in the Dresden Gallery as well as in every other collection, but there are so many master-pieces here, that the inferior or ordinary pictures are soon forgotten.

Dresden, the capital of the Kingdom of Saxony, first came into notice in 1206, and has been the residence of the sovereigns since the latter part of the fifteenth century. It was greatly extended and embellished by Augustus II., and now has a population of two hundred thousand or more. Its beautiful suburbs and magnificent gallery of paintings and other art collections attract numerous visitors from all countries.

## CHAPTER VIII.

*From Dresden to Prague and Vienna.*

OCTOBER 13 we left Dresden, with its treasures of art, for the ancient and memorable city of Prague or Praha, in Bohemia. The route was very interesting, both on account of its fine scenery, and its historical associations. The region through which we passed has been called the "Saxon Switzerland." The rocks, of a soft yellow sandstone, rise to a great height from the Elbe, in the form of castles with towers and bastions. The river is very sinuous in its course, but its graceful curves add a charm to the landscape which is continually changing, while occasionally an old castle is seen reposing upon a high and precipitous cliff, which seems inaccessible to wingless creatures. The Elbe is not a large river, while its waters are a muddy green, at least in Bohemia. The foliage of the region we passed through presented in its autumnal dress different shades of yellow; but there was an absence of the bright reds, seen in the forests of the United States. The trees of Germany are generally of small size compared with those of some other countries.

The railway to Prague passes through, or near, several places of historical interest, comprising the scene of the battle of Dresden, fought in 1813, in which Moreau fell, and to whom a monument is erected; Pina, on the Elbe, captured by the Swedes in 1639, and by the Prussians in 1758; Mt. Lilienstein, 1,293 feet in height, situated on a great bend of the river, where Frederick the Great captured the Saxon army of fourteen thousand men, and not far from here, was the battle-field of Kulm where, August 30, 1813, the French forces, forty thousand strong, surrendered to the Allies. Other places of note were Aussig, the birth-place of the painter, Raphael Mengs; Labosity, where the first battle of the Seven Years' War was fought, October, 1756; Randnitz, where Rienzi, the last of the Tribunes, was imprisoned by Charles IV. in 1350. As we approached the city, the face of the country became less rugged, and indeed seemed almost level.

Bohemia, named from the ancient Boii who emigrated from Gaul in the second century B. C. and settled here, is a country around which cluster many interesting as well as tragical associations. The early settlers were conquered by a king of Moravia who introduced Christianity, and after his death it was governed by the "Dukes of Prague" who subsequently received the title of king. Prague, its ancient capital, was founded by Libussa, the first Duchess of Bohemia, and is very picturesquely situated on both sides of the Moldau, between two hundred and three hundred miles north of Vienna. It is distinguished for its imposing situation, its interesting buildings, towers, palaces, and cathedral, but more especially for the part it has taken in the important events of history. The city is nearly nine miles in circumference, and, at the present time, has a mixed population, occupying four distinct sections. One of these is devoted chiefly to the government offices; another, called the Hradschin, is distinguished by an extensive imperial palace; a third is known as the Jews' Quarter, with its synagogues, churches, and schools, and lastly, what is designated "The New Town," with its streets, squares, and places of public resort. The population comprises Bohemians, Germans, and Hebrews, each speaking his native language, while the types of the different nationalities are quite marked.

The Jewish quarter or Josephstadt was formerly occupied by the Hebrews only, but later, a large number of the lower class of Christians have resided here. One of the synagogues, according to tradition, was founded by fugitives from Jerusalem, after its destruction by the Romans. The University of Prague, founded in 1348, is the oldest of the German universities, and during its most flourishing days it received thousands of students from foreign countries, and still remains a well-endowed institution with various departments of study. The Church of the Hussites of the fifteenth century, contains the tombstone of Tycho Brahe, the Danish astronomer, and a professor in the University of Prague, who died in 1601. This city was the home of Jerome of Prague and the place where John Huss was educated, both distinguished reformers and Christian martyrs; and here, two centuries later, was decided the fate of the Reformation in Bohemia by the battle of White Hill. When in Constance we visited the Council Chamber where Huss, sent thither under the safe conduct of the Emperor, received his sentence and suffered death at the stake, in 1415, and his friend Jerome suffered in the same way the following year.

The Rathhaus recalls some of the terrible scenes of the Reformation, for, in front of this palace after the disastrous battle of White Hill, twenty-seven of the Protestant leaders, mostly Bohemian nobles, were executed, in 1621, and in the same place, in 1633, eleven officers of high rank, in Wallenstein's army, were executed for cowardice at the battle of Lutzen. A column stands in the Grosse Ring, to commemorate the defence of the city against the Swedes, in 1648, where the citizens on pleasant evenings, often assemble to sing hymns. A bronze statue of Charles IV., the founder of the University of Prague, was erected in 1848, on the five-hundredth anniversary of that institution. Numerous bridges span the River Moldau, one of these, the Carlsbrücke, is sixteen hundred and twenty feet in length, and is supported on sixteen arches, with defensive towers at each end; the tower called the Aldstadt contains the statues of the Emperor Charles VI., and his son Wenzel IV., while the heads of Bohemian nobles executed in 1621 were exposed to public view for ten years on this fortress. This stronghold was maintained against the Swedes during a bombardment of fourteen weeks, in 1648, and when the Prussians assailed the city, the Carlsbrücke was the scene of the fiercest struggle. During the uprising of 1848, the University students seized the place, for the construction of their strongest barricades. The buttresses of the bridge are covered with thirty statues and groups of saints; a suspension bridge across the Moldau, fifteen hundred feet in length, is called the Kaizer-Franz-Brüke.

Among the monuments of Prague are an equestrian statue of the Emperor Francis I., seventy-five feet in height, and the Radetzky column, representing the Marshal with a baton and flag, borne on a shield carried by eight soldiers. War has always been the chief business of nations, if we are to judge by their number of soldiers, the strength of their fortifications, and other proofs of a hostile character. The heights about Prague afford excellent facilities for defence, therefore, they are covered with fortifications. From the terrace near the Imperial Palace are obtained fine views of the city, with its broad river spanned by numerous bridges, and of the range of hills on both sides.

The Hradschiner Platz, a high eminence on the northwest side of the river, might properly be called the citadel, which is enclosed by several public buildings, as palaces and a cathedral. The Burg or Imperial Palace, situated on the Platz, has been the theatre of many important events, especially in the Middle Ages. The Imperial Councillors were thrown from the window in an upper story of the Council Chamber, by order of Count Thun, which was the immediate occasion of the Thirty Years' War. This palace was once occupied by the Empress Maria Theresa. Near the Burg are the palaces of the Archbishop and Count Sternberg; the latter contains a small picture gallery of about three hundred and fifty paintings.

With some difficulty, we found the Palace of Wallenstein, and, on the payment of twenty kreutzers, were admitted, but to our disappointment, we saw only the Audience Chamber of the redoubtable warrior, with its marble walls and beautiful doors; there was nothing else to be seen in this apartment. However, we saw the cabinet of the hero and a small room containing the figure of a horse covered with the skin of the animal he rode in battle; the palace belongs to the present family of Wallenstein. Many of the public buildings show signs of neglect and decay.

The Cathedral, begun in 1344, has a tower three hundred and twenty-three feet high, while the nave contains the "Monument of the Kings" where the Bohemian sovereigns were buried. Each chapel has some monument, relic, or other memento of the past; but the most conspicuous object was the shrine of St. John Nepomuc, made in 1763, of solid silver, with very elaborate workmanship, and adorned with statues; the shrine is said to contain one ton and a half of silver. The Saint was thrown into the Moldau, by order of the Emperor Wenzel, for refusing to reveal what the Empress had confided to him in the Confessional; he was afterwards canonized and became the patron saint of Prague. The Wenzel Chapel is inlaid with Bohemian precious stones, and decorated with ancient frescos, and the Cathedral contains some paintings, and other works of art, curiosities and relics of doubtful antiquity.

While wandering about the town, we met some of the American tourists left at Dresden, and in company with them visited several places of interest. One of these was the Museum which contained, among other cherished objects, illuminated MSS.; the sword of Gustavus Adolphus, and the MSS. of John Huss. The specimens in the Geological Department were valuable and well arranged.

Leaving the Museum, we started for the Jews' Quarter, and after passing through the crooked streets, guided by a young Hebrew, we came to a very ancient synagogue, called the "Altneuschule," the most gloomy and repulsive place of worship we had seen. The Palace of Count Steinberg contains a small picture gallery, with paintings by some of the celebrated masters. The Belvedere is a large villa built by the Emperor Ferdinand, for the use of the Empress; the great Hall is adorned with frescos illustrating the history of Bohemia. The Capuchin Monastery is said to contain a monstrance in the form of rays, decorated with sixty-five hundred and eighty precious stones.

Our party engaged a carriage, and we rode about the suburbs for two hours, crossing some of the bridges which constitute one of the peculiar features of the city. The most notable, the

IMPERIAL PALACE.

MONUMENT TO THE ARCH-
DUCHESS CHRISTINE.

## VIEWS IN VIENNA.

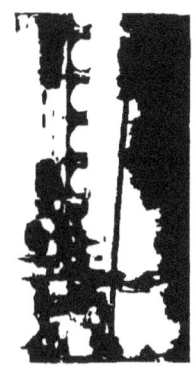

VIEW OF PRAGUE.

DER GRABEN.

Carlesbrücke, previously mentioned, is said to have been erected between 1357 and 1507, by money extorted from the Jews. One visiting this quaint city, in order to understand and appreciate its remarkable career, should be familiar with the history of the Reformation, and the severe conflicts following, as well as the struggles of later times, which have taken place on the fields of Bohemia.

Bidding farewell to the interesting city of Prague, we began our journey to Vienna, which was to be our next stopping-place in our wanderings.

The route afforded scenes of little interest except battle fields; namely, those of the conflict which ended the Hussite war in 1434; the field of Kolin, where the Austrians under Marshal Daun defeated Frederick the Great, 1757; Austerlitz, the scene of the "Battle of the Three Emperors," 1805: the field of Wagram, 1809; of Höingratz, 1866, besides battles between Bohemians and Hungarians in the thirteenth century. Brünn the capital of Moravia is the place where Baron Trench died in captivity, in 1749, and where Silvio Pellico was imprisoned eight years. Beyond Brünn is the place where Napoleon's reserves under Davout, after the battle of Austerlitz, proved dangerous foes to the retreating Austrians. Nikolsburg, a small town on the route, was the place where an armistice between the Prussians and Austrians was concluded, July, 1866. Near the village of Stupnay occurs a geological marvel, viz., a fossilized forest.

Arriving at Vienna late in the evening, we went to the Hotel Metropole, on the Franz-Josephs-Quai, and the next day paid a visit to the Burg or Royal Palace, to see the collections of art. The imperial jewels in the Royal Treasury are numerous, comprising several crowns, sceptre, globe, and other insignia of royalty. The collection contains many diamonds, some of them of remarkable beauty, and very rare, as the famous yellow diamond of one hundred and thirty-three and one-third carats weight and valued at fifty-seven thousand four hundred and forty-nine pounds, or between two and three hundred thousand dollars, and the Florentine diamond once the property of Charles the Bold of Burgundy. An order of the Golden Fleece was set with one hundred and fifty brilliants, and one of Maria Theresa with five hundred and forty-eight. There were crowns composed of diamonds and emeralds, others of diamonds and rubies, and several of different sized pearls, while bracelets and various other kinds of ornaments were formed of diamonds, rubies, sapphires, emeralds, and topazes. The Vienna collection, perhaps equals, if it does not surpass, the Dresden. The specimens of rock crystal seen in vases, pitchers, and other articles, are remarkable for their size and beauty. The collection includes many interesting objects, as curious clocks, watches, goblets, vases, altar-pieces, portrait medallions, ornaments of gold, and enamel, besides coronation robes, crowns, swords, and other objects of the past ages. Here are seen the crown of Charlemagne, the sabre of Haroun-al-Raschid, a talisman of Wallenstein, the insignia of the "Holy Roman Empire," the coronation robes of Napoleon I., as King of Italy, and the cradle of his son, the King of Rome, made of silver-gilt, and weighing five hundred pounds.

The Cabinet of Coins and Antiques in the Royal Palace, contains engraved gems and cameos remarkable for their size. The Apotheosis of Augustus in onyx, is nine inches in diameter and contains twenty figures; it was found in Jerusalem, at the time of the Crusades. There are more than forty thousand specimens of coins and numerous intaglios, but a list of all the curiosities would be tedious.

The Museum of Art and Industry, founded in 1864 on the plan of the South Kensington, England, is a brick building, of the Renaissance style, with two decorated friezes, the lower one containing medallion portraits of thirty-six celebrated artists. The exhibition rooms contain specimens of nearly all branches of ancient art, in gold, glass, ivory, wood engraving, tapestry, pottery wares, tin, iron, brass, bronze, leather, book-binding, etc., besides modern work of superior quality.

Our next point of attack was the Belvedere, or Museum of Paintings, which we had some trouble to find, as it was a good distance from the Royal Palace. The two buildings, formerly the Palace of Prince Eugene of Savoy, stood some distance apart, with a large garden between. The paintings of the old masters were arranged according to the different schools. Many of these we had met before, and they seemed like old acquaintances; among them were Raphael, Corregio, Da Vinci, Tintoretto, Rubens, Veronese, Murillo, Caracci, Guido Rene Perugino, and Rembrandt. We will venture a few criticisms on these works as they appeared to us. Caracci's pictures seemed life-like, while Guido Rene's are wanting in this quality. Perugino paints human flesh in orange brown, quite unlike western nations. The Annunciation, by Rafael Mengs, is fine, in some respects, as in the representation of Mary and the Angels, but the Supreme Being cannot be reverentially portrayed by human skill. The portraits of an old man and woman by Denner were remarkably truthful to nature; there was nothing ideal about them, and for this reason would not be considered to possess the highest artistic merit. The Dutch masters were so painstaking in delineating natural objects, that a close examination of their work was necessary. They were remarkably realistic and thorough, and too conscientious to slight so small an object as the wing of a tiny insect. Their landscapes were painted with great fidelity, while their fruit and flower pieces, in which they delighted, are nature itself. Not a fly, worm, spider, or a drop of dew, not a vein in a leaf escapes their touch, nothing is left for the imagination of the spectator. They could paint what they saw, but their representation of sacred subjects was far below those of the Italian masters. Their Christ and angels were human, nothing more. Rubens is a favorite in every gallery, judging from the number of his paintings. His coloring is rich, but there is a grossness in some of his figures that render them repulsive. His women are sensuous, without intellectuality or spirituality. Both men and women are preëminently flesh and blood; such muscles, such color, belong to those who could afford no pleasure to cultivated people. This is the character of a majority of his works, though there are exceptions to the rule.

The Mineral Collections of the Burg are very large and valuable, and well arranged. They comprised salt crystals ranging from colorless, through all the tints of the prismatic colors; fine specimens of ruby blende, a peculiar mineral of iridescent fibres called by an unpronounceable German name, varieties of arragonite, epidote, Iceland spar which exhibited iridescent reflections and double refraction to the best advantage, a specimen of polished spar of a buff color, representing a plant with stem, branches, and leaves; various combinations of iron, and other metals, and a great variety of marbles, from the different parts of the world, as Italian, called "Fortification marble" with dendritic impressions, looking almost precisely like vegetation growing from crevices of old ruins, marbles from Germany, France, Italy, and Egypt of different colors, and some with peculiar veins. Specimens from Egypt resembled the Mexican onyx, though differing in color, and is designated Algerian, but no marble was so exquisitely beautiful, in our estimation, as the lumachelle, from Carinthia, with its opal-like reflections. One specimen of opal, obtained from Hungary, of exquisite prismatic colors, weighed eighteen ounces, and was said to be the largest known. The collection comprises some very rare and beautiful specimens of granites and porphyries, jaspers, and other minerals, including a bouquet of flowers made for Maria Theresa, of different kinds of gems, comprising a light-green and semi-transparent chrysoprase, a yellowish-green and perfectly transparent chrysolite, a yellowish chrysoberyl, gems that might be easily confounded. It seems to us, that a universal language should be adopted for scientific nomenclature. We were attracted and amused by a specimen labelled, California, Mexico, 1867, and concluded that Austrian mineralogists were more familiar with the natural sciences, than with geography and history.

The absence of almost everything from the mineral kingdom, the fine arts, the industrial arts, of rare objects of interest or of historical value, from the United States, is very noticeable in all the museums of Europe. If this country was erased from the map of the world, it would make but little difference in their catalogues. True, America has not, nor ever

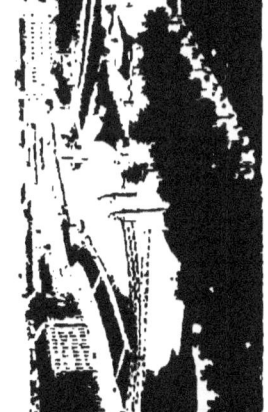
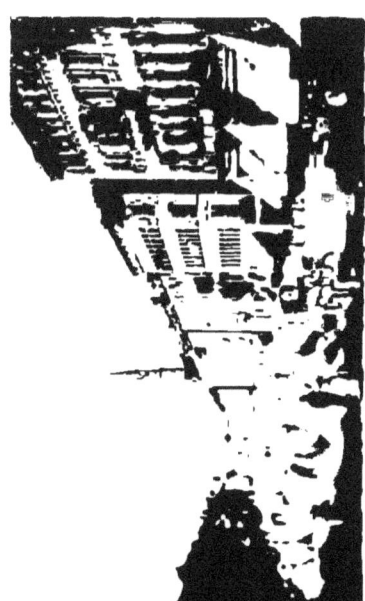

VIEWS IN VIENNA.

can have, the rich treasures of antique art found in Europe. They were, for the most part, collections made under entirely different political and social conditions from those of our own country, and were largely the result of royal or government patronage, or the inheritance of an hereditary aristocracy. Most foreign nations excel in one or more departments of industry, in which a familiarity with the fine arts is essential, and this fact proves the value of free galleries and other places where the masses can be brought in contact with the works of the greatest geniuses of different periods. Therefore, these institutions have a refining influence. Our country needs more such educators, in the character of free museums of art, handsome buildings, monuments, public parks, fountains, gardens, and the like.

We concluded that a visit to the Imperial Stables might be entertaining to a citizen of the Republic, but on our way thither we met with one of those annoyances to which travellers are sometimes exposed. A man who had previously offered his services as guide, but had been rejected, appeared again when it was impossible to get rid of him. He could speak a little English, and said he had been in America, but this might have been a ruse to gain an advantage. He would attend us in spite of all our efforts to elude him, and dictated what fees we must pay the custodians, and even went so far as to order a lunch for himself at a restaurant, at our expense, and after going through the stables, he persisted in accompanying us to our hotel, in order to gain extra fees. Now for the royal stables. Our persistent guide said that the horses numbered seven hundred and fifty, the carriages five hundred and fifty, but the number of groomsmen we have forgotten, a little army, we presume. In one stable the horses were all white with long tails, and were to be used with a particular kind of carriage for special occasions. In another apartment, the horses were all gray with docked tails; in others they were black, bay, or sorrel as the case might be. The carriage room comprises vehicles of all styles, sizes, and ornamentation; gold, silver, and other decorations were profusely employed. Some of these carriages have been used by earlier sovereigns, but a large number were modern, including one used by Napoleon I., and several by Maria Theresa. The walls of the apartment for the imperial harnesses were covered with gold, and silver-mounted caparisons, while in the centre of the room stood the figure of a horse richly equipped, and another animal with the saddle, bridle, and lasso of the unfortunate Emperor of Mexico.

Having seen how the Emperor's horses were domiciled, we were desirous of knowing how his majesty was provided for, therefore we returned to the palace and went through a succession of large rooms, but not so gaudily decorated as some we had seen. The walls of several apartments were covered with tapestry, others were gold and white. The walls of the room containing the bed of Maria Theresa were covered with embroidered crimson damask, another apartment contained the miniatures of royal persons, while others comprised pictures in mosaics. Rich articles of furniture were seen in some of the rooms, including a cabinet inlaid with ivory, two large clocks with cases of tortoise-shells and silver. The floor of all these apartments were in marquetry of different colored woods. One large hall, probably the ballroom, was furnished with galleries, and nearly one hundred chandeliers. A private chapel back of the altar contained a fine painting, representing the death of one of the emperors.

The churches of Vienna afforded some interesting studies We went to the Greek Church where the services were conducted in the vernacular. The churches of this sect are highly decorated, though constructed on a different plan from the Roman. There are no seats for the audience, except the infirm; the men stand on one side, the women on the other, while the area between is left unoccupied. At the end opposite the entrance, a screen separates the body of the church from the place occupied by the officiating priest, who occasionally shows himself to the congregation through a door. The choir occupies a place elevated above the audience opposite the altar; most of the services consisted in singing. The pulpit was elevated on one side, so that considering the official duties of the priest behind the screen, the singing and preaching, far above their heads, it is difficult to understand how the people could be reached. The interior of the church was decorated by gilt bronze, wood, imitation marbles, and paintings, but there was more simplicity than in the Roman churches, with their profusion of statues, shrines, altars, candlesticks, confessionals, etc.

The sacerdotal robes of the Greek clergy are exceedingly rich, consisting of velvet covered with embroidery of gold and jewels, especially those of the higher order. There were no instruments of music, but the singing was good. When the sacrament was administered, each member approached the altar and took from a plate, held by a boy standing near the priest, the consecrated wafer, first the men, then the women; the latter kissed the hand of the priest. During the services the sign of the cross was frequently made by the worshippers, and, in certain ceremonies, it was made simultaneously, which to the spectator appeared like a comical pantomime. The next church we visited was St. Stephen's, said to be the most important one in Vienna. It was founded in the twelfth century, but additions were made between 1300 and 1510. It was constructed of limestone, and is three hundred and fifty-four feet in length; eighteen large columns support the vaulting around which statues, shrines, and various other devices are clustered, giving the interior a crowded appearance. The High Altar is silver with gold ornaments, the columns and architrave are of black marble with silver decorations. The pulpit is of stone with carving; the choir is hung with faded tapestry, while statues, paintings, candelabra, etc., are profuse. Formerly, the members of the Austrian royal family were buried in this church, but for two hundred years their place of sepulture has been the Church of the Capuchins. Prince Eugene of Savoy was buried in St. Stephen's. The tall tower and spire are very imposing. The entrance on the west end called the Giant's Door, is opened only on occasions of great solemnity. Sculptures and monuments embellish the exterior, including that of the

Meistersinger Fricks. St. Peter's Church is a basilica with frescos, paintings, etc., and the Church of St. Nicholas is very ancient having been founded in 1221, but there is nothing remarkable about either, except the unsightly representation of clouds in stucco, in the latter. These clouds look like plates of metal or those disk-like clay formations, familiar to geologists. There is a monument in Grabben Strasse, where clouds were intended to be delineated, and a more ridiculous monument could hardly have been conceived by a lunatic.

There is much that is admirable and beautiful in art, much to elevate the mind and inspire the soul with devout aspirations, but there are also some things that are puerile, even ridiculous and contemptible. Not every subject is suitable for the chisel or the brush, and when a mistake is made in their selection or treatment, art is degraded. What is called the Votive Church, erected to commemorate the Emperor's escape from assassination, was unfinished at the time of our visit, but as far as we could judge, it was designed to become one of the finest churches in the city. It is Gothic with some beautiful frescos and painted glass.

October 22 we met two of our country-women whom we had seen at Geneva, and went with them to the Schönbrunn, the summer residence of the Imperial Family. The royal chateau is delightfully situated in a large and beautiful park intersected by wide avenues, with trees, a la Française, statues and fountains, while opposite the palace, on an elevated site, stands a structure or colonnade called the Gloriette. We visited the chateau and found it decorated with various rich and beautiful designs, and the walls of some of the apartments were covered with large paintings by Rosa. One room was covered with Chinese paintings, another with Japanese, and a third was ceiled with rose-wood inlaid with small panels of paintings, but the most magnificent room had the walls covered with elegant wood and gold. The panels of one apartment consisted of porcelain, and the articles of the room were of the same material. All the cabinets or saloons differed from one another, and no two were furnished alike, and the floors were all of beautiful marquetry. Napoleon I. made this Chateau his headquarters, and his son, the Duke of Reichstadt, died in the same room occupied by Napoleon III. in 1832. There are numerous portraits of Maria Theresa, who seems to have been a favorite of the Austrians. The park, belonging to this summer residence, with its long avenues, its fountains and statues, is a delightful place in which to saunter. Sans Souci has more variety and surprises, but Schönbrunn is more cheerful, while its short distance from Vienna, makes it easily accessible to the citizens and travellers.

Returning to the city we went to the Church of the Capuchins, for the purpose of seeing the royal vaults of the Imperial Family, which contain about eighty sarcophagi mostly of copper, though one was of silver, and all were elaborately ornamented. Here repose the ashes of Maria Theresa and her husband, Francis I., in a magnificent tomb; Maria Louise and her son, the Duke of Reichstadt; Maximilian, the emperor of Mexico, and all the other royal personages of the last two hundred years. Death is no respecter of rank or age, for here are little coffins, showing that royal households have their domestic sorrows.

The collection of the upper Belvedere gallery is not large for a city like Vienna, but there are a number of private galleries open to the public. The Ambras collection found at the Chateau of Ambras, near Innsbruck, contains various kinds of equestrian armor, including that of a life-guardsman of the Archduke Ferdinand which is seven and one-half feet in height, the battle-axe of Montezuma, firearms of all kinds ornamented with inlaid and carved work, garments richly embroidered with pearls supposed to have belonged to the Order of the Golden Fleece ; and two hundred portraits of royal persons of different nations. The Lower Belvedere is divided into two separate departments, one containing antique statues, reliefs, inscriptions, mosaics, etc., most of them found in the Austrian dominions, and the Egyptian collection including various objects in bronze, stone, and clay. Gems are liberally employed in embellishing many of the specimens. Saint

Augustine, the name of the Court church near the palace, is a long, narrow building rich in decorations. The high altar is in the form of a Gothic church, and has several statues and wood carving, but is free from gaudy decorations, and in harmony with other parts of the church. The pure white marble monument of Maria Christina, daughter of Maria Theresa, by Canova, is very beautiful; it is in the form of a pyramid, with a group of several statues, and near the top is a bust of the princess (who died in 1793) in relief, supported by angels. The statue of Francis I., erected in one of the platz of the palace, is of bronze. The emperor is represented standing, while the four corners of the granite base are occupied with allegorical figures of Religion, Peace, Justice, and Bravery. There are groups of statuary near the gates to the platz, delineating the labors of Hercules. In this court, the band performs, when the guard is changed at one o'clock, with military manœuvres. Probably there are several hundred soldiers belonging to the imperial household at every palace. We made a second visit to the Mineral cabinets which contain a very great variety of specimens, from countries all over the world including the United States, then proceeded to the arsenal a long distance off, though unfortunately it was not open to the public only on certain days, but we saw the vestibule where fifty-two marble heroes are arranged about the columns supporting the vaulted roof. The arsenal consists of a series of structures enclosing a quadrangle one third of a mile in length and one fourth in width. The collection of weapons, it is said, is one of the best and largest known; some of them are very curious and others ornamental.

The Prata was the place of the great exposition, and some of the buildings were left standing which made the park seem like a deserted city. Next to Paris, Vienna is the most beautiful town we have yet visited, the buildings are fine, and the streets are wide. The stone generally used in construction, is a light-colored sandstone, producing a cheerful impression similar to that of the Calcaire Grossier, of which the French capitol is built. A number of fine buildings, mostly for public use were being erected and when finished will greatly enhance the beauty of the city.

Having given as much time to Vienna as our plans would allow we prepared to resume our journey for another Italian tour, this time to Venice, Rome, Naples, and other southern towns, where we planned to spend the last part of autumn and the winter.

## CHAPTER IX.

*A Second Visit to Italy.*

OCTOBER 26, a day like a New England "Indian Summer," we left Vienna for Trieste; the route was charming, the scenery exquisitely beautiful, while the Semmering Pass was unlike those we had previously seen. The railroad, a marvel of civil engineering, has a great number of tunnels or galleries of the strongest masonry, many of them with two tiers of arches, one above another. The mountains are not so grand and lofty as the Swiss Alps, but they are very beautiful, being covered mostly with small trees whose foliage is remarkable for richness of color, affording nearly every shade of orange and yellow. The gorgeous red maple of America is wanting, but one species was conspicuous for its brilliant foliage, which, with the sun shining upon it, resembled the Fire Opal. Innumerable shades of yellow and orange, with evergreens and russet browns, combine to make a lovely garniture for field and forest. The color of the rocks varied; some being a light green, and as seen from the train, resembled chloritic slate; the soil was of the same hue. In other places, the rock was a blue-gray limestone. The mountains are generally conical in shape, and with their beautifully tinted foliage, made a charming picture. Never before had we noticed the effect of red color in the general aspect of nature, as we saw it in crossing the Semmering Pass; it was exquisitely softened and blended or contrasted with other hues, and afforded studies in color, over which an artist might become enthusiastic. Add to these, the hue of the rocks, and of the waters of the rivers which, in some is bronze tinted by the pebbles on the bed of the stream, and, in others, as the Save, it is green. The scenery in the valley of this river is grand, with its high and steep mountains on either side, while along the route are villages, cultivated fields, and manufactories.

Gratz, the capital of Styria, the largest town we passed, with a population at the time of eighty-one thousand, is situated on the River Mur; the citadel is four hundred feet above the river. The French, under McDonald, in 1809, blew up the fortifications of this stronghold. Some of the Austrian royal family were buried in this city, which has been the theatre of many historical events. On leaving Gratz, we passed the ruined castle of Wildon, where Tycho Brahe made his astronomical observations. The railway crosses the River Drau, follows the valley of the Save, with its picturesque scenery, then crosses the Laibach, which, it is supposed, may be the same that disappears in the Cave of Adelsberg, and reappears at Planina, though bearing three different names. It is not uncommon for rivers in the Julian Alps, which are a limestone formation, to disappear from the surface, follow a subterranean passage for some distance, and then emerge. We regretted that we could not visit the celebrated caverns of Adelsberg which resemble those of the Mammoth Cave of Kentucky. The remainder of our journey was made in the evening, but we were on the watch to catch the first view of the Adriatic, which was quite distinct, as there was a moon. The sight of the innumerable lights from the wharves and the shipping in the Bay of Trieste was fairy-like. Our journey of three hundred and sixty-three miles made in fourteen and one-half hours was ended, and we found ourselves at the Hotel de la Ville. A few words in regard to the railway over the Semmering will close our account of the journey. It has been said to be the first continuous railway, and the grandest work of the kind in Europe. It is carried through fifteen tunnels and over fifteen bridges, while the cost of twenty-five miles over this part of the way, was more than seven million five hundred thousand dollars. The foundations are so strong that, apparently, it will endure for many generations. The Semmering, comprising three peaks, is sixty-eight hundred and eight feet in height, and the railway station was at an elevation of twenty-eight hundred and ninety-four feet.

Trieste is a very picturesque town; the new and finer streets are along the shore of the bay, but the older parts occupy the sides and summit of a range of hills running parallel with the shore. They are so steep and narrow that no vehicles can traverse them. The approach to the castle, on a high eminence in the new town, is by a paved street as steep as the roof of a building. The harbor is crowded with shipping, and here is seen the bustling activity of a great commercial seaport. The market-places are interesting for the study of the peculiarities and customs of different nations. The native peasant women wear a black garment without sleeves over a white one, and a head covering of white, descending from the back of the head to the skirts below the waist, while the feet are covered in a very clumsy manner. It is surprising to see with what ease these women will carry burdens on their heads. They will balance a large basket or other articles full of their wares, with perfect security. A small cushion or folded handkerchief is placed upon the head, and then almost any burden can be adjusted.

The public squares and wide streets of a town serve as market-places in many of the countries of Europe, and here are collected the vendors of almost every kind of merchandise. Sometimes small booths are erected; but frequently the goods are exposed in the open air. After spending one day in Trieste, we left for Venice by a night boat, and at an early hour the next morning, we had our first view of the distant island city. We passed a long line of fortifications, and when at length we came near the Grand Canal, we caught sight of San Marco. Was it a dream or a reality that the identical St. Mark's loomed up before us, which we had so often heard about and seen represented by art?

The gondolas were crowding about the steamboat, and the gondoliers were clamoring for passengers, in a strange tongue. The Custom House officials were on board our boat, but for what purpose we have never found out, for they did not so much as look at our luggage, but merely asked a question in Italian, which we answered at random in English. It is probable they wished to know whether we had any dutiable articles, but they allowed us to pass without further trouble. After some delay we took our place in a gondola for a hotel, but the gondolier was not quite sure that we knew where we wanted to go, so he hailed a comrade telling him he had as passengers "Inglese," meaning English, and wished him to inquire whether we had a hotel selected. Finally we were landed at the Hotel Italia, near the square of St. Mark.

The following morning we directed our steps to the Piazza San Marco which we had heard so much about, and which seemed like a familiar object, with the Campanile rising above every other object. San Marco with its heterogeneous and pictorial architecture, the Ducal Palace, the tall poles with their flags waving in the breeze, the two columns facing the Grand Canal, the domes, the bronze horses, and the arched doorways of the Cathedral, and even the pigeons moving about the Piazza of San Marco, without fear of their human companions, seemed like familiar objects. We entered the famous Cathedral where several priests were officiating, but the audience did not seem greatly interested in the service, for a part of the worshippers were watching the people, while others were taking snuff and making free use of a piece of checked cloth which, it is presumed, they considered a pocket handkerchief. The entire services appeared very formal and very undevotional, and all seemed pleased when they ended.

The next day we made another visit to St. Mark's for the purpose of becoming acquainted with its special features. When new it must have been a magnificent building, but time has impaired its beauty. The entire edifice, externally and internally, is covered with different colored marbles or with mosaics on a gold ground; some of the marbles are antiques. The Cathedral has five hundred marble columns, and between forty and fifty thousand feet of mosaics, which have retained their colors remarkably well. St. Mark's, like a jeweller's collection, must be studied in detail. It is unlike any other church we had seen, and judged by the rules of architecture, it would probably be considered an exception in the art of building, and belonging to no particular style. The Campanile, or bell-tower, rising three hundred and twenty-two feet makes the Duomo appear quite low, while the Square or Piazza is smaller than we had supposed, and nearly enclosed by buildings. The Palazza Reale or Royal Palace occupies the entire length on the south side, another palace on the north is connected with it, while the Cathedral is on the east side. These palaces were formerly occupied by the Procurators of the Venetian Republic, and subsequently were used for the entertainment of royal visitors. Arcades extend along three sides of the Square, furnishing room for the best shops in Venice, and in the evening, when lighted by gas, present a very brilliant sight, especially the numerous jewellers' stands. The Italians, with their artistic tastes, arrange the shop-windows in a very attractive manner, while the various beautiful objects displayed have the effect of a grand exposition.

Venice may appropriately be called a city of churches and canals, and to continue our study of the former, with our guide book for a "Commissionaire," we started from our hotel, and through the narrow streets, walled on both sides by very high buildings, made our way to some of the churches, and soon met a funeral procession led by a company dressed in red cotton frocks, and with bare heads; each man holding a candle in a bronze candlestick, the two together being probably twenty feet in height. Next came a company dressed in black and white, followed by priests in another kind of dress. One man carried a number of tall candles such as are used in churches, another a bronze figure, and a third a kind of banner like a framed picture. The procession was on its way to the Church of San Zaccaria with the remains. When they arrived there the crowd dispersed; and the officials in red frocks, placed the coffin on a high catafalque. Others with candles arranged themselves around the body, and the priests began the Mass, and went through the ceremony as if they felt no interest in it or in the deceased. The people who came to

ST. MARK'S, VENICE

witness the ceremony comprised many persons very poorly clad, dirty, ragged, and with hard, unsympathetic countenances, as if they had always been accustomed to the dark side of life. This church contains paintings on the walls and ceilings by Tintoretto, Bellini, and other artists; but the light was so imperfect it was difficult to see them. The High Altar is Gothic, and the columns of the interior are covered by brocade with gold borders, while the Choir of the Nuns contains a Madonna, by Palma Vecchio, it is supposed. From St. Zaccaria we went to Santa Maria Formosa, with modern frescos and some rich marbles. The pictures included a Descent from the Cross, by Giovane; a Santa Barbara, by Vecchio; the Last Supper, either by Bassano or Veronese; but the most impressive work in this church is the Dying Christ, supported by angels, a relief in bronze and marble, by Campagna.

The next day we resumed our inspection of ecclesiastical buildings, and passing through Via Merceria, the principal business street, we came to the Church of St. Salvatore, said to be one of the finest in Venice, but found it closed for repairs. The façade is surmounted by three flat domes on a circular vaulting. S. Giovanni Crisostomo, founded in 1483, contains paintings by Bellini and Piombo, and reliefs by Lombards; and the Church of Santi Apostoli contains a painting of the Last Supper, but inferior to that of Da Vinci's, the Fall of Manna, by Paul Veronese, and an imposing tomb to the Corner family.

The Church of S. Felice, on the Corso Vittoria Emmanuele, the broadest street in Venice, is peculiar in some features, comprising an altar very rich in gold ornamentation, a crown of the same rich metal, supported by golden angels, resting on a wreath of gold, while on each side were candelabra, supported by angelic beings with golden wings, and covered with a mantle of gold. The drapery of the High Altar is of crimson velvet, bordered with gold. This church contains a painting of the Virgin with the "Burning Heart." The S. Maria dell' Orto has a fine Gothic façade, a curious tower, and some good pictures, comprising the Last Judgment and the Adoration of the Golden Calf, by Tintoretto, besides the Capella Contarini, with several busts representing members of this celebrated family.

For a change, we took a sail in the afternoon to the Ledo, a place of resort in summer, but at this season almost deserted. With its pleasant drives and shaded avenues, its conveniences for sea-bathing, the fine views of the Adriatic it afforded, would, of course, become attractive. We witnessed here a glorious natural phenomenon — a sunset similar in some aspects to those of New England, but with this difference, that in addition to the celestial splendor, were added the changeable colors of the sea — pink, blue, and gold equal to the glory of the sun itself, while in the clear water were reflected the shadows of the campaniles, the churches, and indeed the entire city of Venice, seated on her island throne like a princess. Besides her peculiar natural surroundings, the Queen of the Adriatic, is very interesting on account of her historical associations. One unaccustomed to the special study of ecclesiastical buildings, might think it would become monotonous and tedious; but while there is a similarity in the more celebrated churches of Europe, generally the work of the Middle Ages, there is also great diversity, no two being precisely alike in style or decorations. Many of them are really splendid exhibitions of the fine arts — music, paintings, sculpture, and architecture, the last being the noblest and broadest of the arts, combining all the others. Without some previous knowledge of the fine arts, a tourist through Europe would fail in securing great advantages from foreign travel. Returning to the churches of Italy, the S. M. Gloriosa dei Frari, one of the largest and most beautiful in Venice, in the Italian Gothic style, was founded in the thirteenth century and completed by Pisano, in 1338. It is remarkable for its sculptures and monuments, comprising those of Titian, Canova, and several Doges, besides other distinguished persons. The beautiful monument of Titian is of light colored marble, with four Corinthian columns and the same number of pilasters, all resting on decorated pedestals, supporting an arch on the top of which is the winged Lion of St. Mark. Figures representing Sculpture, Painting, Architecture, and wood-carving are placed on the columns. Titian is represented sitting by an angel and uncovering the statue of the goddess Sais; and at each corner of the base is a sitting statue. Three of the artist's most celebrated works, the Assumption, Martyrdom of St. Peter, and Martyrdom of St. Laurence, are represented on the walls, in relief, while above the vaulting, are reliefs of his Annunciation and the Entombment. The monument of Canova, directly opposite, is a pyramid of white marble with a doorway in the centre, and is a duplicate, with some modifications, of the one made by Canova, for Maria Christina. This church contains paintings by some of the Venetian masters; the marble screen between the nave and the choir is covered with reliefs, and the stalls are elegantly carved by Marco da Vicenza. A Monastery near contains one of the largest collections of archives known, including, it is said, fourteen million of documents, the oldest dating from 883 A. D.; they occupy two hundred and ninety-eight different apartments.

The church of S. Rococo, near the Archives, contains a picture of Holy Martyrs, by Tintoretto, and of Christ on the way to Golgotha, by Titian, and several other paintings representing Scripture scenes. The Scuola di S. Rococo, containing the council halls of the brotherhood, is adorned by works of some of the masters; as Ecce Homo and the Annunciation, by Titian, and the Crucifixion, by Tintoretto. If it would not be presumptuous to criticise so eminent an artist, we would suggest that too many figures appear in the Annunciation, for we had always supposed that Mary was alone when she received the angelic visitor. The Crucifixion, a large picture with many figures, is a powerful and pathetic scene. The group in the foreground consists of the friends of Jesus, comprising his fainting mother. The cross of the Saviour has already been erected, and on one side of it men are raising, by means of a rope, the cross of one of the malefactors, while on the other side the thief is partly reclining, gazing up at the Saviour, and two soldiers are casting lots for the garments of Jesus. Groups of people, including men, women, and children, are scattered about, some led thither from curiosity, some from hate, and a few from sympathy; the City of Jerusalem is seen in the distance.

Some of the most beautiful wood carving we had yet seen is used in the decoration of the Scuola. Its deep color, smooth and glossy surface so closely resembled bronze, that we were at first deceived by the imitation. The Church of St. Pantaleone presented a very peculiar and repulsive aspect. The interior was covered with black drapery, on which were painted in white, skeletons, skulls, cross-bones, and other funereal decorations. The priests were instructing a class of boys, whom we found were much like American youth, under the same circumstances — inattentive, curious, and noisy. They watched our movements, and became so bold as to call for "centessimi." The churches we had visited were all on the west side of the Grand Canal, but the Church of the Jesuits was on the east side. Like all others of this order, it was highly decorated, and might be regarded as a remarkable quarry of different marbles. The columns, walls, etc., of light colored specimens, were inlaid with verde-antique, representing large vines and flowers. The high altar had ten spiral columns of verde-antique, while the pavement in front of the altar was of mosaics. The chapels were highly decorated, and the ceilings were of yellow marble. The Church of SS. Giovanni e Paolo, founded in 1240, and completed in 1430, may be called the Westminister Abbey of Venice, on account of the number of monuments it contains; it ranks next to St. Marco for its imposing aspect. It contains the burial vaults of most of the Doges, whose funeral rites were performed here. The front entrance exhibits some beautiful architectural designs. The tombs with their wealth of statues and sculptured reliefs are magnificent, especially the Mausoleum of the Valier family, with its statues and yellow marble, representing a curtain with folds, so nearly like woven fabrics that the illusion is almost complete. This monument reaches to the top of the vaulting,

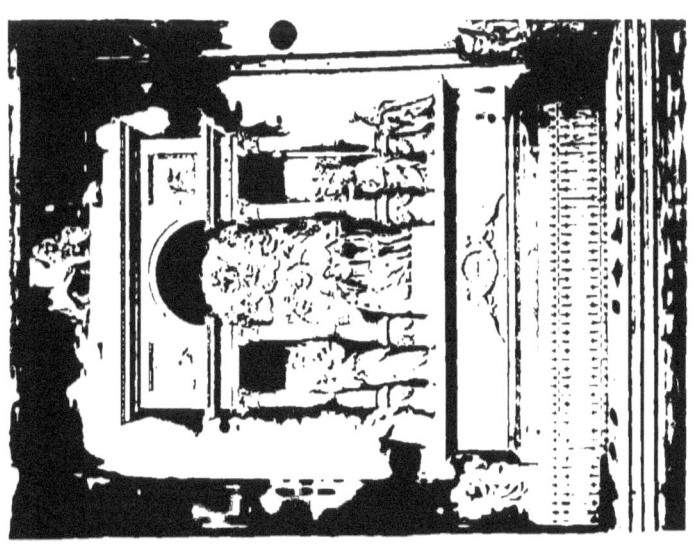

TRAJAN MONUMENT, VENICE.

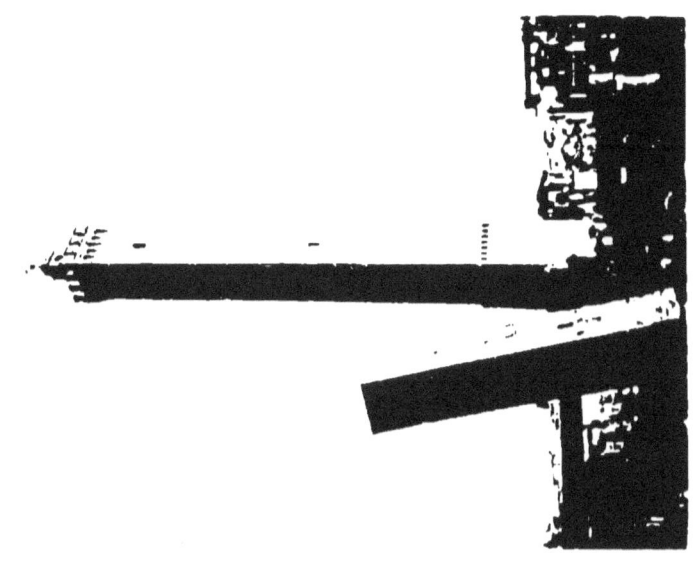

TOWERS OF BOLOGNA.

and though the height of the nave is great, some of the sarcophagi are placed near the top. Several beautiful monuments adorn the choir and chapels.

Many other churches were visited, but a description of them might become tedious. Though on the whole we were edified and delighted with this branch of study, yet there were a few sad lessons taught. Some of the paintings were so discolored by age that they needed the best light to reveal their merits, yet they were often hung in dark, remote corners, as if they were rubbish. Statuary and sculptured ornaments were less affected by age, except the pure white marble which has assumed somewhat the color of bronze, while wood-carving greatly improves by time, making it one of the pleasing features of old churches. The treasures of art these buildings contain bear the marks of decay, and will in future generations be known only as the events of history are known. Nothing can preserve them from utter extinction, while it is different with the works of architecture, they can be repaired, though in Venice there seems to be little inclination to do so. There are signs of deterioration everywhere. The buildings are going to decay, and there is no room to construct new ones. The question arises, will the time come when this renowned city of palaces and churches will become a general ruin?

The paintings in the Academy of Fine Arts are placed in a more favorable light than those in the churches. One of the most striking pictures of this collection is Titian's Assumption which needs no comment except praise. Its rich coloring and fine expression cannot be described. The Madonna, the angels, the apostles, are all remarkable representations of joy and rapture. Some of Tintoretto's best productions are found in this gallery, including his Miracle of St. Mark and the Supper in the House of Levi, for large paintings, and his Death of Abel and Fall of Man, for smaller ones, considered by Ruskin, among his best, while some other critics regard his St. Mark the best. Some of the other celebrated paintings are the Presentation of the Virgin in the Temple, when a child, painted by Titian, and the Fishermen presenting the Doge with a ring, a large painting giving a fine view of the Square of St. Mark. The preaching of John the Baptist, in the Wilderness, is remarkable for rich coloring and the fidelity of the large number of figures represented. The Venetian school is remarkable for richness of color and vividness of expression. The old masters had the power of delineating the spiritual qualities of human beings; they were diligent students of the sacred writings, or they could not have succeeded so well in representing Scripture scenes. A deeply religious and reverential feeling, foreign to most modern works, pervades them. Superstitions they may have had, but they cherished more lofty ideals and a stronger faith than is common in the present age.

We made a visit to the Palace Giovanelli, built in the fifteenth century. The apartments were furnished very sumptuously, but there is little satisfaction in being attended by a guide, who rushes through the rooms without giving one time to see half they contain, much less to examine the specimens, or objects. In going rapidly through the palace we gained a confused idea of some things, very splendid and costly, as a magnificent marble staircase, elegant furniture, fine paintings, splendid glass chandeliers, painted mirrors, floors of beautiful woods, marble mosaics in different patterns, walls covered with tapestry and figured satin, tables of beautiful patterns of inlaid work, rare antique porcelains, statues, elegant woodcarving, and other ornaments of various kinds; these were among the sights of a Venetian palace, which was probably, a fair representation of others in this city of merchant princes. Now for the Doges' Palace.

This historical building was begun in 800 A. D., and during a visit one is carried back in imagination to the time of the Republic, when so many secret tragedies were enacted here and in the dungeons opposite. The palace has been destroyed five times, and as often rebuilt with greater magnificence each time; the present structure was completed in 1442. A few of its striking features are the following: the west and south sides are flanked by two colonnades, one above the other, both together supported by one hundred and seven columns. The upper colonnade or "La Loggia" is the place where the ancient Republic published the sentences of death, and the portal of different colored marbles called the Porta della Carta was so called from the placards exhibited here announcing the decrees of the Republic. The prison of the poet, Count Silvio Pellico, imprisoned in 1822, was in one of the upper rooms of the Court. The coronation of the doge, occurred on the highest landing of the Scala dei Giganti, with their colossal statues of Mars and Neptune, and busts of several Venetian scholars, artists, and doges. The hall of the Great Council, where the highest tribunal of the Republic sat, is a room one hundred and sixty-five feet in length, and contains on the frieze, the portraits of seventy-six doges, while the walls are covered by the pictures of Venetian masters, including Tintoretto's Paradise, said to be the largest painting in the world; but it seemed to us to have little merit besides. The Voting Hall is adorned with the portraits of thirty-nine doges; on the entrance wall is Giovane's Last Judgment. The palace contains the Library of St. Mark's with many rare MSS. and a collection of coins.

The Archæological Museum contains ancient marble sculptures of Greek and Roman art, brought to Venice during her foreign wars. The Sala della Bussola, formerly the ante-chamber of the "Three Inquisitors of the Republic," contains an opening in the wall, called Bocca di Leone, or Lion's Mouth, in which the documents of secret information were placed. There are the rooms of the Council of Ten, and of the Three Chiefs of the Council, with walls decorated with paintings, besides various other apartments memorable in the Republic. The east side of the palace is connected with the Carceri, or Prison, by the lofty Ponte dei Sospiri, or Bridge of Sighs, over which so many unhappy victims were led to execution. There were also prisons called Piombi, located under the lead roof of the palace, but they were destroyed in 1797, and the famous dungeons on the opposite side of the Canal have not been used since the seventeenth century. To close the day, we ascended the Campanile, in the Square of St. Mark. This tower, with no architectural beauty, is three hundred and twenty-two feet in height, and built of brick, and has no ornaments except in the vestibule. The ascent is by an inclined plane and some steps, and before reaching the top we pass many times around it. From the summit we had an extensive view of the entire city, the beautiful Adriatic, with its gem-like islands, and in the remote distance the majestic Alps, while near, stands the Cathedral, the Doges' Palace, the Royal Palace, and scattered all over the islands are seen numberless spires and domes of the churches.

November 5 we made preparations for leaving Venice, the city of wonders, but first we paid a visit to St. Mark's, not without a feeling of regret that we should see it no more. Before leaving we passed through the Grand Canal, and had a fine view of the famous palaces on its borders; many of them appeared like miracles of architectural beauty. A number of them are faced with colored marbles, generally stained by age, though some have retained thier beauty. What a splendid picture the Grand Canal must have presented in the prosperous days of Venice!

Our route to Padua, a little more than twenty miles southwest from Venice, afforded but few objects of special interest, except the railway over the bay. We arrived at our place of destination in the afternoon, and went to the hotel Albergo Croce d' Oro, but found no English-speaking attendants, therefore were obliged to make French the medium of communication, since our Italian was quite limited in the use of words.

Padua is said to have been founded by Antenor, the brother of Priam, both prominent characters in the Trojan War; it was called by the Romans Patavium, and was an important city of Northern Italy. As early as 302 B. C. it had acquired such strength that its citizens were able to resist the Spartans under Cleomenes, who were defeated with great loss. This ancient city, like so many others, has passed through great changes and misfortunes. It was plundered by Attila, and subsequently razed to the ground by other brigands, therefore the modern town has fewer antiquities than some others. It has a celebrity for having been the birthplace of Livy, the historian. It is surrounded by walls, ditches, and other means of fortification, and took part in the wars of the Guelphs and Ghibellines during the Middle Ages.

The University of Padua, founded by the Emperor Frederick II., in 1238 A. D., has been a celebrated seat of learning in the past, and at the present day has sixty or more professors and teachers, and one thousand students. Some of the other objects and places of interest are the Botanical Garden, among the most celebrated in Europe, the Museum of Natural History, Observatory, Chemical Laboratory, Library with one hundred and twenty thousand volumes and fifteen hundred MSS., besides numerous churches, palaces, theatres, hospital, and celebrated works of art. The present population is estimated to be from sixty thousand to seventy thousand.

The school of painting established here attracted artists from other places, and exercised considerable influence on that of Venice, and even some of the Florentine masters were allured thither. The churches, like others of Italy, are, in fact, museums of art. The Basilica of St. Antonio, begun in 1256 A. D., to which additions were made at different times, was entirely rebuilt in 1749, after its destruction by fire. It has seven domes, and is larger than St. Mark's at Venice. The paintings and frescos which adorn this church are the works of some of the celebrated masters, and represent chiefly Scripture scenes and characters, and events in the lives of the saints. In and about the church are several monuments of notable persons, including admirals and generals. An Augustinian church of the Middle Ages is peculiar for the absence of aisles, columns, and pillars; but here are seen two monuments of the Carrura princes, ancient lords of Padua. Near one of the gates is the monument to Petrarch, erected in 1874, the five hundredth anniversary of his birth.

Several monuments are dedicated to graduates of the University who have distinguished themselves, while statues of Dante and Giotto, and a double row of figures, adorn other places. The Cathedral, built the latter part of the sixteenth century, has no special attractions, though the baptistery, of the twelfth century, is adorned with ancient frescos. The palace, now the Municipio, erected in the eleventh century, is remarkable for its great hall, two hundred and seventy-three feet long, ninety broad, and seventy-eight high, claimed to be one of the largest in the world.

The Piazza Vittorio Emanuele, through which a small stream flows, is of considerable size, while around the centre are arranged the statues of several distinguished Italians, including Tasso, Ariosto, Petrarch, and Galileo, all bearing the marks of decay. We were disappointed in the University Building, which was situated in a narrow street, and enclosed by other houses, while the ground floor was occupied by shops. Before leaving Padua we made another visit to the Church of St. Antonio, November 7, when roses in the gardens were in full bloom, reminding us we were in a southern climate. This church has some beautiful modern painted glass, not often seen in Northern Italy. One rose window was exquisitely beautiful, and the sculptures were very profuse.

The journey from Padua to Bologna was through a region of considerable historical interest. The railway passes a small town said to have been the home of Petrarch, and also of Este, with the ruins of the ancestral palace of the distinguished family of the same name; Rovego, with its leaning towers, built in the tenth century, and Ferrara, raised to eminence by Duke Alphonso II., the patron of Tasso and Guarini. The sad and romantic story of Tasso has invested this city with peculiar interest. Alphonso was the last of the noble house of Este, whose dukes were ardent admirers and collectors of the paintings of Raphael and other masters. Titian painted his Cristo della Moneta, now in the Dresden gallery at Ferrara, the birthplace of Savonarola.

We passed Monti Euganei, a volcanic chain of hills with warm springs and mud baths, and quarries of trachyte. Arriving at Bologna we went to the Piazza Vittorio Emanuele, a rather small square adorned with a fountain and a bronze statue of Neptune. In the vicinity are some noted buildings, namely the Palazzo Publico and the Palazzo del Podesta, where the young poet Prince Henry, son of the Emperor Frederick II., having been taken prisoner at the battle of Fossalta, 1249, during the sanguinary struggle between the Guelphs and the Ghibellines, was detained a prisoner the remainder of his life, a period of twenty-two years.

On one side of the Piazza stands the Church of St. Petronio, the largest in Bologna, and of the Tuscan Gothic style; it is three hundred and eighty-eight feet in length and one hundred and fifty-six in width. The twelve massive columns of the interior, with their plain capitals, harmonize with other parts of the building, which is less decorated than many others. A few of the chapels are worthy of note, especially that of the Bacciocchi, containing the monuments of this family. On one side is the monument of the Princess Elisa Bacciocchi, sister of Napoleon and grand duchess of Tuscany, who died in 1820, and also of her husband Felix. It represents an angel, and the statues of the deceased, one on each side, while a crown and shield supported by two figures, is placed above. Opposite to this monument is that of two of their children, with a weeping female figure at one end, and that of an angel at the other. This church —St. Petronio— contains some paintings, frescos, and sculptures worthy of note, and a double-faced clock, one side giving the solar, and the other the mean time, while on the pavement is a meridian line drawn by Cassini, the astronomer. The Emperor Charles V. was crowned in this church by Pope Clement VII.

The Church of St. Domenico is more highly ornamented than St. Petronio, and contains the tomb of the saint, with its reliefs representing scenes in his life by different artists. Some of the inlaid stalls of the choir are said to be the finest in Italy. The tomb of the captive Prince Henry, before mentioned, is on one side of the choir, while in the left transept are those of Guido Rene, and the female artist, Elisabetta Serani, who was poisoned in 1665, at the age of twenty-six; some of her paintings adorn this church.

The Madonna di St. Luca, the pilgrimage-church, is comparatively modern, having been erected, in 1731, on a fortified eminence two miles southwest from the city. We decided to make a visit to this church, and to the Campo Santo at the same time; therefore passing through the arcades of the Via di Saragozza to the gate of the same name, on the west side of the city, we were directed by a guide who had followed us with the hope that he might be engaged to conduct us to Monte della Guardia, a fortified hill on which the Church of St. Luca stood. Arcades lead to the top, a distance of one mile, over a pebbly walk, and comprise six hundred and thirty-five arches. Our persistent guide was very serviceable, and perhaps indispensable, though at first we considered him superfluous. Fine views were enjoyed from the summit of the hill of the city, and adjacent regions covered with beautiful villas, trees, gardens, terraces, etc. The church is reached by a very long succession of steps, and is decorated in the interior with rich marbles of various kinds. One specimen was of different shades of green, with delicate tints of pink and other colors. The marbles of the Church of the Jesuits in Venice were more numerous, but those of St. Luca were more beautiful. There is a tradition that this church contains a picture of the Virgin painted by St. Luke, which was brought from Constantinople in 1160. The view from the top of the hill extends from the Apennines to the Adriatic. The Campo Santo is reached through another arcade; but the way is level and less fatiguing than to the church. It was formerly a Carthusian monastery until 1801, when it was devoted to its present use; a small church is connected with it, containing some pictures by Elisabetta Serani and other painters. The cloisters contain ancient tombstones taken from suppressed churches, as far back as the thirteenth century, while the arcades contain monuments of white marble, the work of modern times, generally very beautiful; that of Letizia Murat Pepoli, who died in 1859, is especially fine. The statue of Christ occupies the centre, and the two angels poised on the corners look as if they were hovering in the air; it seems a mystery how they preserve their balance. The monument of her father, King Murat, is a very elaborate piece of sculpture. In the rotunda are seen the busts of several distinguished professors of the present era, as Mezzofanti, the celebrated linguist, Galvani, the scientific discoverer, Costa, and others.

The Leaning Towers of Bologna attract the notice of strangers on account of their novelty. The Torre Asinelli, erected 1109 A. D., which is finished, is two hundred and seventy-two feet in height, and is three feet five inches out of perpendicular; the unfinished Torre Garisenda, begun 1110 A. D., is one hundred and thirty-eight feet, and leans eight and one-half feet. It is supposed these towers were purposely constructed in this manner; but there is no pleasure in viewing a structure that threatens to fall. The University of Bologna, founded in 1119 A. D., next to that of Salerno, is the oldest in Italy, and one of the most celebrated in Europe. It numbered nearly ten thousand students in the thirteenth century; but at the present time it has only about four hundred, with fifty professors. The anatomy of the human body was first taught here during the fourteenth century, and here galvanism was discovered. This university has numbered among its professors several ladies, including Novella d'Andrea of the fourteenth century, Laura Bassi, professor of mathematical and physical science, Mme. Manzolina, professor of anatomy, and from 1794 to 1817, Clotilda Tambrone, professor of Greek. The library, of one hundred thousand volumes, had for a time the celebrated linguist, Joseph Mezzofanti, of Bologna, for librarian. At the time of his death, in 1849, he was familiar with forty-two different languages.

We were shown some of the recitation-rooms of the university, with uncushioned benches, and a narrow shelf or rest in front for the book. The desk, or what answered the purpose, was covered with ink spots, and decorated by carvings of caricatures of the professors, doubtless illustrating the fact that college students are much the same everywhere.

The Accademia delle Belle Arti, or Academy of Fine Arts, comprises the Pinacoteca or Picture Gallery, with paintings chiefly of the Bologna School, as Rene, Caracci, Guercino,

Francia, Perugino, Domenichino, and others. Probably the best known painting was the original St. Cecilia, by Raphael, in which are the traces of the great master's hand. It occupies the centre of a group, consisting of SS. Paul, John, Augustine and Mary Magdalene. There is an exalted idealism in the figures, verging upon the supernatural or seraphic. Raphael's figures are never gross, like those of some of the old masters, who evidently believed in a literally muscular Christianity, for some of their saints might pass for a Hercules, in their physical development. The artists of such pictures certainly exhibited a thorough knowledge of anatomy, however greatly they may have failed to represent the spiritual nature of their subjects. Their little cherubs are almost always bulky, and look like plump babies, with about as much developed mental faculties as infants display.

Bologna is both ancient and modern; some of the buildings are very old, while others have been renovated and appear new. It may be, *par excellence*, called the city of arcades, since nearly all the public passage-ways have them, at least on one side, and many on both, while the streets are broader than those of most other Italian towns. With one hundred and thirty churches and twenty monasteries, and the addition of a celebrated university, the citizens should be among the most enlightened in Italy; but there are a great many poor and wretched people found here, as in all other Italian cities.

St. Stefano is an architectural pile, comprising seven different churches, with ancient columns and mural paintings, and, according to an inscription, was founded on the site of a temple to Isis; it is supposed to have been built in the fifth century. The numerous churches are not all on the same level, and were constructed at different periods. Each one in this ancient town has some peculiar feature, either in its structure, decoration, or works of art, which is true of those of other cities. We will not leave Bologna without mentioning the Piazza Vittorio Emanuele, one of the most interesting in Italy, which occupies the centre of the city, and is adorned with a fountain, and a bronze statue of Neptune.

## CHAPTER X.

*Florence, Perugia, Terni.*

EARLY in the morning of November 10 we left Bologna for Florence. The scenery along the route was interesting, with its beautiful valleys and attractive villas. The Apennines are crossed at Pracchia, forty-five and one-half miles from Bologna, at an elevation of two thousand and twenty-four feet, and nearly fifty tunnels are passed, some of them being of considerable length; the longest was twelve and one-third miles. Pistoja, one of the largest towns on the route, is very ancient, and noted for its manufacture of guns and iron wares. Pistols are said to have been invented here, and received their name from the town. Prato, the next place of importance, is known for the manufacture of straw-plaiting; while at Monteferrato, three miles from the latter town, are the quarries of serpentine, called Verde di Prato, used in the construction of some of the public buildings of Florence and other cities of Tuscany.

As soon as possible after our arrival in Florence, we went to see the famous Duomo, which far exceeded our expectations in regard to size. Its immense dome rising from the centre vastly enhances the magnitude and grandeur of the building, which has just been cleansed by acids to give the marbles a fresh look, corresponding to those of the façade now being finished. The architectural designs of beautiful tracery and mosaics about the windows are exquisite, while the interior is very impressive, with its immense size and grandeur; but many visits must be made before its beauties can be understood.

The Campanile — who that has read Ruskin does not remember it — is indeed a gem in architecture, and near is the Baptistery, with Giotto's Bronze Doors, copies of which are so familiar. We exchanged our hotel for a pension in Via

Maggio, near the Picture Gallery, where we found both American and English guests. Our first visit to the gallery was for a general idea of the collection, to be studied afterwards in detail. Many of the paintings being originals of some we had examined in other collections, seemed like familiar objects. Thanks to the arts of engraving and photography for even the imperfect knowledge they impart; their study, with suitable descriptions, is a good preparation for travel.

A second visit was made to the Cathedral, which deepened our impressions of its grandeur and the beauty of its decorations. It was begun in 1294, and was not completed at the time of our visit; it is in the Italian Gothic style. The dome exceeds in size that of St. Peter's at Rome, being three hundred and fifty-two feet to the top of the lantern. The church is five hundred and fifty-six and one-half feet in length, and three hundred and forty-two across the transepts. The façade, when completed, will add greatly to the beauty and magnificence of the exterior. The Cathedral, Campanile, and Baptistery form a group of remarkable buildings, of which any city might be proud. We ascended the dome of the Cathedral by four hundred and sixty-three steps, a feat less difficult than one would suppose, considering its height, which is three hundred and fifty-two feet from the pavement, and were favored with a prospect not soon forgotten. The morning, December 10, was perfect; the sky so clear that we could see the regions about the city a long distance off, while Florence itself, with its streets, piazzas, palaces, and churches, reposed at our feet, encircled by hills crowned with lovely villas and olive groves, and in the distance arose the snow-crowned peaks of the Apennines. Near the Duomo the Campanile rises towards heaven, a marvel of architectural beauty. Its exquisite tracery and lovely tints could better be seen from the dome of the Cathedral than from any other point of observation. This bell-tower begun by Giotto, in 1334 A. D., is a square structure two hundred and ninety-two feet in height, and consists of four stories, the lower one being decorated with reliefs and statues by some of the celebrated masters.

GIOTTO'S TOWER, FLORENCE.

UFFIZI PALACE, FLORENCE.

The Pitti Palace is interesting for its ornamental marbles and other stones. Some of the doorcases were made of showy breccias of various colors, while a room called the Hall of Venus contains several tables of different kinds of stones, including marbles, alabasters, breccias, and others of a great variety of colors. In the Hall of Apollo, the Hall of Mars, and the Hall of Jupiter were articles of very rich marbles and other ornamental stones, including gems; mosaics of shells, pearls, and corals were almost perfect imitations. Some of the other apartments similarly decorated were the Hall of the Iliad, the Hall of the Stufa, the Hall of the Bath, the Hall of Ulysses, and the Hall of Prometheus. Almost everything in the vegetable kingdom is imitated here by art. One table, with a foot of bronze, representing the four seasons, made in the royal manufactory of Florence, required fourteen years for its completion, and is valued at fifty thousand dollars.

The Poccetti Gallery contains three beautiful tables, two of oriental alabaster, and one of Siberia malachite. The "Corridor of the Columns" has two exquisite columns of white oriental alabaster, crowned with a porphyry vase. The Hall of Flora contains the celebrated Venus, by Canova, and two tables of rare, light-green alabaster, with mosaics. There were other galleries or halls, with their rich treasures of art, besides those designated. The one for works in Pietra Dura contained some fine specimens of mosaic-work, of large size, made of stones exceedingly beautiful, and very costly.

The porticos of the Uffizi Palace have twenty-eight modern statues of eminent Florentines. The building contains the celebrated gallery founded by the Medici, the National Library, and the Archives. The Gallery contains between three hundred and four hundred statues and other sculptures, and more than thirteen hundred paintings, while the corridor leading to the palace contains about ten thousand engravings, and a large number of original drawings, selected from thirty-three thousand belonging to the Gallery. Besides these collections there are six hundred tapestries, forming a part of the Uffizi Gallery, some of which cover the walls of the corridor. The

Hall of Portraits contains the likenesses of distinguished painters executed by themselves, and occupying two rooms. In the Tribune are seen some of the most valuable works of the collection, comprising Raphael's Farnarina and Madonna of the Goldfinch. The Madonna of the Well has been attributed to him, but the authenticity is doubtful. For statues there are the Venus di Medici, found at Hadrian's Villa, the Wrestlers, the Dancing Fawns, and a small statue of Apollo. The room of the Venetian School contains two tables of verde antico, which are worthy of notice, and in the Hall of Baraccio are four tables of Florentine mosaic, one of which is exquisitely beautiful, consisting of various precious stones, arranged to represent shells, flowers, leaves, fruit, and other designs, on a ground of black marble. Another table affords landscapes in mosaic, bordered with silver and gems, while the other two are ornamented with various devices, one of them with a string of pearls and a ribbon of lapis-lazuli, and pink and white chalcedony. The scales of marine animals are very correctly imitated. Other rooms contain specimens of the Flemish, German, and Italian schools. The Cabinet of Gems affords a study for these most beautiful objects of the material world, but we will only mention a table with the centre of Persian lapis lazuli covered with a view of ancient Leghorn, in mosaic.

Before leaving Florence for Rome we paid another visit to the Cathedral and Baptistery. The latter has a great antiquity, having been built in the seventh century; its most noted feature is the bronze doors. The one on the south was the work of Pisano, and contains bas-reliefs representing the life of St. John; the other, facing the Cathedral, was made by Ghiberti, who devoted twenty years to the work, and contains the history of Christ's incarnation.

The new façade of the Cathedral is unfinished, though at the time of our visit workmen were busy in completing it. The material used corresponds to that of the other parts of the building, namely, white marble from Carrara, green serpentine from Prato, and a dark-red stone which the workmen said was from Siena; the doors have some fine wood carving.

Though Florence cannot claim so great antiquity as some other Italian cities, yet it is one of the most beautiful and interesting, and forms one of the great art centres of Europe, and the "focus of Italian intellectual life," while its historical reminiscences are intensely interesting; but with its inestimable treasures of art, its palaces and piazzas, its churches and other historical buildings, the traveller cannot always tarry here, and this is one of the unpleasant incidents we must meet. It is not surprising that tourists have pronounced so decided eulogiums upon "la bella Firenze," though we must confess that the frequent rainy days somewhat marred our pleasure.

On a fine morning, December 17, we left Florence for Perugia, on our journey to Rome. The scenery between the two cities is agreeably diversified by mountains whose summits are covered with snow, while the valleys afford cultivated fields and olive orchards, with their light-green foliage presenting an agreeable harmony with the dark-purple and russet-browns of the surrounding objects. We passed several towns noted as being the birthplaces of distinguished men, as San Giovanni, the native place of the painters Massicio and S. Giovanni, Arezzio, an ancient town, the birthplace of Macenas, the patron of Virgil and Horace, and, later, of Guido Aritino, the inventor of musical notation, 1000 A. D., of Petrarch, Aventino, the satirist, Aretino, the painter, Vasari, painter and architect, besides several other eminent men. The railway passes Cortona, "a city on a hill," in the vicinity of Lake Trasemene, and is one of the most ancient cities of Italy, the birthplace of the painter Signorelli. The region of Lake Trasemene, the ancient Lacus Trasimenus, is classic ground, having been the scene of the sanguinary struggle between Hannibal and the Romans under the Consul, C. Flaminius, 217 B. C., in which the latter were utterly defeated and their commander slain. Ruined castles, suggestive of the civilization of the past, are seen at intervals along the route.

Perugia, delightfully situated on a hill, or rather a succession of hills, is a quaint walled town, a charming and romantic place where poets and artists might love to linger among its antiquated buildings, its fertile valleys, and distant snow-covered mountains. It was known in ancient history as Perusia, the arena of obstinate conflicts both in ancient and mediæval times. Charming views are afforded from different points of the fertile valleys of Umbria. The narrow, winding streets of Perugia are walled on both sides by high, irregular, and peculiar buildings, that denote a great antiquity; on the whole, it is the most picturesque Italian city we have yet seen. The Cathedral of San Lorenzo, of the fifteenth century, is yet unfinished outside, though the interior is very showily decorated, the ceiling being covered with frescos, and the columns with marble imitations, while the chapels are ornamented with beautiful and elaborate wood carving, said to be from designs by Raphael. This Cathedral contained the celebrated Sposalizio of Perugino, until it was removed to Caen, Normandy, in 1797. Among the objects of interest are an altar-piece by Signorelli and a sarcophagus with the remains of three popes. The Collegio del Cambrio, or Chamber of Commerce, contains frescos by Perugino, the master of Raphael, who, it is said, was assisted by his illustrious pupil. The Palace Constabile formerly contained a gallery of paintings in which was a celebrated Madonna by Raphael, sold in 1871 to the emperor of Russia for three hundred and fifty thousand francs, or seventy thousand dollars. The Arco di Augusto is an ancient gate dating from the Etruscan period. The University of Perugia, established in 1320, contains a picture gallery, mostly the works of the Umbrian school of art. The Chapel of San Severo, formerly a monastery now a college, contains the earliest frescos of Raphael, and are thought to resemble his Disputa in the Vatican.

The Perugians evidently regarded us as objects of curiosity, for they watched us closely — old men, young men, priests and women — as if they had never seen foreigners before. Perhaps they never had seen any from America; but we thought we were conducting with strict propriety when we issued forth from our hotel with our guide-books under our arms, even if we did gaze at every old, peculiar building, every quaint bit of ornament, and every time-worn stone. The natives plainly considered us very *green* or very peculiar. Before leaving for Terni, we took another view of the charming landscape adjacent to the town. Those travellers who give their attention exclusively to cities lose a great deal of pleasure, for the natural scenery of Italy combines the grand and the beautiful in agreeable variety.

The route to Terni was no exception to the general rule; besides, we passed towns on the crests and slopes of hills, some of them surrounded by walls and defended by fortifications, while all along the way groups of dwellings, scarcely deserving the name of village, and single habitations were scattered, to complete a fascinating picture. As we approached Terni, the scenery became more grand and rugged; the road passed over a limestone region, sometimes between precipitous walls and sometimes through tunnels. Our train moved very slowly until the summit of the pass was reached, when it descended and moved some distance before reaching Terni. This old Roman town stands on a hill or mountain, and is protected by walls and other defences. The streets are very irregular and the buildings very ancient; but there is a good walk along the ramparts, from which remarkably fine views are obtained of mountains, valleys, and towns of the surrounding regions. There are many agreeable walks shaded by trees in this old town, and in the Episcopal Palace are seen the remains of an ancient structure believed to have been an amphitheatre; while portions of stone columns were scattered about. The Cathedral is quite large and contains a number of paintings and frescos.

Two of our party, that originally comprised four tourists, left us at Perugia, to go direct to Rome, while the other two, including the writer, stopped at Terni in order to visit the celebrated Falls, about four miles from the town. The day for our visit was fine. We had previously made arrangements for a carriage and driver, not intending to engage a guide, as we had been told it was quite unnecessary but when we were ready to start, behold, a guide stood waiting to mount the seat beside the driver. We remonstrated and insisted we did not need his services, but our self-elected cicerone as strenuously affirmed we did. Finally, the waiter coming to his aid, we at length yielded, partly from compassion and partly to be rid of his importunity. He asked three francs for his services, not a very large sum to be sure.

The road to Terni Falls lay through a wild, grand, and picturesque region, bounded by high cliffs of limestone, rock, and rugged mountains, with the rich green ilex growing at their bases, while olive and orange trees were on the hill slopes. On our right was seen the picturesque village of Papigno perched upon a high rock.

The Velino, a tributary of the river Nera, forms the celebrated falls called the Cascate delle Marmore. The descent is about six hundred and fifty feet; but the falls are broken into three cataracts, the first being three hundred and thirty feet, while the other two are much less. As the Velino is thoroughly impregnated with lime, the water has a greenish-milky color, and the entire region contains extensive petrefactions. The deposition of lime is gradually raising the bed of the stream, which threatens the adjacent regions with inundation. To avoid such a catastrophe, the Romans built a tunnel 271 B. C., which is used at the present time, though it has been necessary to construct several others in addition. The quantity of water is small at this season; it descends sometimes vertically, and then it dashes over the rocks, breaking into spray, while at one point the cascade is divided by the projecting precipice.

During the afternoon of December 19, we left Terni for Rome, where we intended to spend some time. Our journey was through a region of beautiful and picturesque scenery, varied by mountains clothed in rich purple, whose steep acclivities presented ruined castles. The day of our memorable ride to the "Eternal City" closed very appropriately with a glorious sunset and a clear Italian sky. We did not arrive there until evening; but the bright, full moon enabled us to see distinctly all near objects, so that we had a pretty correct idea of that part of the city through which we passed from the railway station, opposite the Baths of Diocletian to our hotel, the Milano, in Via Santa Chiara, where we joined our friends.

We have now before us the most interesting scenes of all our travels, which carry us back to the remote past, and are connected directly or remotely with nearly all the nations of the world.

We intend to spend several months here, studying its antiquities and its treasures of art, before we proceed to Naples, the end of our journey towards the south, when we retrace our steps, and visit some of the Western Italian towns on our return to Paris.

## CHAPTER XI.

*Rome.*

THE first place to visit in this city of wonders was the Colosseum; therefore after dinner, our party started for this purpose. The Colosseum by moonlight! What associations are linked with this historical building! We had often seen it represented by art, but now we actually stood in the arena, and saw the lofty walls crumbling to ruins, but still vast and majestic, and under the magical effect of moonlight fascinating and awe-inspiring. We passed the Forum on our way; but the view of the Colosseum was sufficient for our first attempt at sight-seeing. The next day, December 20, was given to St. Peter's, the Castle of St. Angelo, and the Pantheon, the last two being relics of old Rome.

St. Peter's is grand and spacious, and surpasses any representations of the pen or brush. It is rich in marbles, statues, pictures, and architectural decorations, yet it is not to these alone it owes its inexpressible power, but it is its magnitude, combined with these, that renders it so conspicuous. The size of the building, as seen from the front, is at first disappointing, inasmuch as it appears far less than the reality; but viewed from the interior, after some effort of the imagination, its immensity begins to be appreciated. When contemplating any grand and beautiful object, in the first glow of enthusiasm, criticism or even a calm judgment seems cold; language fails to express the emotions at such a time. Many and prolonged visits must be given to the study of this memorable church before it can be understood.

The old Castle, associated with some of the most tragical events of the past, stands as an outpost to guard this wonderful temple. The Pantheon, a monument of ancient Rome, with its immense walls and columns, though denuded of their decorations, still bears witness to the grandeur of the city in earlier times. The streets of the older parts of the town are narrow and without sidewalks; but one is constantly reminded of the magnificence and departed glory of the "Eternal City," for extensive and remarkable ruins bear witness of the fact.

The weather being unfavorable for outdoor explorations, we made a visit to some of the notable buildings, particularly the churches. That of Santa Maria is Gothic, the only one of any importance of this style in Rome. The exterior is neither grand nor beautiful, but the nave is fine, with high and massive columns, and the building contains much colored glass and numerous monuments, comprising those of Leo X. and Clement VII., both popes belonging to the Medici family. Here is the Christ of Michael Angelo, which has a bronze shoe on the advanced foot to prevent the devout from wearing it away by frequent kissing. The Dominican Monastery, near the church, is the place where Galileo was compelled to retract his statement that the earth moves round the sun. This monastery contains the largest library in Rome, after that of the Vatican, and comprises two hundred thousand volumes and one thousand manuscripts. A bridge over the Via St. Ignazio connects this library with the Bibliotheca Vittorio Emanuele, in the Collegio Romana.

The Piazza Navona, in the form of a parallelogram, encloses two large fountains and one small one; that in the centre, made of Pentelic marble, contains the statues of the river gods, of the Danube, the Ganges, the Nile, and the Rio della Plata, all the works of Bernini. The obelisk formerly in the Circus Maxentius is placed on the top. At one side of the piazza stands the Church of St. Agnes, decorated with frescos and sculptures representing events in the life of the saint.

In the afternoon we went to the Piazza del Popolo, and the Pincio, a hill laid out in gardens, walks, and carriage drives. Grand views are afforded from the terraces and the top of the hill; the best view of the dome of St. Peter's is had from this eminence. To the north are the Albion Hills, while all along the Tiber, and crowning its numerous hills, reposes the celebrated city, the scene of the memorable events of twenty-five centuries, and is to-day restless with the on-rushing tide of the nineteenth century. "It bears in its bosom the buried relics of an effete culture, and upon its surface the activities of a new civilization." Rome is both ancient and modern; it has one hand on the past, and the other on the present. Before leaving the Pincio, December 21, we gathered a rose growing in the open air, which describes better than words the climate of this latitude.

The site of the Church of Santa Maria del Popolo, founded 1099 A. D., was the burial-place of the Emperor Nero, and tradition says it was haunted by evil spirits until a church was built on the spot. It contains a large number of monuments, some of which are magnificent. The vaulting of the dome is decorated with eight mosaics by Della Pace, after the cartoons of Raphael, representing the creation of the heavenly bodies. One of the chapels is supported by columns of Sicilian jasper, and is very rich in marbles of divers kinds. The church is contiguous to the Augustinian monastery where Luther resided during his visit in Rome.

The gallery of paintings in the Corsini Palace comprises selections from a number of the old masters, as Carlo Dolce, Titian, Caracci, Rubens, Rembrandt, Claude Lorrain, Murillo, the two Poussins, Vernet, Salvator Rosa, Fra Angelico, and others, but not all of the paintings possess great merit. The landscapes were generally good, and some of them excellent. One room contains the celebrated Corsini Vase in chased work, representing the atonement of Orestes, while in another apartment Christina, Queen of Sweden, died in 1689. The library of the palace occupies eight rooms, and contains one of the largest collections of engravings in the world. The gardens in the rear of the palace extend to the Janiculus, and afford from their heights excellent views of the city.

Returning to the churches, the Santa Maria dell' Anima, the German national church, is very peculiar, with the façade extending a considerable distance above the roof. It contains a monument to Hadrian of Utrecht, preceptor of the Emperor Charles V. Santa Maria delle Pace, near the German church, contains Raphael's Sybils, ranked among the greatest of his compositions, and also the most admired of his frescos. They comprise the Sybils of Cumæ, of Persia, of Phrygia, and the aged Sybil of the Tiber, recording the revelations concerning Christ. Above the Sybils are the Prophets, by Timoteo della Vite. A very ancient Madonna, with a sweet and pensive countenance, is placed over the high altar, and is held in great reverence. Newly married couples celebrate their first Mass after the wedding in this church. St. Andrea della Valle is interesting for its monuments and rich marbles. The Strozzi Chapel has some of the works of Angelo and Domenichino, and the monuments of Popes Pius II. and Pius III., and the Barberini Chapel has several statues. SS. Luca e Martina, near the Marmatine prison, consists of an upper and a lower church, with several monuments. The tombs of the saints are of bronze, with some fine work.

The Capitoline Museum, on the left of the Capitol, contains antique statues, including some of the master-pieces and celebrated works well known to lovers of art, as the Dying Gaul, the Venus of the Capitol, the Satyr of Praxitiles, Flora, taken from the Villa of Hadrian, a Boy struggling with a Goose, the busts of many Greeks and Romans, reliefs in marble and fragments of sculptures and architectural ornaments. A fountain in the court contains a colossal statue of a river god, with a shell in one hand, where the answers to Pasquino were placed. Santa Maria in Campitelli, it is claimed, has a miraculous image of the Virgin to whose influence the cessation of the plague in 1656, has been ascribed. The frescos of Pozzi adorn the Jesuit church of St. Ignazio.

The Colosseum, Arch of Constantine, Arch of Titus, the Basilica of Constantine, the Temple of Venus and Roma, are all relics of the past glory and magnificence of this enchanting city. The ruins of Rome constitute its chief attractions, and carry one back to the time of the Republic and of the Empire. The Colosseum, with its immense arches and buttresses, its walls and flights of steps, its arena, and everything connected with it, was on a grand scale. The broken columns of marble and granite, the beautifully carved capitals strewn about, convey some idea of its magnificence. The ancient Church of SS. Cosma e Domino, erected 526 A. D., contains mosaics of the sixth century, thought by some to be the most beautiful in Rome.

The Palace of the Conservatori, near the Capitol, is a museum of antique bronzes and the Proto Moteca or Picture Gallery of the Capitol. Many of the ancient works of art, found in the excavations on the Palatine, are placed in this museum. The busts of several Italians distinguished in art, science, and literature, together with those of a few from other nations, are arranged along the corridor leading to the Picture Gallery. These Italians present a fine type of the human family, and would be noticed as remarkable men. Italy has taken good care to perpetuate the names of her distinguished sons, of whom she has had a large number, by statues, busts, paintings, and monuments scattered throughout her cities.

Among the more notable bronzes of the Conservatori are the "Wolf" in the early Etruscan style, perhaps the same as that of 296 B. C.; the Thorn-Extractor, and the bust of Junius Brutus, the first consul. The collection of paintings is neither large nor very celebrated; some of the more notable were an unfinished painting of a Redeemed Spirit, by Guido Rene; a Magdalen, by the same artist; the Cumæan Sybil, by Domenichino; a Persian Sybil, by Guercino; Madonna and Saints, by F. Francia; David and a St. Cecilia, by Romanelli; Madonna in Glory, by Garofalo; Europa by Guido Rene, several portraits by Van Dyck, Titian, Tintoretto, and other masters. The art collections of Rome are scattered instead of being concentrated, as they are in some other cities, therefore more time is needed to study them. Many of the celebrated works are found in the private galleries of Italian nobles, either in their town palaces or their country villas outside the walls.

We made another visit to St. Peter's; but as it was a festal day, we could not ascend the dome, therefore we examined the

CHURCH OF ST. PETER, ROME

FOUNTAINS AND OBELISK, ST. PETER'S

interior. It is well lighted, which cannot be said of many other churches, hence the pictures in mosaic were seen to advantage. There is the idea of space, magnitude, and grandeur suggested to the mind; nothing is confused, no crowding of different objects often seen in other similar buildings. The gilding and ornaments of the ceiling and the marbles are rich and sometimes gorgeous, but even this renowned church is not faultless. The baldacchino under the dome seems out of place, and not in harmony with other parts, while some of the decorations are paltry; the statues in the niches of the columns are not considered the best of their kind, and though some of the monuments are good, others are wanting in taste. The Church of Santa Maria Maggiore, one of the oldest in this city, if not in Christendom, a basilica, and one of the fine patriarchal churches of Rome, over which the Pope presides, was, according to tradition, founded by order of the Virgin, and contains several boards of the Manger. The nave, marble columns, and mosaics are claimed to be a part of an original edifice, built 432 A. D. The interior is two hundred and seventy-nine feet long and fifty-seven wide; the nave has forty-two Ionic columns supporting an architrave adorned with mosaics of the fifth century. The high altar has a canopy supported by four columns of red porphyry. This church contains the tombs of several popes, and was selected, it is said, by Pius IX. as his final resting-place.

The Sistine Chapel is particularly gorgeous in marbles, bronze, and sculptures, and the Borghese Chapel opposite highly decorated; it contains an ancient picture of the Virgin, painted, according to tradition, by St. Luke.

Near Santa Maria Maggiore stands the church of St. Pressede, 822 A. D., remarkable for the Orto del Paradiso, or chapel, in which is placed the column at which Christ was scourged. (No incredulous person should visit the Roman churches.) Ladies are not allowed to enter the sacred precincts except on special occasions. A spot is pointed out where St. Praxedis collected the blood of the martyrs, who suffered in the early persecutions of the Christians.

St. Paolo Fuore le Mura, or St. Paul's beyond the walls, is between one and two miles from the gate, and is one of the most beautiful of the Roman churches; it was founded 388 A. D., and was connected by subterranean arcades with the city. A large part of the building was consumed by fire in 1833, therefore the present structure is largely modern. It is three hundred and ninety feet in length, one hundred and ninety-five in width and seventy-five in height, in the interior. The double row of columns in the nave, are made of granite from the Simplon; six columns of oriental alabaster were presented by the Viceroy of Egypt, and the beautiful malachite pedestals were given by the Emperor Nicholas of Russia. The nave and transepts contain mosaic portraits of all the popes, each five feet in diameter, while colossal statues of SS. Peter and Paul are placed in the nave. The rosso and verde antico which decorate the Confessio were brought from the ancient quarries of Greece, recently discovered. One of the chapels contains a statue of St. Stephen, and two paintings representing his revelation and martyrdom. A monastery connected with the church affords beautiful columns and mosaics.

The Church of St. Paolo is exceedingly costly and magnificent, yet it is situated in a sparsely settled region on the compagna, occupied by a rural class, generally poor and ignorant, hence, the question, why were all this wealth and decoration lavished upon it? The splendor and magnificence of most Italian churches are beyond description, and in painful contrast to the poverty and wretchedness of the lower classes, many of whom depend upon alms for a living.

The Baths of Diocletian (the ruins are still to be seen) enclosed a circumference of six thousand feet. One of its circular buildings is now used for the Church of St. Bernardo, while a large vaulted hall was converted into the Church of Santa Maria degli Angeli, by M. Angelo, but since altered; the painters Maratta and Rosa are buried in the latter. It contains sixteen granite columns, forty feet in height.

The Barbarini Palace is an imposing building with a court in which is placed the statue of Thorwaldsen, by Wolff. The gallery of paintings contains Raphael's Fornarina and Guido Rene's Beatrice Cenci, both of which are well known by copies and engravings. We were little interested in the former, but our attention was arrested by the sweet, sad face of the Cenci. It is said to be a correct portrait of the beautiful captive whom the artist visited in prison the day before her execution. It is a countenance that bears the impress of suffering, more mental than physical, though Beatrice had been subjected to indescribable torture; it expresses a resignation to her fate, and an innocence that refutes the foul calumnies that have been circulated, to excuse, doubtless, the injustice and cruelty of her execution. In the same room are the portraits of her own mother and step-mother Lucretia Cenci, who suffered the penalty of death at the same time. The Fornarina is unlike that of the Uffizzi gallery except, perhaps, the eyes. The Barbarini painting is thinner in flesh and less voluptuous, while the figure is nearly nude; the one at Florence is clothed, but neither conveys any other idea than that of a woman possessing physical beauty. From the Barbarini palace we went to see Guido Rene's Aurora.

The Palace of Rospigliosi, erected on the site of the Baths of Constantine, is said to contain valuable works of art, but it is not easy to get access to the rooms of the palace, though the Casino containing the celebrated painting is open to visitors during two days of the week. The exquisite fresco is on the ceiling which renders its study more difficult. Apollo is represented as driving the chariot of the sun, attended by seven hours preceded by Aurora scattering flowers, while a small divinity is bearing a lighted torch. Language is inadequate to convey a full idea of the beauty of the painting. The admirable disposition of the figures, the exquisite blending of the colors, the glorious effulgence of the rays of light diffused over the figure of the Apollo and imparting a deep warmth to the drapery of those near him, the soft clouds, the sleeping earth below, with the intense blue of the sea, the dark grays of the land, the spirited horses, the grace of the nymphs, in fine, the beauty and gorgeousness of the entire painting, all combine to make it one of the most charming frescos known. The colors have retained their freshness in a remarkable degree.

Another interesting picture was Guido Rene's Andromeda. The beautiful princess is chained to a rock looking down at the hideous monster coming to devour her, and does not see Perseus, her deliverer, mounted on Pegasus, and just on the point of killing her dangerous foe. Domenichino is represented in this gallery by several pictures, one being the Fall of Man; while Rubens has some fine paintings representing the Apostles.

Sabbath on the continent of Europe is very different from that of New England. Here church services are observed for a part of the day, while the remainder is given to pleasure and business. Where form and ceremony constitute the essence of religion, less importance is attached to the spirit of christianity or the character of its professors provided they observe its outward forms. This is to a greater or less extent true in all countries where there is a "state religion."

Rome is so full of wonders it will require weeks and months to gain a tolerable idea of them, for there is always something *new* that is *old* to be studied, either historical or artistic. Every palace, street, and ruin has its tale of romance, its deed of noble daring or of murder, of great suffering or of great luxury. The old Romans were eminent in almost everything; their buildings, their wars and conquests, their vices and crimes. To close the year we made a visit to the Vatican, the most conspicuous object of Mediæval and Modern Rome.

The Vatican of the early period was built near the last of the fifth century, but has been rebuilt and enlarged since at different times. Pope Alexander VI. during the last part of the fifteenth century completed it, and as it now exists, it is eleven hundred and fifty-one feet in length, and seven hundred and sixty-seven in width, and contains eleven thousand rooms of all sizes, eight grand staircases, and twenty courts. The Sistine Chapel contains many celebrated works of art, such as numerous frescos by distinguished masters, comprising those of Michael Angelo, representing the Creation, the Fall of Man, with the Sybils and the Prophets, and the Last

Judgment. One apartment is called the Raphael Stanza and Loggie, but, unfortunately, the frescos after the designs of the great master are more or less injured by time or exposure.

Thus closed the most eventful year of our personal experiences, full of useful lessons, designated to improve the mind, to broaden and deepen the human sympathies, and inspire the heart with gratitude for Divine protection and guidance.

## CHAPTER XII.

*Rome Continued.*

JANUARY 1 we called upon some friends and visited a few churches, including San Pietro in Vincoli, which contains the Moses of Michael Angelo. This is a grand subject by a grand master, one just suited to the genius of the great artist. Of all his sculptures, it appears to us the most impressive; it is sublime. His David is fine, his Pieta is tender, but his Moses is awe-inspiring, a fit embodiment of the Law. Its colossal size, the majesty of the features, the wealth of beard, the penetrating eye, the sternness of countenance, the pose of the figure, give to the statue the similitude of an Olympian Jove. Indeed, he seems more like a divinity than a human being. It is difficult to imagine that this majestic man was one of the meekest of the human race. The Moses was intended for the monument of Pope Julius, to be placed in the church of St. Peter, near the Vatican, but the design was never completed. On the right of the statue, is one of Rachel, and on the left, that of Leah, by the same artist.

The ancient Church of San Lorenzo in Lucina contains the painting of the Crucifixion, by Guido Reni. The Divine Redeemer is on the cross, and with no other being in sight. He is turning his eyes to heaven in his agony, as if suffering from a sense of desertion, which wrung from him the agonizing cry, "My God, my God, why hast thou forsaken me?" Darkness is on all the earth, except the rays of light descending from heaven upon the dying Saviour. This is the most affecting and impressive representation of the tragical scene we have ever beheld. In most paintings of this subject the attention is diverted from the Sufferer by many other objects. Numerous figures are introduced representing different ideas, but here, nothing turns the attention from the mournful event — the death of the Son of God. The Church of SS. Trinita di Monti, situated on elevated ground, is reached by long flights of steps from the Piazza di Spagna, where extensive views of the city are obtained. In front, stands an obelisk, and among the pictures is a Descent from the Cross, by Volterra, considered his master-piece. The nuns perform choral service at this church during vespers.

The gallery of the Borghese Palace has a large and fine collection of paintings, by different artists, said to be the best in Rome, after the Vatican, and contains a greater number of master-pieces than any other gallery. A few of these are the following: Madonna Vase, by Credi; St. Stephen, by Francia; Descent from the Cross, by Garofalo, who has been called the Raphael of Ferrara; Earthly and Heavenly Love, by Titian; Circe, by D. Dossi; the Entombment of Raphael; the Four Seasons, by Albani; and the Holy Family, by P. Vecchio. The Colonna Palace contains a collection of some of the eminent masters, comprising landscapes in water colors, by Gasper Poussin, thought to be his best works. The rooms were painted in frescos; in one of them the paintings were in commemoration of Pope Martin V., who built the palace, in the fifteenth century; in another room, they were to celebrate the battle of Lepanto, 1571, in which a Colonna led the papal troops. On a staircase leading to one of the halls there is left a cannon ball, where it fell in the revolution of 1849. The gallery contains portraits of the ancient and noble house of Colonna, including one of Vittoria Colonna, taken in her youth. Marble tables, rich inlaid furniture, tapestries, painted mirrors, antique statues, etc., are seen in this once celebrated palace, now occupied, or part of it at least, by the French Ambassador.

St. John Lateran, formerly the leading church in Rome, was founded by the Emperor Constantine. It has been destroyed several times as in 896, by an earthquake, and in 1308 and 1360 by fire. It is one of the Roman basilicas, and has been the place of meeting for five important ecclesiastical councils. There are twelve pillars in the nave, with colossal figures of the Apostles, and on each side are double aisles, with chapels, monuments, and paintings. Some of the chapels are highly decorated, especially that of the Torlonias, which contains a Descent from the Cross in marble relief, and the chapel of the Corsini, which is exceedingly rich in antique marbles. The vault below the chapel contains a beautiful Pieta in white marble, illuminated by a burning lamp. The Madonna has an expression of deep, maternal grief, while the features of the Christ are traced in delicate lines. The group has been attributed to Bernini, though its authenticity has been questioned. The canopy over the high altar is very beautiful and is said to contain the heads of SS. Peter and Paul. The Pope alone reads Mass before this altar. At the left is the great altar of the Sacraments, with its four ancient columns of gilt bronze. The Baptistery, for a long time the only one in Rome, is embellished after the manner of other ecclesiastical buildings.

January 3 we ascended to the top of the dome of St. Peter's, and had a magnificent view of all Rome, — the campagna and the distant mountains, some of whose peaks were covered with snow. On the north were the Sabine hills, and on the south the Alban; while the Vatican, with its appendages, lay at our feet, and resembled a fortress in some of its features. Including its courts, it covers a very large space. The ascent to the top of St. Peter's is not difficult, and one is well paid for the trouble, on account of the fine views obtained; it gives one an idea of the magnitude of the building, which covers an area of seventy-eight thousand four hundred and eighty square feet. The length is six hundred and thirty-nine feet; height of the nave, one hundred and fifty; height from the pavement to the top of the cross, four hundred and thirty-five feet, or nearly one hundred less than the Cologne Cathedral; the dome rises three hundred and eight feet above the roof, which is reached by an inclined plane, and short flights of steps.

The palaces of the Cæsars occupied the Palatine Hill; their extensive ruins convey some idea of their magnitude and splendor. Judging from the solid walls of brick, these buildings must have been remarkably strong, and it seems almost incredible that they should ever have been in the ruined condition they now present. They were literally buried for years, until uncovered by modern explorers. The remains of statues, the rare and beautiful marbles, porphyry, and granite, the brilliant paintings on the walls, and the mosaics of the pavements, all show the luxurious habits of the "masters of the world." There are few objects in this city of wonders so interesting as its ancient ruins. They teach us lessons about the personal habits of the nation that for centuries occupied the first place on the pages of history, as well as the instability of human greatness. One is very forcibly impressed with this latter truth by travel, for there are few places that do not have their ruins, their deserted castles and palaces, their dilapidated walls, and unoccupied fortresses, which so emphatically tell the story of decline and ruin. Many European cities combine both the antique and the modern; they are perpetually dying and perpetually renewing their existence. This is emphatically true of Rome, where new buildings are erected on the sites of those belonging to earlier periods. It is like an old tree sending out new shoots to take the place of decayed branches. A large number of villas and palaces are seen in most ancient countries either quite deserted or only partly occupied.

The Church of the Capuchins, founded by Cardinal Barbarini, contains a monument of Alexander Sobieski, son of King John III. of Poland. Its most remarkable features are the four vaults containing the bones of about four thousand Capuchins, arranged in clusters, festoons, or other decorative forms; while between the arches are the ghastly skeletons of deceased monks, dressed in the costumes of their order. The graves are filled with sacred soil taken from Jerusalem. There is a small chapel in these vaults, where the living monks may come and meditate on their prospective destiny. Such repulsive sights would naturally make death fearful to contemplate, while, on the contrary, the tombs should be as attractive as art can make them, for the consolation of friends.

The Church of San Pietro, in Montorio, was founded by Ferdinand and Isabella, of Spain, in 1500 A. D., on the spot where tradition records St. Peter suffered martyrdom. It is situated on an elevation one hundred and ninety-seven feet in height; and the prospects from the Via Garibaldi, which winds around the southern side, are superb, affording numerous commanding views, comprising the entire city, with its palaces and churches, the Campagna, the villas, the Alban and Sabine mountains, with small villages scattered about, and the ruins of *old* Rome like ghosts of the past. Add to these the blue sky above and verdant fields below suffused in the rays of a tropical sunset, and we have a charming picture which carries the imagination through nearly thirty centuries of the past. The church was closed at the time of our visit; but an aged monk admitted us to an open court of the monastery connected with it, where the Tempietto, a small circular building with sixteen granite columns, stands on the spot where, it is said, St. Peter's cross was erected. Inside the temple is a chapel with a sitting statue of the Apostle, and below this is another chapel with an opening in the floor. Our guide, a pleasant little fellow about ten years old, took some of the yellow sand as a relic for us to carry away. After the return of the custodian of San Pietra in Montario, we were admitted to the interior, which is decorated by frescos designed by Michael Angelo. Until 1797 it contained Raphael's Transfiguration. The unfortunate Beatrice Cenci was buried in this church, though there is not a single memento to mark her grave.

Following the broad street along which are public grounds with trees and fountains, we come to the Acqui Paolo, the ancient Aqua Trajana, which flowed from a lake thirty-one miles away. The fountain has five separate mouths pouring water into an immense basin. The façade, an imposing structure, is adorned with portions of columns taken from the Temple of Minerva, in Trajan's Forum. Trastevere, once a suburb of the city, but annexed by the Emperor Augustus, is connected with Rome proper by three bridges. The inhabitants of this region, comprising the working classes, claim to be the most direct descendants of the ancient Romans, and their character and dialect which differ from those living in other parts of the city, seem to give them some right to the claim. The Janiculus is an eminence in this vicinity, rising two hundred and seventy-five feet, and was once the site of an ancient castle.

January 6. The Festival of the Epiphany began last evening with all sorts of strange noises and curious antics, lasting nearly all night, and the same performances are to continue for some time. The Romans and, indeed, most other Italians, seem to be a mirth-loving people and fond of childish sports. Our relaxation came with the Sabbath, a day of rest to mind and body, which was much needed, for sight-seeing, especially in Rome, is no light task. Walking, which is absolutely necessary to a great extent, over pavements of cobble-stones — sidewalks are rare — is very tedious. One cannot explore ruins and examine churches in carriages. But how soon the novelty of travel passes away, and we come to look at remarkable objects with cool and critical indifference. This is to be regretted, for the greatest pleasure in travel arises from the new ideas and emotions it awakens and stimulates. Yet, with all its fatigue, expenses, and annoyances, who would forego its advantages? True, many persons travel for the distinction of having visited foreign lands, others, to divert the mind from unpleasant experiences, while another class are influenced by a desire for knowledge and prepare themselves for such an object. With how much greater interest and profit will the *travelled* reader return to the pages of history, poetry, or general literature, after having seen the places and works referred to by different authors.

The Vatican Museum must, of course, be visited many times before its priceless treasures can only be partially studied. It contains the largest collection of statuary and other sculptures in the world, and most of the specimens are antiques belonging to different periods. Casts or copies of many of these works we had seen in the museums of other countries, but copies do not possess the same interest as the originals. The oil paintings of this museum are few in number, compared with some other galleries of Europe, or even in Rome, but they include some of the best works of the old masters, including the Transfiguration, Raphael's last effort, his Madonna of Foligno, his Annunciation, Adoration of the Magi, and some others. Besides these are the Communion of St. Jerome, by Domenichino, pictures by Murillo, Perugino, Titian, a Madonna by Fra Angelico, as well as works by other artists. The fresco paintings are celebrated. The collections of this gallery are more difficult of access than most others, since they are farther removed from the populous sections of the city.

The Doria Palace, one of the most magnificent in Rome, has three façades, one on as many different streets, and contains a gallery of fine paintings, with some statuary and antique relics. The different schools of painting are represented, comprising two portraits by Raphael, one of Innocent X., by Velasquez; the Nativity of Christ, by Garofalo; landscapes, by Claude Lorrain, considered among his best; the Moneychangers Disputing, by Quentin Martyn; landscapes, by Caraccio, Rosa, Poussin, and others; portraits by Rubens, Giorgione, Titian; and a Faun, by Rembrandt. The Sacrifice to Apollo, by Lorrain, is especially interesting. The time is evening, and a temple of Apollo, probably the one at Delphi, is represented, while in the foreground are seen several human figures. The "Mill," by the same artist, is an exquisite landscape, in which the charming effect of a skilful arrangement of distance is very effective. Trees occupy the foreground, the middle distance is gradually shaded off, while in the remote distance are seen the faint outlines of snow-covered mountains. The Herodias, by Pardenone, is a fine painting, though the subject is treated in a different manner from the usual method. The countenance of Herodias wears a look of tender pity for the murdered prophet whose head she holds in a charger, with the long hair of the martyr falling over her arm, while at her side a female attendant, probably, is looking at the spectacle, touched with a feeling of compassion. Murillo's Magdalen is quite unlike that of Titian.

St. Carlo al Corso is the national church of the Lombards, and the resort of the fashionable world; the altar-piece is considered one of the finest of Maratta's works, but the interior is very showy; the ceiling is covered with frescos and gilding, and the walls and columns are painted in poor imitation of marble. The Piazza di Pietra contains the Dogana di Terra or Custom House, with a façade of eleven marble Corinthian columns belonging to an ancient temple, probably that of Neptune; this structure is sometimes erroneously designated the Temple of Antoninus Pius. It once had twenty-three columns, while those that remain are defaced and some of their capitols are broken. January 9 King Victor Emmanuel died, after an illness of a few days, therefore the museums and places of business are closed, but we paid a visit to the Mausoleum of Augustus, the burial-place of the Roman emperors from his time to that of Nerva. The structure contains mortuary chambers, over which arises a mound of earth in terraces planted with cypresses and connected with a park in which is placed the statue of Augustus.

The Vatican Museum being opened on the 11th, we visited the Nuovo Braccio or galleries of statuary. At the entrance are two columns of black and white granite, supporting the busts of Augustus and Trajan, while many others of distinguished persons rest on half columns of Egyptian granite. Here are seen many celebrated works of antiquity, including statues of Augustus and Silenus in Parian marble, of Euripides, Demosthenes, the Apoxyomenes, and a Wounded Amazon in Pentelic marble, the Nile, Julia, daughter of Titus, in Luni marble, Minerva, supposed to be a copy of the one in gold and ivory, by Phidias, and a Mercury considered one of the finest of Greek art. There is a great variety of granites, marbles, and alabasters comprising rich and rare species. The gallery of paintings is, perhaps, less interesting than many others, but it contains some master-pieces. The battle of Constantine and Maxentius, by Romano, is full of action, and represents a remarkable combination of the different scenes witnessed on a battle-field. The victor and the vanquished, the wounded and dying men and horses, and the weapons of war, are all mingled in confusion and, to add horrors to the scene, the contest occurred on the bridge and banks of a river, therefore some of the combatants are in the stream. Maxentius with his horse is endeavoring to save himself from sinking in the waves, while Constantine is advancing triumphantly in the midst of the terrible carnage.

After making another journey to the Vatican Museum, we went to the Quirinal Palace, where the king lay in state, but the immense crowd prevented our entering; the next day we gave to rest, a necessary precaution after a week of constant strain on the physical and mental powers. Rome is a city of wearisome, if not "magnificent distances," and it requires much time and "hard travel" to see all the places of interest, but few cities in the world are so full of attractions to the antiquary. Visiting the Vatican Museum under the present regulations is attended by delay and fatigue. Tourists are obliged to get a new "permisso," or ticket of admission, every time they go, instead of using one a second time, and in place of entering through the court, formerly used, they must go around St. Peter's, nearly three quarters of a mile, over the rough pavement. It is said these regulations are partly due to the political differences of the pope and the late king. Rome at present is full of people from other Italian cities, to attend the obsequies of Victor Emmanuel, who had won the hearts of his countrymen by his patriotic devotion to their interests.

The Church of Santa Croce in Gerusalemme is a very ancient basilica, said to have been founded by St. Helen; it is decorated by the frescos of Peruzza, and is situated near some of the notable structures of old Rome, particularly the Amphitheatre. This building was one hundred and seventy-one feet in the longest diameter, but there are only sixteen arches remaining, and these are included in the city walls. St. Giovanni in Laterano is connected with the old palace of the popes, occupied from the time of Constantine until the removal of the papal see to Avignon, France. This palace, in 1843, was appropriated as a museum of heathen and Christian antiquities. The statue of Sophocles, said to be the best portrait statue known, and one of Neptune, are among the most noted sculptures. The collection comprises a large number and variety of architectural specimens of ancient art. The Christian department was founded by Pius IX., consequently it was not complete. The few paintings are mediocre; one of them, of a large size, is a copy of the fresco of Domenichino, and represents the martyrdom of St. Andrea. On the whole, the Church of St. John Lateran is highly decorated, and its monuments, statues, and reliefs are rich and numerous.

Trajan's Forum comprised several magnificent edifices, designed, it is thought, by Apolodoras, of Damascus, and erected by the Emperor Trajan, 111–114 A. D. The statue of the emperor stood in the centre, and on the north side was Trajan's Column, one hundred and forty-seven feet in height, with a spiral band three feet in width, running around the shaft; the figure of St. Peter, on the top, has been substituted for that of the emperor. The reliefs on the column represent scenes in the wars of Trajan with the Dacians, and comprise twenty-five hundred human figures. The forum contains Trajan's Triumphal Arch, a temple dedicated to him, and a library. Some of these sculptured reliefs have been removed to embellish the Arch of Constantine, while some of the latter have been used in churches.

January 17 the funeral ceremonies of the late king were observed. The procession was very long and required many hours to pass a given point, and, on the whole, was magnificent, comprising, as it did, only persons of rank and official station, and foreign ministers with their attaché. The military was largely represented by officers, and the navy by marines, though fewer in number than the soldiers. The Italian nobles are very fine looking and splendidly uniformed, but their marching was open to criticism. In regard to the "rank and file" of the Italian army, it can be said that they are inferior in personelle and in the style of their uniform, to most other

European soldiers. Some of the banners, on this occasion were very beautiful. The funeral car, the riderless charger of the dead hero, the veterans who served under him, and the tattered battle flags, afforded a solemn and affecting sight. A large number of Italian cities, if not all of them, with their special banners, were represented in the procession. The foreign ambassadors and ministers, covered with decorations, afforded an interesting spectacle, in striking contrast to those from the United States, who were conspicuous for the absence of any such emblems, being dressed in black, without a single decoration. A vast concourse of spectators thronged the public streets, balconies, windows, monuments, and indeed every available spot, where the procession was to pass, but there was the greatest good humor and decorous behavior, which proves that the Italians have a keen sense of propriety. We have always found them courteous and obliging, and cannot recollect an instance where they were otherwise. In our journeys we have sometimes been amused at the prejudices of race, a fault as old as nations themselves, the result of narrowness and ignorance which travel will modify, if not eradicate.

For more than a week little has been accomplished in the labor of sight-seeing, and many tourists, whose time is limited, are feeling impatient at the closing of nearly all public institutions. This should teach them that Rome and other Italian cities, and indeed those of nearly all other countries of Europe, confer upon foreigners very great favors by opening their museums free of charge.

Another " festa " April 18, therefore the galleries were closed. There were so many people in the city from abroad, that it was difficult to obtain carriages, and some of our party were obliged to defer a visit to the Baths of Caracalla; but after some effort, we secured seats in an omnibus for St. Trinita de Pellegrini, which contains an altar-piece by Guido, and a Crucifixion in which Christ is represented on the cross. This church was erected in 1614, and near it is a hospital for convalescents and pilgrims, providing accommodations for several hundred persons at one time. Pilgrims are entertained here at Easter for a number of days.

In the Crucifixion at St. Trinita, two angels stand at the foot of the cross, two are above, while the Father is represented in the clouds of heaven. The other pictures we did not see, as the church was undergoing repairs. Santa Maria, in Monticello, consecrated in 1101 A. D., is remarkable for its decorations of rich marbles, while the Church of St. Carlo Borromeo, in the form of a Greek cross, contains paintings by some of the celebrated artists.

The Cenci Palace, situated on a small piazza of the same name, is associated with the beautiful princess Beatrice. It is now dilapidated and occupied by poor families; but entering a small court, we saw evidences that the building was undergoing repairs or being taken down. A staircase could be seen from the court which probably led to the different apartments. Up and down these steps, the young girl, the heroine of so many romances, had passed in the joyousness of childhood. It was in this palace that the unfortunate brother took an affectionate farewell of his wife and children, when on his way to execution. There is scarcely a building in Rome that has a sadder history. It was here that the fiendish Count Cenci tortured his family with an excess of cruelty too repulsive to be related, and yet they were powerless to obtain redress or protection from the government of Pope Clement VIII.

The Pincio was the "Hill of Gardens" in ancient Rome where were the Gardens of Lucullus and the scene of Messalina's orgies and death. A magnificent view of the city and distant mountains is obtained from the terraces of this hill. The obelisk erected by Hadrian to Antoninus stands on the Pincio. From the lofty walls on the north side, we look down on the Villa Borghese, with its fine park and beautiful trees, including the rich green ilex and the Italian pine. The Piazza del Popolo contains an obelisk brought from Heliopolis, Egypt, by Augustus, after the defeat of Mark Antony. The shaft is seventy-eight feet in height; and the entire monument, including base and cross, is one hundred and eighteen feet.

The Casino, with its works of art, is nearly in the centre of the grounds, and its different apartments are adorned with statues, paintings, frescos, and marbles, including a Meleager by Rossi, a colossal bust of Hadrian and of Antoninus Pius, a Juno, Ceres, Venus, Hercules, Mercury, and Apollo, an Amazon on horseback, and many other interesting subjects. The statue of Paulina Borghese, sister of Napoleon I., representing a reclining Venus, is exquisitely graceful; and the statue of Paris, that might have been taken for an Apollo, deserved special notice. On the walls are three large paintings of scenes in the Trojan War, namely, the meeting of Paris and Helen, the Abduction of Helen, and the death of Achilles.

January 20 we attended services in the church of St. Andrea della Fratte. Being the occasion of a festival, the church was draped in crimson and gold, while numerous candles were burning in the different chandeliers suspended from the ceiling. Near the Tribune are the statues of two angels, by Bernini, originally intended for the Bridge of St. Angelo. A reclining figure of Lady Falconnet, by Harriet Hosmer, is placed in this church. The statue holds a rosary and cross in the hand.

Among the tombs of distinguished persons are those of Angelina Kauffmann and Schadow, a Danish archæalogist; here also is one of a prince of Morocco, whose only fame is his title. The Academy of San Luca, the oldest in Italy, was founded in 1595; its first president was Federigo Zuccaro, and its present director is Professor E. Wolff, the German sculptor. The gallery contained some good pictures and some of little merit, while portraits of artists adorned the walls. Following the Via Bonella, in which the Academy is situated, we come to an ancient gateway, a remnant of old Rome. Three Corinthian columns support a very beautiful entablature, all of which belonged to the Temple of Mars in the Forum of Augustus. In regard to this forum, about four hundred and fifty feet of its lofty walls remain standing, while its original level was about sixteen feet below the street. Near the Forum of Augustus was the Forum of Cæsar, with a Temple of

Venus. During the intervals between visits to other places of interest, we made frequent excursions to the Vatican Museum, with its inexhaustible treasures of art.

January 22. To the Baths of Caracalla we next gave our attention. These were begun by the Emperor Caracalla, in 212 A. D., and completed by Alexander Severus, in 222; they could accommodate sixteen hundred bathers at once. The high and thick walls, the immense arches, and the extensive apartments, whose remains are now seen, prove that they were on a magnificent plan. The area comprised one hundred and six square feet, and like other public buildings, it had warm and cold baths, a stadium, and numerous chambers. The richness and magnificence of Roman baths added to the grandeur of the ancient city. It has been said these baths caused the overthrow of Roman supremacy, as they were so sumptuous, that the citizens spent most of their time in them, and by an excess of luxury became effeminate, and when internal dissensions and foreign invasions assailed the nation, they were powerless to resist. The Baths of Caracalla afford many interesting relics, in the form of broken columns, with ornamented capitols, friezes, mouldings, pedestals, reliefs, statues, and mosaic pavements, with their abundance of beautiful marbles.

On the Cælian Hill stands St. Stefano Rotondo, a circular church without spire, façade, or any other distinguishing feature of ecclesiastical architecture. It is the largest circular church known, though smaller than the original one built at the close of the fifth century; fifty-six granite and marble columns support a wooden roof, while the interior contains frescos representing the martyrdom of the saints, by every conceivable form of torture, a very repulsive scene, as any one can imagine. A marble episcopal throne occupied by Gregory the Great stands in the vestibule. The church is seldom, if ever, used for worship. The Palace Spada alla Regola was built by Paul III. of the Farnese family, in 1540, but it subsequently came into the possession of the Spada family. In this palace is seen the colossal statue of Pompey, claimed, by some antiquaries, to be the one mentioned by Shakespeare, at whose base Cæsar fell. The custodian pointed to a dark spot on one of the limbs of the statue said to have been caused by the blood of Cæsar's wounds. Portraits of the Spada family that has furnished several cardinals, and other paintings, adorn the walls.

The Farnese Palace is one of the most magnificent in Rome, but at present is closed to the public, though the court and main entrance can be seen. The vaulting of the archway is very elaborately ornamented with carving designed by Michael Angelo; the entrance has a triple colonnade. The court contains two sarcophagi, one being that of Cecilia Metella, and beautifully ornamented. This palace formerly held three famous groups, — the Farnese Bull, the Hercules, and the Flora, now in the Museum of Naples. It was begun by Paul III., and for several years prior to 1872, it belonged to the kings of Naples, but now it is owned by the government. In visiting Rome, one should not be too fastidious about the want of cleanliness in the public streets. We were obliged to pass through the Ghetto, which is not remarkably neat, in order to reach the Arch of Janus, called Janus Quadrifrons, on account of its four façades formed by four arches, constituting a square structure of grand and fine proportions. An ancient church, founded in the fourth century, stands near, and not far off is the Cloaca Maxima, the oldest arch in Rome, built more than two thousand years ago.

At the foot of the Aventine is the church of Santa Maria in Casmedin, which has in the portico, the Bocca della Verita, the mouth of an ancient fountain into which, according to tradition, the Romans were accustomed to insert the right hand when pledging themselves by an oath. The church dates from the third century, and was built on the site of an ancient temple; ten of the columns are enclosed in the walls of the modern edifice. The pavement consists of mosaic work called Opus Alexandrinum.

In this part of the city is seen the Temple of Vesta or of Hercules Victor, it is not certain which, a circular building surrounded by nineteen standing columns (one having been removed), of the Corinthian order; the temple has been christened Santa Maria del Sole. Not far from the Round Temple is a church of the Ionic order, and near stands the brick house of Crescentius or Casa di Rienzi, one of the oldest existing specimens of the domestic architecture of the Middle Ages. Almost every church has some special characteristic or some relic of peculiar interest, but it would require volumes to delineate their distinctive features. They are really museums of art, and must be studied as such.

The weather was so fine January 24, that a party of tourists from our hotel decided to take a drive to the Campagna by the Appian Way, as far as Casale Rotondo, about six miles from the gate of St. Sebastian. The Via Appia, famous both in sacred and secular history, was begun by Appius Claudius Cæcus, 319 B. C., for a military road, and in 1860 it was repaired or excavated for the distance of eleven miles, and merits the ancient title of "queen of roads." On this thoroughfare are some of the most interesting remains of pagan and Christian Rome. Ruins of ancient tombs, broken statues, and marbles, reliefs, and architectural ornaments are scattered along the way, while on the left are seen the remains of the aqueduct built by Claudius, 52 A. D., and in the distance the Alban Hills and the town of Frascati. About a mile from the gate are the Catacombs of St. Calixtus. We were met by the custodian, who conducted our party across an enclosure of ground to a staircase that descended a number of feet below the surface, perhaps fifteen or more, then gave to each one a lighted taper, when we began our subterranean exploration in single file, our guide preceding us. We were conducted through passage after passage, some of them being very narrow, with niches all along the walls for the bodies of those buried here. Occasionally we passed a small chapel, and in one were two skeletons in coffins. The chapel where the early popes were buried contains the remains of Sixtus II., who suffered martyrdom in the Catacombs 258 A. D., besides inscriptions in commemoration of persecuted Christians.

The remains of St. Cecilia were removed to the church in Trastevere. These Catacombs, originally designed for tombs, afforded an asylum to the Christians during the persecutions by pagan Rome, hence the chapels found in them. As we wandered through these narrow passages running in all directions, there was danger of being lost in the perplexing maze of these subterranean streets; therefore we kept near our guide, to avoid so fearful a doom. The Church of St. Sebastian, on a site above the Catacombs, and containing the remains of martyrs, includes a stone which, tradition says, bears the footprints of the Saviour.

From the Appian Way we see the ruins of the Circus Maximus, ten hundred and fifty feet by two hundred and eighty-five feet, built in 311 A. D.; but the Tomb of Cecilia Metella, wife of the Triumvir Crassus, forms the most conspicuous object and serves as a landmark. It is a circular monument sixty-five feet in diameter; the frieze is adorned with wreaths of flowers and the skulls of oxen, a curious decoration. At one time it was furnished with turrets or pinnacles, and used as a tower. The visit to the Catacombs and the Campagna formed a memorable event in our sojourn at Rome. After our return, we went to the Villa Medici, and from the Belvedere obtained excellent views of the surrounding scenes. This building in 1801 became the seat of the French Academy of Arts; its collections of casts comprise some copies from the Parthenon at Athens and the Louvre at Paris.

We made frequent visits to the Vatican Museum, and during one of these went to the Church of St. Onofrio, founded in 1439, and the burial-place of Tasso. It is built on the Janiculus, and contains the poet's monument of white marble erected by Pius IX. The statue of Tasso occupies a niche, while below it are reliefs on a frieze representing his funeral procession, with the deceased poet borne through the streets wearing the laurel wreath, which was not conferred upon him until after his death. On a declivity of the highest peak of the Janiculus, stands the oak, partially destroyed by lightning, under which Tasso used to sit when a resident of the monastery near the church. The cell he occupied, together with some relics, including his desk and a specimen of his handwriting, brings to mind the history of this gifted but unfortunate poet, one of the most eminent, if we except Dante, of the Italian poets. His immortal work, "Gerusalemme Liberato," will be studied with deeper interest after having seen these mementos.

Visits were again made to the Sistine Chapel, the Stanze of Raphael, and the Picture Gallery. In examining the faded frescos, one must give full play to the imagination; doubtless they were very fine when fresh. Michael Angelo is the prince of artists for sublimity, but it seems to us he lacks grace. As a skilful anatomist, he has perhaps no equal; his figures are nearly all very muscular, but not gross like those of Rubens; he lacks warmth of color, while Raphael endows with grace everything he touches.

The Villa Albani, just outside the Porta Salara, was built in 1706 by Cardinal Albani, hence it is new for this venerable city. It was formerly enriched by admirable works of art, but two hundred and ninety-four specimens were carried off to Paris by Napoleon I., and afterwards sold. The villa now belongs to Prince Torlonia, who has removed several of the best works to his private museum, so that the collection at present is greatly inferior to the original one. The Casino has a number of frescos, statues, and busts representing classical scenes, and a fine relief of Antoninus, the only one returned of those taken away by Napoleon. This villa is rich in rare and beautiful marbles.

January 31 we made another unsuccessful attempt to get a "permisso" to visit the Vatican Mosaic Works. Signor "Somebody" did not bestow favors on Thursday, we must apply some other day. This is a specimen of the arrangements at this celebrated museum. We contented ourselves by making a visit to the Villa Ludovisi, with its alluring walks and groves, fine views, and treasures of art. The Casino contains the Aurora by Guercino, much inferior to that of Guido, in the Casino of Rospigliosa. The coloring, the grouping, and the figures of the former are inferior to those of the latter.

The Church of St. Clemente, between the Colosseum and the Lateran, belongs to Irish Dominicans. Prior Mullooly has recently made excavations under the building, leading to some interesting discoveries. The crypt of the present church was an early basilica, mentioned by Jerome as early as 392 A. D. It was nearly destroyed in 1084, and in 1108 the present edifice was built on its ruins. A third ruin was discovered under the crypt, supposed to date from the second century, and some portions even from the Republic. The Church of St. Clemente is very interesting, both on account of its great antiquity and its rich marbles. St. Clement was the third successor to St. Peter, and, in honor to him, the church was founded on the site of his house, it is claimed. It is richly decorated by frescos, marbles, etc., and has a pavement of remarkably fine "opus Alexandrinum," of various designs, made of beautiful marbles of different species. The red granite obelisk, erected sixteen centuries before the Christian era, in front of the Temple of the Sun, at Thebes, in Egypt, now stands in the Piazza of St. John Lateran. It is one·hundred and four feet in height, or, including the pedestal, one hundred and fifty-three feet.

Returning to the Colosseum, we ascended this remarkable structure, or what is left of it, nearly to the top. The vastness of the building is almost inconceivable, while the views from every point were very extensive. From one side are seen the ruins on the Palatine Hill, and in another direction those of Nero's Palace, or rather its locality, since the remains are under ground, and the Baths of Titus. We continued our study of churches, including San Marco, said to date from Constantine; the present edifice was erected in 833 A. D., and is decorated in the usual rich style of Roman churches. Another, on the Corso, contains the monuments and busts of Joseph Bonaparte and his wife, while the Bonaparte Chapel is very rich in decorations.

The Museum Kircheriano contains many ancient relics, including a toilet casket of bronze, found near Palestrina, in 1774. It is in the best style of Greek art, the figures on it representing the Argonauts and the victory of Polydences. They are drawn by a single fine white line, but with the perfection of Greek workmanship.

We made another effort to obtain a "permisso" to the Collection of Mosaics, but were unsuccessful. We went through various passages and rooms, ascended several flights of stairs, and finally found the sacristan, to inquire what was necessary to obtain our object. This official was curt even to rudeness, an unusual thing for an Italian, and declined giving us any information, and we were obliged to abandon our attempts. While pondering what next to do, some German tourists, waiting to enter the room of the Œcumenical Council, invited us to accompany them. As we could not enter the Room of Mosaics without a special "permisso" from the aforesaid Signor T——, we were very glad of the opportunity.

The transept used by the Council in 1872 remains the same as then, with rows of seats for the members, while the walls of the room are covered with large frescos, representing the transactions of the Council. A fine monument of Clement XIII., with the figure of the pope, and a crouching lion, by Canova, is seen here, while in the chapels are the works of celebrated masters. We finally succeeded in getting access to the Mosaics by purchasing a "permisso" for two francs, besides a fee to the official.

The manufacture of mosaics is a special privilege of the papal court, at least those carried on in the Vatican. The pictures were fine, and some of them very large; but the most beautiful specimens were in a small show-room. The most interesting were a marble table top, with a wreath of flowers in the form of a circular garland, and views of places in Rome and Tivoli, besides several small works of different patterns. Only a few workmen were employed, and the exhibits were not what we expected. A large quantity of material used was placed along the sides of the rooms, and paintings frequently taken from galleries were arranged for copies.

We paid one more visit to the Vatican Museum, this time to the Library; but, strange to say, there were no books or

MSS. to be seen, though it contains twenty-four thousand of the latter. They are all hidden from sight in close-locked cabinets. The numerous apartments are highly decorated, and contain art treasurers; as a marble table from the Catacombs of St. Calixtus, and one from the ruins of the Palatine. In one room was a large figure of Pius IX. in painted glass, made at Aix-la-Chapelle. Illustrations of magnificent bindings of books and illuminated MSS. are kept in the library. The Church of the Gesù, the principal one of the Order of the Jesuits in Rome, is one of the richest in decorations; not a square inch is unadorned. The costly marbles were given by Prince Alexander Torlonia, in 1860, though the church was built in 1568.

February 6 we visited the Castle of St. Angelo, in company with some American travellers. This historical building was originally Hadrian's tomb which he built for himself, and which became the burial-place of the emperors to Septimius Severus, 193 A. D. It was made of travertine, and encased in marble, but the outer covering has all been removed. The tomb was converted into a fortress during the Siege of Rome by the Goths, 537 A. D., when the statues that adorned the top were hurled down upon the enemy. The bronze angel that now crowns the summit was placed there in 1740. The castle has been in possession of the popes ever since Boniface IX., 1389, and in 1500 the covered passage was built, connecting the castle with the Vatican. We were conducted by an accommodating guide through many winding passages and large rooms, over several bridges, to the apartment where Beatrice Cenci received her sentence, and into a dungeon where she was imprisoned for nearly a year, with a very low doorway, so that we were obliged to stoop in order to enter. No light was admitted except through a small grating above, while the prisoner's food was lowered through another aperture. The places on the walls to which her bed wsa attached still remain.

February 7 we made another visit to the Palatine Hill in company with some English travellers, when, conducted by a guide, we descended into a low, dark, grotto-like region with pitfalls, deep wells, or cisterns of water, into which one was liable to fall unless very cautious. The dark and dangerous passages and the smoke of our torches made a return to the outside world very agreeable. The beautiful marbles taken from the Palaces of the Cæsars on this hill, are under the control of the Italian government. Large piles of these stones are scattered about or still cover the walls yet standing, and strangers are not permitted to carry off any specimens. To prevent such plundering, a special police or guard is kept there; and if he sees any one doing so, he says gently, with genuine Italian politeness : " It is not permitted to take these marbles." Travellers, however, can purchase specimens of nearly all the varieties of the marble workers for a trifling sum. Returning from the Palatine we went to the studio of Miss Edmonia Lewis, the American sculptress, where we saw specimens of her works, including Cleopatra, Hagar, and busts of Hiawatha and Minnehaha.

Pope Pius IX. has just died after an administration of nearly thirty-two years. Italy has lost her two most distinguished men within a very short time: the king, Victor Emmanuel, January 9, and Pius IX., February 7. The weather has been, on the whole, all that one could desire for visiting any part of the city and its suburbs, so that very little time has been given to rest; but a change of scene is refreshing both to the physical and the mental powers, and that is what every one may have in this city of wonders. We could not leave Rome without visiting the studios of some of the artists; therefore we accompanied a friend to the rooms of two eminent Italian painters — De Sanctis, a portrait painter, and Vertuni, whose studio was a museum of mediæval art. He had several rooms furnished with tapestries, brocades, Turkey carpets, rich antique furniture, porcelains, and numerous specimens of interesting objects. His paintings were very beautiful, comprising landscapes representing Italian and Egyptian scenery. It seems to us that modern artists excel the ancient masters in landscape painting. Rogers, the American sculptor, had a large number of works, including the Blind Girl of Pompeii, one of his most attractive productions. The studio of Miss Hosmer, who was absent in England, displayed a great number of finished and unfinished works. A large group comprising several figures was intended for a fountain in San Francisco, California.

The closing day of the week was given to rest and reviewing our Roman adventures during this interesting visit. Travel affords excellent opportunities for studying human character. Some persons are frivolous, some disagreeable, some talk too loud, others, too low, some laugh too much, others seldom smile; some are brusque in manners, others are too gentle, some are too familiar, others are repellent, and so the catalogue might be extended. It teaches the lesson that no one is faultless, therefore we should be charitable and forbearing towards others; yet it is the fortune of most travellers to meet with more agreeable than disagreeable persons.

February 11 we went to St. Peter's, to see the deceased pope lying in state. He looked as his pictures represent him, though bearing the marks of suffering in his countenance. There was a very great crowd, and in the throng some expert thief stole our purse, fortunately containing only a few francs, and, what was a greater loss, our note-book.

Before leaving Rome for Naples, we made another visit to Santa Maria Maggiore to examine the beautiful marbles. The Confessio, in which Pius IX. is to be finally buried, after the death of his successor, is very rich.

## CHAPTER XIII.

*Rome to Naples.*

ON the beautiful morning of February 13 we started for Naples. The railway for a long distance runs nearly parallel with the ancient aqueduct which, for many miles, has been well preserved, but as we proceeded there were evidences of decay and ruin. As we leave the Campagna the region becomes more fertile, while olive orchards and cultivated fields, with rugged mountains in the distance, give variety to the landscape. Farmers were at work ploughing and sowing, and in places, grain and certain vegetables were in a greater or less state of advancement. At length Mt. Vesuvius came in sight, with its dense column of smoke and scattered tracts of snow. The ascent looked steep and difficult, though it is frequently made by tourists. On arriving at the railway station in Naples, we found it was a good distance from the hotel we had selected, but it gave us an opportunity of seeing much of the city while going to it. The next day we began our customary task or pleasure of sight-seeing, by a visit to the Museum, a long distance from our hotel on the Riviera di Chiara. The collection is large and has some features different from all others. It contains numerous specimens from Herculaneum and Pompeii, but no description will be given until future visits are made.

The streets of Naples are well paved, and the buildings look fresh and cheerful, while near our hotel, once a palace, is the Villa Nazionale, which is a public garden. The Riviera is the " Rotten Row " of Naples, where may be seen the élite of the city, taking their daily drive with their splendid teams. We took a pleasant walk on the shore of the charming blue Mediterranean, where we had a view of Vesuvius, the royal palace, and San Carlo, an immense theatre. A party was formed of some of the guests at the hotel for a visit to the Island of Capri. The day, February 16, was fine, and we had a delightful sail of three hours down the bay, first to Sorrento, thence to the Blue Grotto, passing near Vesuvius, whose perpetual column of smoke, illuminated by the sunlight, looks like a pillar of silvery clouds. All along its base, villages quietly repose as if insensible to the dangers of sudden destruction. A few years ago several were destroyed by an eruption, and the ruins of some of them still remain. For some distance, towns and villages are scattered along the route, but farther south the coast is rocky and precipitous. Sorrento is picturesquely situated on a high cliff, while passages are cut through the steep rocks from the sea to the hotels and villas above. The natural wall, with these openings, give the town the appearance of being fortified. The rocky promontory, on which the city is built, is covered with olive orchards, and orange trees flourish in the valleys. We sail around the cliffs and promontories in going from Sorrento to Capri, a distance of eight miles.

The Island of Capri consists of limestone of a reddish color and contains grottos, the most celebrated being the Blue Grotto, the principal object of our visit. Leaving the steamer we entered a small rowboat under the direction of a guide; and as the arch to the grotto is low, we seated ourselves in the bottom of the boat, in order to avoid a contact with the rocks; but after entering the cave, we found the vault quite high. What an enchanting scene was revealed, after our sight had become accustomed to the dim light! The water was a heavenly blue, clear and transparent like the sky, or more, perhaps, like the sapphire, while objects below the surface were of a silver white; the roof of the grotto was of a deep shade of blue, and the effect of the whole scene was magical and beautiful beyond expression. The cavern was quite dark at a short distance from the entrance, which inspires one with a sense of danger, especially as there were nearly a dozen other boats near, and we were glad to emerge into daylight. The sides of the rocks were covered with a bright red coral, mixed with a purple substance which may have been coral or a vegetable production. The changeable colors of the Mediterranean are remarkable; near the rocks and beach, it is a beautiful green, sometimes of a deep shade, and sometimes of a clear emerald hue, while distant from the shore the color might be compared to turquoise blue.

It is impossible to describe fully the beautiful and diversified scenery of Naples and its vicinity. The colors surpass everything artists have represented, varying from the deepest and richest shades to the softest and most delicate tints, suffused by an indescribable haze.

Sunday in Naples is a gala day, and the most exciting of all the week. Business and pleasure are blended, though in the morning services are attended in the churches. The desecration of the Sabbath on the continent of Europe is shocking to one born and educated in New England; but it is a danger that threatens our country at the present time, due largely to the great number of immigrants.

We went to the Chapel of San Severo, which contains some fine statuary, the most interesting being the reclining figure of the dead Christ, entirely covered by a marble veil, the work of Sammatino; a veiled figure of Modesty; and Disillusion, representing a man escaping from a net of cords, besides several other statues; the ceiling was covered with frescos of no great merit.

February 18 the weather was very warm. In the forenoon we visited the Royal Palace, and were hurried through the numerous apartments at the rapid pace at which guides usually conduct visitors, only a little more so; and in the afternoon we went to the Palace of Capodimonte, a summer residence, situated on an elevated site surrounded by beautiful grounds. The palace contains a large collection of paintings, considerable statuary, arms, and porcelain of the old Capodimonte manufacture, now very rare. One room is entirely covered with porcelain ornaments.

February 19 was a memorable day in the history of our

travels, for a visit to Vesuvius. A party of tourists was formed, but those who made the arrangements had secured too many passengers for one carriage. In consequence the driver objected, and then ensued an altercation such as can be known only in Naples. Several cabmen came in for a share, and actually came to blows among themselves. Finally, it was decided to appeal to the hotel-keeper, who had furnished the team. He thought the carriage could take all the company, and after an hour's delay we all started with our youthful driver, who had been roughly handled by his burly associates. We had plenty of "runners," and before we had gone far we began to understand the character of Neapolitan beggars. One ragged fellow persisted in accompanying us all the way to the Hermitage, and was very officious in procuring specimens of lava for us. As some of them contained crystals, we bought them, when he obtained more and placed them in our carriage; but we took good care to put some of the best in our pockets, which was a timely precaution. After arriving at the Hermitage, we left our carriage, and on returning we could find nothing of our specimens, for the rogue had sold them to other travellers during our absence, and then came with a gracious smile for us to purchase more specimens. Neapolitan beggars are the dirtiest, sauciest, best-natured, and most persistent class we have yet seen, and perhaps the most contented. It does not seem to disturb their equanimity to be refused alms, and they are rather surprised to be treated otherwise. In going to Vesuvius we passed through sections of the city occupied by the poor classes, whose almost only home is the street. Various kinds of work, including household duties, are performed in the open air, such as washing, ironing, cooking, mending clothing, arranging the hair, etc., and even macaroni was drying on poles by the side of the street.

Naples, with its suburbs, extends along the sea for a considerable distance, in the direction of the volcano; but finally we began to ascend a slope not very precipitous, leading past fields of lava, at first of no great depth, but as we continued, the volcanic matter increased until scarcely any other object was to be seen. For miles vast heaps of lava and volcanic ashes were piled up, and also scattered about in wild confusion, covering the sides of the mountain and adjacent plain, while the rocks assumed the most fantastic forms, such as coils like ropes, and shapes resembling human and animal figures in all sorts of positions. The prevailing color of the lava is gray or brown, but it is sometimes inclined to yellow and sometimes to green, and not unfrequently a brick-red. It has different degrees of porosity and sometimes contains crystals of different minerals. The lava jewelry, so called, of various light shades, is said to be made of clay found in the region. The utter desolation seen here is beyond description. There is no animal or vegetable life, nothing but a vast sea of lava or rocky billows; no motion except the columns of smoke perpetually ascending from the crater. One can hardly conceive of a more grand and fearful object in nature than an active volcano. The eruption of 1872, which lasted about a week, is said to have been terribly grand, and calculated to inspire every one living in the vicinity with consternation. The stream of lava flowing down the mountain on that occasion destroyed or laid waste two villages and killed many people.

An observatory has been erected on a spur of the mountain for scientific observation in regard to the condition of the volcano. The Hermitage, a small building at the end of the carriage road, is near the observatory; at this place donkeys are used to carry visitors to the foot of the crater. A few of our party walked some distance over the rough path towards the cone; but the day was not favorable for an ascension, and we did not attempt the perilous task. On our return to Naples, our heavily loaded carriage broke down, and we were compelled to seek other methods of conveyance. The next day was spent in a quiet way, at our hotel and in calling upon some fellow-travellers who had just arrived from Rome.

The Cathedral of Naples was built on the site of a temple to Neptune, and was destroyed by an earthquake, but rebuilt. It encloses the tombs of Charles I. of Anjou and Charles Martel, King of Hungary. The richest chapel is that of St. Januarius, the patron of Naples, and is decorated with paintings, statues, marbles, etc., besides bronze figures of the saints. The treasures of the church comprise a great amount of silver plate, together with the crown of the saint, containing thirty-six hundred and ninety gems. Among the silver articles were about twenty-eight figures of saints, besides candelabra, crosses, platters, flowers, and other things in silver. These treasures were, for the most part, given by the different conquerors of Naples, to conciliate the inhabitants and reconcile them to the tyranny of their rulers. Most of the churches in this city have a dilapidated appearance externally, but in the interior they are covered with ornaments. The marbles are very showy, but the frescos are not particularly noteworthy. There is such a medley of costly and cheap decorations in many Italian churches, that the tourist hardly expects to find one fitted up in good taste; this is especially true of those in Naples. Images and *dolls*, as they may be called, are profusely scattered about, making one feel that he is in heathen lands.

February 23 an excursion was made to the ruins of Pompeii. So much has been written about this uncovered city, that all description seems superfluous; but a few sentences relating to its history may assist the memory. Pompeii was a very old city, founded, it is claimed, in 600 B. C., on a bed of trachyte, at the mouth of the Sarno, on the south side of Vesuvius, perhaps at the distance of two or three miles. It seems to have been exposed to great dangers from early times, for in 63 A. D. it was nearly destroyed by an earthquake, but was soon rebuilt, though not completed, when the awful catastrophe of 79 A. D. completely buried it, and the city remained covered with a bed of lava until 1748, when excavations were begun by Charles III., and continued at intervals until the present time. They are still going on, and new discoveries are constantly made; some of the frescos recently brought to light are as fresh and bright as if just painted. Until 1860 not more than one third of the town had been uncovered; but since 1863 the work of excavation has been vigorously prosecuted under

Fiorelli. In this deserted place are seen roofless houses, with occasional columns, courts, fountains, small rooms without windows, kitchens, servants' apartments, etc., more or less decorated with bright-colored frescos. Most of the designs the public are allowed to see are classical subjects, very beautiful and graceful, and are copied by modern artists. The bright tints must have given cheerfulness to rooms without windows. The streets were paved with large blocks of lava, and had very narrow sidewalks. Stepping-stones were placed across the streets at intervals for the convenience of pedestrians, but it was not possible for carriages to pass one another, as in modern cities, on account of the narrowness of the streets; therefore it is probable they were compelled to move only in one direction. Comparatively few skeletons have been found, which proves the larger part of the inhabitants escaped before being overtaken by the onflowing stream of lava. The Museum contains several human figures in whole or in part. The scenes at Pompeii are exceedingly impressive. A depopulated and ruined city is a melancholy sight; but one suddenly buried beneath melted lava, when the citizens were engaged in their customary daily pursuits, either of business or pleasure, is terrible beyond expression. We returned to Naples greatly impressed with the sights we had witnessed in this memorable region.

What is called "The Institution of Fine Arts" in Naples is a picture gallery containing a small collection of paintings and plaster casts by modern artists. Some of the views of the city and bay were faithful representations; but the paintings, generally, were open to criticism. The Gesù Nuovo, built in 1584, like other Jesuit churches, is highly decorated: the high altar is adorned with precious stones, and the pavement is formed of both antique and modern marbles. The Church of St. Severino is a fine building, with paintings in oil and frescos, and decorated with rich marbles. It is near the University, which contains a collection of minerals, it is said; but we were not successful in gaining admission, therefore we engaged a cab for San Martino, near the Castle of St. Elmo.

The price was decided, but after we arrived at the church the driver insisted upon our paying more fare; and rather than dispute the point, we yielded, but we refused to return in his cab, which left him without a passenger. "Honesty is the best policy" is a maxim he ought to have learned by the incident.

The Certosa of San Martino, founded in the fourteenth century, ranks among the first in Italy for the works of art it contains, including paintings by Guido Rene and Spagnoletto, and frescos by Bellisario and others; but the mosaics of wood, marble, and precious stones were the most interesting objects, and were displayed in the pavements, walls, balustrades of altars and chapels, and the covering of the columns, upon which were placed twelve large vases in Egyptian stone. The elevated site of San Martino, which is ascended by flights of steps, commands a magnificent view of Naples and the sea.

The last days of February were mostly given to rest and study. At our hotel there are only four guests whose native tongue is English; but of the many nationalities nearly all speak French, which seems to be an international language. It is amusing to a quiet listener in the drawing-room to hear Italians, French, Germans, Roumanians, Russians, Greeks, and English all speaking at once or by turns, representing a perfect Babel. Travelling is an excellent school for the study of human character, as one meets with almost every variety.

March 1 we took a long walk, and saw flowers in bloom, lemons and oranges ripening upon the trees, and vegetation in general in an advanced stage, corresponding to the last of May or the first of June in New England, though the weather here is much warmer. On the 2d inst., after many delays, we made a journey to Pozzuoli and Baia. Our route lay through the "Grotto of Posilipo," a tunnel cut through the native rock for the distance of half a mile, by the ancient Romans, for a passage to Puteoli. It is paved and lighted by lamps, and on the Naples side is the reputed tomb of Virgil. Leaving the Grotto of Posilipo we traverse a low and uninteresting region until we come to Lake Agnano, now nearly dry.

Near this lake is the celebrated Grotto del Cane, a sort of cavern, on the bottom of which the carboniferous acid gas is fatal to dogs, and would be to all animal life, did the deadly vapor rise higher. Our guide took a small dog to try the experiment, but we persuaded him to desist, and were satisfied with seeing a lighted taper suddenly extinguished in the blue smoke, for such the gas seemed to be. Near the Grotto del Cane, or dog grotto, is another called Grotto dell' Ammoniaca, because the lower part contains ammonia in a gaseous state. Not far off are the Thermæ Angoulanæ, or Baths of St. Germano with the heat in one of the apartments equal to a hot vapor bath. In the neighborhood of Lake Agnano are the White Mountains, which furnish edible earth, and decomposed trachyte used in the manufacture of alum. The road between this lake and Pozzuoli passes the thermal mineral baths, while along the shore fine views are obtained of the Mediterranean, the Island of Nisidia, Mt. Olibano, composed entirely of volcanic rock, and the Flegean Fields.

As soon as we reached the town we were importuned by a host of would-be guides, but refused all of them except a lad who conducted us to the Solfatara. This is the crater of an extinct volcano, from which sulphurous fumes are constantly issuing and if a stone is cast upon the bottom of the crater, there is an echo along the ground, proving it is hollow beneath. The only eruption of lava occurred in 1198, which left an empty crater from one half to one mile in diameter. The bottom is covered with a fine white powder or dust, the puzzolano, from which a hydraulic cement is made, used for stucco. This extinct volcano resembles a very deep basin with walls of stone, lava, and pulverized volcanic matter, partially covered with vegetation. In one part of the crater there is a cavern, from which are constantly issuing hot fumes with a strong smell of sulphur, which, as the gas escapes, makes a gurgling sound much like the boiling of any thick substance. Small streams of hot vapor frequently issue from different parts of the ground. Doubtless this crater communicates with Mt. Vesuvius, though they are many miles apart, since the phenomena in this vicinity are affected by the eruptions of the distant volcano.

Some interesting ruins are seen in Pozzuoli, — ancient Puteoli, — as the theatre, the amphitheatre, and the Temple of Diana and Neptune ; but to the geologist the Temple of Jupiter Serapis is the most remarkable, on account of the alternate subsidence and elevation of its site. Some of its columns have been taken away to be used in the royal palace at Caserta, but three are left standing.

On the route from Pozzuoli to Baia we pass Mt. Nuovo, thrown up in forty-eight hours during a volcanic eruption in 1538, on the spot occupied by a village ; and a short distance from the road is Lake Averno, rendered famous by Virgil. It is a beautiful sheet of clear water, reposing in the basin formed by surrounding mountains, while near its banks is a cavern called the Grotto della Sibilla, though it is not certain that it is the one named by the poet. After leaving Lake Averno we pass the Thermæ Neronianæ, or Baths of Nero, near Lake Lucinus, famous in Roman times for its oysters, as it is now for its fish. All along the road are ruins which, if exhumed, would rival those of Rome. The temples of Venus, Diana, and Mercury were especially rich in decorations of marbles and other ornamental works; but the most conspicuous object was a large castle standing on a high promontory. Baia is really a thing of the past, the famous watering-place of the ancient Romans, and the whole region from this place to Pozzuoli was crowded with the palaces of the emperors and the nobles.

In returning to Naples, our route lay along the seashore except when it crossed the mountain by the artificial Grotto of Sijanus, built before the Christian era. The masonry seems fresh and substantial ; but as it is not used for public travel, it is not illuminated. It is said to have been constructed by Lucullus for a communication between his villa called Pausily Pou — without care — and the Island of Nisidia. The whole region is volcanic, and the different geological formations are very distinct. Arriving in the city, we made another visit to the Museum, which contains about eight hundred paintings, a fine Pompeian collection, about four thousand Italio-Greco vases of different forms and sizes, and a collection of ancient bronzes said to be the largest in the world. The engraving on rock crystal is very beautiful; the specimens from Herculaneum and Pompeii were especially interesting.

There are few cities that afford so many excellent views as Naples. The elevated hills, the sinuosity of the coast, and the unrivalled Mediterranean, while in the distance Mt. Vesuvius with its adjacent villages, Sorrento, Castellemare, and Capri, are all seen from the Corso. The stone used largely for buildings, called "volcanic tufa," gives an air of cheerfulness to the city, as the "calcaire grossier" does to Paris. We spent a few days in rest and study before attempting another excursion.

March 8 we rode to Frisio, the terminus of the tramway, and then walked a long distance farther. The views in every direction are charming, interspersed with romantic villas scattered along the road. The shore on which Naples is built may be compared to amphitheatres opening to the sea, and the terraced hills may be called the tiers of seats, one above another. This peculiar conformation affords a pleasing variety to the aspect of the city, while Vesuvius and the high cliffs of volcanic rocks add to its grandeur. Unite to these characteristics the effect of the most exquisite tints in sky, clouds, sea, rocks, and all distant objects, and we have a paradise for artists.

We went with a friend to call upon Count Gigliano to see his collection of autographs, comprising a large number, including those of sovereigns, statesmen, generals, literary men, and artists of different countries and periods. It was interesting to see the remarkable chirography of many of these eminent persons; here were all styles of writing, except a correct style, of which there was hardly an example.

Our linguistic family at the hotel remains unchanged, unless, it may be, some new members have been added. Europeans have a remarkable talent for conversation; it seems they only needed to begin, and words flowed spontaneously; perhaps it arises from their acquaintance with many different languages. The continental nations are brought into so close contact, it is important, if not essential, to understand one another's language.

We met a friend who came to Italy some years ago to perfect her musical education, and who is now fulfilling an engagement at Naples. As she has married an Italian, she will probably spend her life here. In the evening we went to hear this American sing in the opera as a prima donna representing Lady Macbeth. The weather for two days has been very cold for this region, and snow partially covers Vesuvius, while the more distant mountains are completely enveloped in their white mantles. Stormy and unfavorable weather affords an opportunity for rest and the study of Corsi, an interesting work on antique marbles, written in Italian. The houses of this country are ill adapted to cold weather, and it is surprising to see how the natives seem to thrive on so few comforts in lodging, food, and raiment.

Another visit to the Museum which contains three remarkable works, the Farnese Bull, the Hercules, and the Flora, mentioned before. The Farnese Group is considered the largest known cut from a single block of marble. In the room of the Flora, the pavement contains a mosaic representing a battle of Alexander the Great. Beautiful columns of different kinds of stone are placed in the various apartments. From the ramparts we had a fine view of the Bay of Naples. Thence we proceeded to the northeast part of the city, where are the Botanical Gardens and the Reclusorio. The Via Cavour is a wide and pleasant street, but the Strada Cabonara is probably the broadest thoroughfare in the town, while the Toledo presents the busy life of Broadway, New York, or Washington Street, Boston. The cold weather induced us to postpone our return to Rome until the next week, and in the meantime we visited Portici and Resina; the latter town is built over the buried city of Herculaneum. The excavations were not extensive, and to be reached one must descend flights of steps and explore by torch-light. The ruined town was built at a remote period, and was the home of many distinguished Romans. The buildings of the present town of Resina must be removed before Herculaneum can be uncovered, a work requiring great labor and expense. The day after our return we were gratified by another long walk on the shore of the beautiful Mediterranean, which has wonderful fascinations; the views never tire, they never lose their charms. "See Naples and die" has deeper meaning than can be comprehended by any one who has never been there.

March 24. The storm of last night has passed away, but its effects are seen in the surging waves which roll over the high sea wall. We took our last walk by the sea and had our last view of Vesuvius, then called upon our friend to bid her good by, and take her parting message to America. One must feel at times a sense of isolation who has left friends and country forever. The ties of nationality are fortunately very strong in most natures. On the beautiful morning of the 25th, we left Naples for Rome, accompanied by American friends as far as Caserta, where we made a short stop to visit the palace and park at this place.

An hour's ride brought us to the station, where an amusing incident occurred. A duty is levied on certain articles passed from one part of the country to another, wine being included. One of the passengers had taken a bottle along with him for lunch, when a custom officer espied it, and insisted on the payment of duty. The traveller, whom we will call Mr. A., paid no attention to his remonstrances, when another officer came to the aid of the first one. Mr. A. walked on between the two officials quite unconcerned until, seeing he could not escape from his captors, he dashed the bottle on the ground, which summarily ended the contest. The wine cost only fifty centimes, or about ten cents. The disconcerted officers immediately retraced their steps, and left us to continue our journey; but the affair gave amusement to the crowd of cabmen, hotel porters, and boys found at railway stations. As our hotel was near the station, we declined offers from porters, and insisted on having our own way, which required much heroism, as they followed us to the inn. Many of these people have no means of subsistence, except what they can get from travellers. Even railway officials sometimes resort to dishonest methods by demanding fees, over-estimating the weight of baggage, and in making change.

On arriving at Caserta, after making arrangements with the hotel clerk for accommodations, we made our first visit to the royal palace, now unoccupied, an immense structure, built of travertine, with some brick-work in the upper stories; the ground story comprises large arcades, with immense clustered columns of travertine and marble. From the portico a magnificent staircase of unpolished lumachelle marble ascends to the upper story, while the walls of the building are covered with different species of marble arranged to represent grotesque human figures; one is said to resemble that of Napoleon, but it requires a vivid imagination to detect the similarity, while other figures might easily pass for ogres, giants, chimeras, and the like. The ceilings of the different apartments were decorated by frescos, but there was little furniture left in the spacious rooms.

This palace afforded an excellent study of ornamental and precious stones employed in its decoration, though it comprised only a few statues. The theatre contains twelve columns, which are said to be alabaster, and taken from the Temple of Jupiter Serapis, at Pozzuoli. Passing through the palace, we came to a wide, straight avenue, with fountains and rows of oaks covered with dense foliage on either side. Through the centre of this avenue, for the distance of nearly two miles, the water flows and forms artificial cascades and small lakes, then disappears in subterranean channels, and finds an outlet somewhere. The source of this peculiar channel is a mountain on the farther side of the park, where the water falls in several small streams down the steep side, then over a large artificial cascade, besides several other streams of inferior size. The long avenue is lined with statues, single or in groups, representing heathen characters and animals. In the upper cascade are seen those of Diana and her nymphs, comprising nine figures, and Actæon, who is passing through his transformation into a stag, and is surrounded by twelve dogs, while statues are scattered about everywhere with a lavish hand. This celebrated avenue passes directly through the palace, and is five miles in length, thus affording a royal driveway over a smooth road between rows of shady trees. We spent the night at Caserta, and during the time there was a storm of thunder, rain, hail, and snow, attended by cold, and the next day we made preparations to return to Rome, after an absence of six weeks in Naples and its vicinity.

## CHAPTER XIV.

*A Second Visit to Rome. — Other Italian Cities.*

TRACES of the storm of last night, March 26, were observed on the route from Naples to Rome, both on the mountains which were covered with snow, and in the plains where traces of the tempest remained; and on arriving there, we learned the weather, for the most of the time during our absence, had been cold and stormy at the capital. We returned to the Hotel Milano, but found all the guests, including Americans, strangers; therefore we had to form new acquaintances. Almost immediately we resumed our visits to the public buildings, notably the churches, for the purpose of studying the works of art and antique marbles. On the 27th we examined six churches, and the next day the Churches of Santa Maria in Ara Coeli, and Santa Maria Liberatrice, thence we proceeded to the Roman Forum. There are few objects more interesting and instructive than the ruins of a once magnificent city, and it is from these that we are more forcibly impressed with a sense of the grandeur of the former "Mistress of the World." The Church of Santa Maria in Transtevere is very rich in decorations, and has twenty-eight large granite columns, with bases and capitals more or less ornamented, besides four pilasters incased in Cipolla marble, while the high altar is supported by four red porphyry columns. The Tribune is covered with antique mosaics of different periods, and on some of the walls are paintings representing saints on a gold ground, while mosaics ornament the façade, and early inscriptions are seen in the portico. This church is a basilica, and was first constructed in 499 A. D., but was subsequently rebuilt.

The Church of St. Cecilia in Trastevere was originally the house of the saint, and a stone in one of the chapels is claimed to be the one on which she suffered martyrdom. Before the high altar, is her shrine, with a reclining statue of St. Cecilia in white marble, representing her as she was found on opening her sarcophagus in 1599. The shrine is ornamented with rich marbles, alabasters, and gems. Her remains, together with those of other saints, were taken from the Catacombs of St. Calixtus, and buried in the crypt. This church has some ancient paintings, including a Madonna by Annabali Caracci, a Crucifixion, by Fra Angelico, and frescos by Pinturicchio, and other masters. Some of the churches we had seen on our first visit to this city were revisited. That of St. Prasede has the pillar, according to tradition, to which our Saviour was confined for scourging, but no allusion to a pillar is made by the scriptures. It is, however, considered important that every church should have some sacred relic, to inspire the languid devotions of the worshippers, and spurious mementos answer the purpose if the deception is not found out. No woman is allowed to enter the chapel except on Sunday, or in the season of Lent; but men, being remarkable for their superior sanctity, can enter at all times. We made a third visit to the Capitolini Museum, and the next day, April 1, went to St. Peter's and the Vatican Collection, a visit that was repeated several times. April 3 found us in the Gallery of the Candelabra; but before we had made much progress an unwelcome custodian appeared with authority to drive us all out, as if we had been intruders. As the gate was open, we could not understand the reason for the act, and inquired the cause, when the custodian told a long story, from which we inferred that the guardian of the department was absent, and it was necessary to close it, lest, perhaps, some visitor might carry off a statue, a vase, or a column.

Though we had visited St. John Lateran on a former occasion, we took another opportunity to study this interesting church, one of the most important in the city, on account of its early connection with the papal palace. The Court of the Monastery contains two carved columns from Solomon's

Temple, and in the court stands the frame of a well, made of white marble covered with carving, said to have been brought also from the Temple. The stalls in the Choir Chapel contain statues in wood, and the Sacristy has a painting of the Annunciation, by Venusti, from the drawing of Michael Angelo. Near this church is the Scala Santa, which the Saviour ascended; it was brought from Pilate's palace, and was constructed of Tyrian marble. Not far off is the oldest obelisk known, one hundred and four feet in height, first erected at Thebes, in Egypt, 1600 B. C., or nearly thirty-five hundred years ago. The Colosseum, the Arch of Constantine, and the Arch of Titus received another visit.

The forenoon of April 5 was spent in the churches studying the beautiful marbles, and in the afternoon we went to the Villa Doria Pamfili, said to be one of the most charming of Roman villas; but we felt disappointed, and regretted the time and trouble it cost us. In our visit to the Church of St. Andrea della Valle, we were shown the hand of St. Catherine of Sienna, though to confess the truth, we were more interested in the marbles. Another visit was made to St. Pietro in Vincoli, which contains the magnificent statue of Michael Angelo's Moses. Other churches received our attention, including Santa Maria del Anima, which contains two imposing monuments, one of Pope Hadrian VI., and the other of Prince Charles Frederic; but the most elaborate "deposito" is in a small church adjoining; it is of white marble, with carving, statues, and reliefs, and two sarcophagi with reclining figures; here is also the tomb of one of the Gregorys. St. Luigi de Francesi is very gaudily decorated, and contains several monuments of eminent Frenchmen, and also that of Claude Lorrain. The Church of San Marco, with its showy columns and pilasters, has a peculiar appearance, but, like most others, contains some beautiful marbles. We called upon an Italian lady for a "permisso" to visit the Palace Torlonia, not open to the public, and were promised that one should be left at our hotel, but we did not receive it, therefore concluded it was not sent. A Scotch family of six persons, who for some time have been our fellow-travellers, leave Rome to-morrow, so we shall be quite isolated as regards our native language.

April 11 we made what is probably our last visit to St. Peter's and the Vatican. We have been there so many times, they seem like familiar objects, yet they never tire, and one can always find in them something new. Thoughts of preparing for another journey are occupying our time, when we shall revisit Paris and London, before embarking for America. In the meantime we shall be occupied with new scenes or in reviving recollections of old ones. Sunday, April 14, we went to hear a sermon in English, by an Irish priest. The part of his sermon on the atonement we could accept; but when he introduced the papal doctrine of transubstantiation, we were not in sympathy with the speaker.

It would not be the proper thing to leave Rome without visiting the Tarpeian Rock, therefore we took some pains to get there. Passing into a garden through a gate opened by a custodian, we were shown a very steep rock that looked like a wall on which buildings were erected. The place was so enclosed by houses that it was impossible to get an accurate idea of its height, but it did not seem great; perhaps, like other parts of Rome, the present land has been elevated by the accumulation of soil and débris of the centuries. It is so near the Capitol and the prison, that criminals did not have far to go from their dungeons to death. The Marmatine prison or the Carcer Marmatinus of the old Romans, is a place of great tragical interest, connected with ancient Rome. It is near the Capitol, and consists of a deep pit or well into which prisoners were let down by a rope. The bottom was covered with water to a considerable depth, into which the accused was plunged. His food was lowered to him unless he was left to starve, as was the case of an eminent Roman. Here Paul was incarcerated when a prisoner in Rome. A church is now built over it.

April 15 we walked to the Piazza de Spagna and through the Corso for the last time. We have spent nearly three months in this wonderful city, but its treasures of art and its numerous antiquities have not lost their fascinations. Rome, though less beautiful than many other cities, has nevertheless a power over the imagination which no others have. It was the centre of the old Roman power, as it now is of the papal; hence its ruins and churches are the most interesting in Europe if, perhaps, we except the ruins of Greece.

April 16, a warm and pleasant day, we left Rome for Sienna, by the way of Chiusi, through a region not particularly interesting, and arrived at our destination late in the evening. As our stop at Sienna was to be short, we were obliged to make the most of our time, in spite of the rain, and made our first visit to the Church of St. Dominico. This edifice is peculiar, lofty and massive, and in the Gothic style with an open roof, that is, with no covering for the rafters, and is undecorated. The Chapel of St. Catherine of Sienna is adorned by some good frescos illustrating events in the life of the saint, by Sodoma, while her heart is contained in a silver reliquary. The high altar is of white marble; the ciborium is generally ascribed to Michael Angelo. From the church we went to the Instituto delle Belle Arte. A large part of the paintings are by Siennese masters, consisting of Madonnas and saints, and a more gloomy company of saints it would be difficult to find. If these figures represent the men and women of the times, there must have been a great improvement in the physical type of the race since those days. They were painted with very dark complexions and melancholy features expressing no emotions of joy. There were, however, a small number of pictures worthy of notice, comprising a copy of Raphael's Madonna della Perla, at Madrid, the Morra-players by Caravagio, SS. Catherine and Magdelina by Fra Bartolommeo. The Church of St. Giovanni is conspicuous for its marble front with bronze reliefs. A baptism occurred at the time of our visit; and the young candidate, like a little heathen, protested with all his might against the ceremony; he evidently belonged to the "church militant." The Duomo, in the Gothic style, is built of white, red, and black marble, and is ornamented with sculptures, while the walls of the interior afford alternate stripes of black and white; the effect of such an arrangement is not altogether pleasing. The vaulting has a dark ground, with gilt stars and bright colored frescos; but the absence of antique marbles is conspicuous, and in striking contrast to the churches of Rome and Naples. The famous pulpit by Nicola and Giovanni Pisano, of white marble, covered with high and low reliefs, is supported by granite and marble columns. Four of these rest on the backs of lions, and four on white bases, while a column in the centre has a base with figures in relief. The wood carving in the choir and on the reading-desk, and also the intasio of inlaid wood are very elegant. Statues and monuments are seen in this Cathedral, but it differs from most others in Italy, in its stained glass windows. The library contains a large number of illuminated books, with beautiful paintings and designs. The pavement of the building consists of mosaic-work of different patterns and representations in marble, which is called "graffito," though some of the pavement was covered. The Cathedral of Sienna is open to criticism; its parti-colored interior and exterior do not seem in good taste, while the stucco busts of the cornice do not add to its architectural beauty.

The Palazzo Publico, with the Tower del Mangia near, reminds one of the Vecchio of Florence, and some other structures. The Del Campo being depressed in the centre affords a peculiar aspect, which might be compared to a large dish, while at one side is the Fountain Gaga, with its white marble basin carved in relief. Sienna is built on a series of hills, therefore the streets ascend and descend. Most Italian cities occupy hills or rocky heights, with castles and other fortifications. The houses are near together, very high and with small windows, a necessity in past ages for defence against the lawless condition of society, but they now appear like a mass of dingy stone walls, without regularity, beauty, or comfort.

Our route to Pisa lay along a region of picturesque towns, generally built on hills, and with fertile valleys and olive orchards along the way. A town on a high eminence, named Sinalunga, is the place where Garibaldi was arrested on his march to Rome, 1867. At Empoli a change of train was made for Pisa, where we arrived about noon, April 18. We soon found our way to the Duomo and the celebrated Leaning Tower. The Cathedral, built in 1063, is of white marble which has a yellowish tint, the result of age, but the trimmings are of colored stone. The Baptistery and Campanile, or Tower, have the same appearance. The church is three hundred and twelve feet in length, with nave and double aisles, and the transepts are also flanked with aisles. The façade is very beautiful; the lower story contains columns and arches attached to the walls, while there are four tiers of open galleries diminishing in height towards the top. On each side of the principal door stands a white marble column, with beautiful carving. Indeed, the entire façade is ornamented with exquisite mouldings, mosaics, and reliefs. The three bronze doors, with borders of vines and leaves, are sculptured with scenes in relief, from Scripture. These doors were substituted for those of an earlier date, but one belonging to the twelfth century, is placed at the opposite end of the church. The sixty-eight ancient Greek and Roman columns of granite and marble, taken by the Pisans, the gilded and coffered ceiling, the stained-glass window, the lofty triforia, with gilded ceiling, the transepts that seem like separate churches, with imposing altars and statues, the famous carved pulpit and bronze lamp, the rich carving and tasio of the choir, the high altar of lapis-lazuli, and other valuable stones ornamented with figures of angels, the mosaics of the apse, by Cimabue, the number and size of oil paintings, the mosaic pavement, and other rich decorations render the Cathedral of Pisa one of the most beautiful and interesting in Italy.

The Baptistery is a circular building, a little more than one hundred feet in diameter and, with the dome, rises one hundred and ninety feet. The building rests on nine columns, standing on the backs of lions; in the centre is the font. Every part is highly ornamented with sculptures, mosaics, etc. This building is celebrated for its wonderful echo, of which the custodian gave us an illustration by singing a few strains, when there seemed to be two voices in different keys, but there was perfect harmony. It is said that if discordant notes are given the echo will be harmonious.

The Campanile, or Leaning Tower, is one hundred and seventy-nine feet high, and is thirteen feet out of perpendicular. Viewed from the exterior, it seems insecure, while its architectural beauty is diminished by its inclination; but the details are very graceful and admirable. It rises in eight different stories, similar to the Cathedral and Baptistery, by two hundred and ninety-four steps. We ascended the tower, and the prospect gained from the different openings was peculiar. We felt that the tower was upright, while all the objects about us were leaning. This fact might point a moral: " We are right, the *rest* of the world are wrong." The only compensation we had for our trouble was to say that we had been in the Leaning Tower. These three buildings are remarkable instances of harmony in designs and ornaments, as if they had been the work of a single mind; but the Duomo was begun in 1063, the Baptistery in 1153, and the Campanile or Bell Tower in 1174, all by different architects.

The Campo Santo of Pisa, begun in 1278, is a quadrangular building, comprising a series of Gothic arches opening upon a court, similar to cloisters. The walls are covered with frescos, and the monuments, both ancient and modern, are arranged along the covered gallery or passage. In the open space is the sacred soil brought from Mt. Calvary. There are few memorable places that have disappointed us more than this Campo Santo of Pisa. We had expected to see a large number of fine monuments, while, on the contrary, there are very few in any way remarkable. Pisa, though founded before the Christian era, has a more modern appearance than some other Italian cities. The Lungano reminds the traveller of Florence, while the Arno is about the same in both cities.

The journey from Pisa to Genoa was memorable, on account of the picturesque scenery, save the fifty or more tunnels through which the road lay. We passed along the coast of the sea, and caught a view of the silver waters, as we dashed out of the tunnels, and glimpses of the steep, rocky promontories on the left, and mountains of marble, with scattered villages, on the right. Nature was smiling in a profusion of beautiful flowers, green fields, and olive orchards. The daisies and heath, with clusters of yellow blossoms, remind one of England and Scotland later in the season than April 19. Soon after leaving Pisa we passed clusters of peasants' cottages made entirely of thatch, differing from the English thatched-roof cottages. They have no windows; but a door of boards, placed generally in one end, serves not only as a means of ingress and egress, but also for light and air. These habitations, which resemble haystacks, have become blackened by long exposure to the weather. The region of the quarries was indicated by the blocks of marble along the route, and sometimes by a ledge on the sides of the mountains.

As we approached Genoa, the parti-colored and frescoed buildings presented a novel appearance. These peculiar decorations are occasionally seen in other places, but here they seem to be the general type. Finally, we reached the city once so famous in maritime history.

In regard to the churches of Genoa, that of the Annunziata is one of the richest in marbles, frescos, and gilding in the city. St. Siro, St. Ambrogio, and the Cathedral St. Lorenzo are all highly ornamented. The old palace of the doges and the monument to Columbus were objects of interest. The Palazzo Ducale, or Doge's Palace, is reached by a very broad staircase. We were admitted to the hall of audience, it is presumed, with walls, pilasters, and pavement covered with marble called Brocatello di Spagna. The ceiling was frescoed, and there were a few paintings; but for a state building of the powerful Republic of Genoa, it was very plain.

The Palazzo Pallavicini, now belonging to the Durazzo family, has a collection of very good paintings comprising some of the celebrated masters, — Caracci, Guido Rene, Domenichino, and others of the Bolognese school. One room contained paintings representing scenes in the life of Achilles, a pleasant change from the oft-repeated Madonnas and saints. Besides

PULPIT, PISA.

PULPIT, PISA

STATUE OF LEONARDO DA VINCI.

CATHEDRAL, PISA

those masters just named, Van Dyke, Titian, Rubens, Albert Dürer, Del Sarto, Veronese, Tintoretto, Guercino, with others, were represented in this gallery.

The Terazzo di Marno is a broad promenade, built of marble, above a series of arcades, affording an excellent view of the harbor with its shipping, while beneath the walk are the railway and docks; the neighborhood, however, is not altogether agreeable for the pedestrian. To reach the Terrace, one must pass through the part of the city appropriated to the business of shipping and railway transit. Viewed from this place, the Church of Santa Maria in Carignano did not appear very far off, therefore we concluded to visit the building, but we were deceived in regard to the distance. Several narrow streets and steep ascents in the neighborhood of wharves had to be traversed before reaching the Ponte Carignano, a bridge over a street one hundred feet below. This led to the church, which was closed; but after ringing a bell, and waiting some time, the custodian finally opened the door. The site on which the church stands is one hundred and seventy-four feet above the sea level, and affords a good view of the Mediterranean and the semi-circular coast line of hills covered by the city. The highest gallery of the dome of the building is three hundred and sixty-eight feet above the sea.

The situation of Genoa resembles that of Naples, only less beautiful and varied, at least from this eminence. The great number of its palaces seems to be its most striking feature; some of the streets are crowded with them, which is a proof of the wealth and luxurious habits of the citizens of the Republic. There appears to be considerable business activity and love of commercial pursuits, that characterized the early inhabitants. About six miles from Genoa, on the coast, is the Villa Pallavicini, which is an interesting place to visit. It affords many charming views and many agreeable surprises, in the various winding paths that conduct the visitor from one eminence to another. Here are seen flowers in great profusion all along the pathways,— camilias, azalias, oleanders, violets, roses, etc., permeating the air with their sweet perfumes. Besides, these are kiosques or summer-houses in different styles, fountains, tiny cascades, lakes, grottos, and other imitations of nature. The grounds are on the slopes receding from the sea; and on the highest point stands a tower overlooking the water, the mountains, and villas on their sides. One of the most interesting objects in these grounds is a large grotto of natural stalactites brought from the Island of Sardinia. It has many intricate windings, some of which are filled with water from a small artificial lake, and deep enough to sail a boat. We were conducted through several dark passages to one of the boats, evidently waiting for a passenger. The guide then said "embarké," and having obeyed, he wished us a "bon voyage." The boatman, by some dexterous manœuvres, brought his craft around several sharp angles, and emerged into an open sheet of water. After sailing about for a little time we were landed on a small island, where our guide met us to complete the tour of the grounds. We returned by a different way, thus giving one a greater variety of scenery. This villa has not so many works of art as the Roman villas, but it surpasses them in natural beauty. The gardens are very extensive and varied in their tropical productions, — coffee, vanilla, cinnamon, pepper, sugar-cane, camphor, and others.

The park called Acquasola, in the north part of the city, contains nothing of special interest except its small trees, which make it an agreeable place for walking and resting in pleasant weather, and for the fine view of the bay and the adjacent hills covered with dwellings; the best prospect is obtained from the Villa Negro, on the summit of a hill which is reached by winding promenades. The magnificent buildings of Genoa form a special feature, while its commercial activity distinguishes it from some other Italian cities, notably Naples. The art collections are generally found here in private palaces, most of which are open to the public. The fine arts do not seem to thrive so well in a commercial city, though Genoa has produced some distinguished masters or has been the home of those from other places, hence some of their works are seen here.

April 25 we left Genoa for Turin, a distance of one hundred and three miles. The first part of the journey was over a hilly region, and the railway passes through several tunnels, one being two miles in length. After reaching Alessandria, the region is level. Many places of historical interest are passed during the entire journey; as Novi, the scene of a battle between the French and the Austrians August 15, 1799; Marengo, not far off, where the great battle of 1800 was fought, and Asti, the birthplace of the poet Alfieri. On arriving at Turin we went to the Cathedral and found the Capella del St. Sudario open, which, it is said, contains the linen cloth in which the body of our Lord was wrapped after his death. The chapel back of the high altar is very peculiar; the ascent is made by thirty-seven steps, and the top is crowned by a dome. The circular walls are covered with a very dark marble, which in the dim light appears black, in striking contrast to the white marble monuments. The Dukes of Savoy are buried here, also Maria Adelaid, the queen of Victor Emmanuel, who died in 1855. From the church we went to the Monastery of the Capuchins, on the east side of the Po. After walking through the Via di Po, with arcades on both sides, and the Piazza Vittorio Emanuele, and crossing the Ponte di Po, we saw before us on an eminence the monastery and church.

The road to the summit winds around the hill, from which a charming prospect was enjoyed, broadening at every turn as we ascended; and when we had gained the terrace in front of the church, it was magnificent. Below was the city, with its fine streets and piazzas; beyond, fertile hills and plains, and, above all, the snow-crowned Alps, forming an outer barrier for this amphitheatre of nature and art combined. Views from these hills are seldom surpassed for extent and magnificence. Near by was the Superga, with its church, the sepulchre of the royal family.

Though Turin cannot boast of its ancient and mediæval palaces, found in most other Italian cities, yet it surpasses all others for its fine, wide streets, its numerous piazzas, and handsome buildings. It has a public garden, inviting promenades, and extensive driveways, and seems to be preëminently a modern city for this venerable country. The most peculiar public building was the Jewish Synagogue, not completed, of immense height, ending in a structure half dome, half tower. At eleven o'clock, the time for opening to the public, we were at the palace, when the guide, as usual, hurried us through a series of apartments, so that we could hardly tell what they contained. Palaces are wonderfully alike in general features; and after having seen hundreds before, it was a needless waste of time, strength, and money in fees. It contains rooms with beautiful marquetry, some pictures, and other objects of interest. The queen's reception-room was decorated with Chinese vases of different sizes, and other Chinese ornaments. The Royal Armory contained a fine collection of ancient armor, some of the weapons being rich in gems, gold, silver, and inlaid work. The mounted horsemen looked very formidable; one of the most interesting weapons was the sword of Napoleon, worn at the battle of Marengo.

Walking through the streets we saw a large number of statues, but the finest monument was that of Cavour. Having paid our silent homage to the great statesman, we entered a church in the Piazza St. Carlo, and heard a sermon in Italian, a language which seems adapted to the uses of persuasion, at which the natives are adepts. There is something very captivating in their tones and gestures and rising inflections, seen and heard everywhere, which makes it difficult to refuse a street beggar. The Cathedral, like other similar buildings, was decorated with marbles, frescos, and gilding. The Academy of Art has a very good collection, and the Egyptian Museum contains interesting specimens of papyri. The paintings occupy a number of rooms, and include many fine pictures.

As we are about to leave Turin for Paris, we will close our journal of six months' travel in this fascinating land with some remarks on the country and its people as they appeared to us. Italy affords inexhaustible sources of interesting studies; its treasures of art and antiquities are perhaps unsurpassed, and, in most cases, are open free to travellers from every part of the world. The natives are civil, polite, obliging, and agreeable; they appear happy, and temperate in their habits; they are never brusque, dictatorial, or assuming. The lower classes appear to be very poor, and are sometimes repulsive in their personal appearance; they are dependent largely upon what they can obtain by begging; therefore it is not strange they should sometimes practise deception, to obtain a small gift from strangers. The business habits of the Italians are unfavorable for themselves. They charge foreigners a higher price for their goods or their services than their real value, and the same is true of hotel accommodations; but after considerable bickering, they recede from their first demands. No one of any experience in travel would be so injudicious as to accept the terms first offered; indeed, they do not expect it.

Poor Italy! for so many centuries divided into petty sovereignties, oppressed and robbed by her rulers, has just begun to know the advantages of a united country, and to awake to a progressive activity; but the great need seems to be want of resources, more money, and more avenues of business for her teeming population. Travellers often condemn the practice of public begging so common in this country, in spite of the royal interdict, as well as the custom of feeing the servants. They are nuisances, to be sure; but on the other hand, one should not forget what Italy gives in return, what treasures of art are free to the tourists, what collections are found in her palaces, churches, and ruins; and if these places were closed, or made difficult of access, what a loss to the world it would prove. Let us give our help and sympathy to a struggling people who seem grateful for trifling gifts; and though some of them may be unworthy objects of charity, suffering probably made them so, and does not the kind Father of all bestow his blessings upon the evil and the good? And does he not pity the erring with a divine compassion, though undeserving of his favor?

## CHAPTER XV.

*From Turin to Paris.*

APRIL 29 we left Italy for Paris, and journeyed through an interesting region, in sight of the snow-covered Alps, sometimes directly at their base. These grand mountains were like familiar objects which had been lost to our view many months, until we arrived at Turin. The scenery between this place and Modane is fine and sometimes magnificent, though there are not many important towns on the route. Of the few notable objects is the Abbey of S. Michele della Chiusi or La Sagra, near San Ambrogia, with its tombs, which possess the quality of petrifying deceased bodies. A great number of tunnels are passed before we reach the celebrated Mt. Cenis tunnel, which, by the way, is not under Mt. Cenis, but another mountain, the Col de Fréjus, eighty-three hundred and thirty-eight feet in height. The passage is eight miles long, with a descent from the Italian side of three hundred and sixty-one feet; and the depth below the top of the mountain is four thousand and ninety-three feet; hence we had that amount of solid earth or rock over our heads during thirty minutes, the time required to pass through it. The tunnel, twenty-six feet wide and nineteen feet high, was begun in 1861, and finished in 1870, and cost seventy-five hundred thousand francs, or fifteen hundred thousand dollars. Mt. Cenis, which gives the name to the tunnel, is seventeen miles east of it. This remarkable work has rendered useless the famous Mt. Cenis military road, built by Napoleon 1802–05.

At Modane, France, the custom-house officials pretended to examine our baggage, but they barely looked at it, and sent it forward to be inspected in Paris. We were obliged to change

RAILWAY STATION, PARIS.

THE MADELINE, PARIS.

railway carriages at this place, a disagreeable experience which was repeated four times during a journey of five hundred miles, and in a rainy night. Few objects of interest were passed, unless it be the stone quarries, which yielded a light-colored stone, some of which resembled that of the Paris Basin. As far as we could judge, it was a calcareous rock, extensively used for building in that region.

It is always a disagreeable experience to arrive at a railway station in a large city, especially early in the morning. Travelling in France was not so agreeable as in Italy; the railway officials are less accommodating; there were no porters at the stations except in a single instance, and on arriving at Paris we were obliged to wait a long time before we could get our luggage, and then the cabmen did not seem ready to attend to passengers, or anxious to be employed. The rain was pouring in torrents, and by the time we had secured our baggage, there was no carriage to be had, and we were obliged to go in an omnibus to our "pension," or boarding-house, in the Rue de la Sorbonne, a long distance from the station. At length our temporary home was reached; and though our rooms were not altogether what we could wish, in other respects our accommodations were comfortable, and the family kind and agreeable. During this, our second visit to Paris, we hope to gain a more extended knowledge of this famous city and its environs than was possible during our first acquaintance in the preceding year.

May 1. The Paris Exposition is to be formally opened to-day, and though the morning was stormy, yet towards noon the rain ceased, and the sun came out bright and warm. A party, comprising our hostess and her daughter, with a number of her guests, went to see the procession, which comprised many distinguished persons, including the Prince and Princess of Wales, the Prince of Denmark, the president of the Republic, and other notables, attended by an escort of soldiers well mounted, though we did not admire the uniform of the French army. The carriages of the more distinguished persons in the procession, with their attendants in white livery, made a fine appearance. Every one seemed happy, notwithstanding frequent showers of rain occurred at intervals. In the evening the buildings were illuminated, and the youth were alert all night with shouts and trumpets, fireworks and firecrackers, pretty much as American boys are accustomed to amuse themselves — we will not say their adult friends — on the nights preceding and succeeding the celebration of the Fourth of July. We have seen nothing that reminds us so forcibly of our native land as the events connected with the opening of the Exposition.

Having witnessed the grand parade, we spent the next day in attending to our personal affairs, such as collecting our scattered baggage, some of which had been left in the care of our banker, who charged us no *trifling* sum for its storage. One effectual lesson is taught by travel: that human nature is much the same the world over, that greed is the controlling passion of the race, and that the majority are unscrupulous in the use of means to secure this object. It would not be the proper course to pursue to leave Paris without making some purchases at dry-goods stores, therefore we walked a long distance to Au bon Marché and the Magasin du Louvre, which are of themselves great expositions; but we found that goods, even in Paris, are not bestowed gratuitously upon purchasers.

We resumed our visits to ecclesiastical buildings, and paid another to the famous Notre Dame. It appears to us that the churches of some other European countries are superior in architectural beauty to those of Central and Southern Italy, though less rich in decorations, especially the interior. There is no style so noble and magnificent as the Gothic, which admits of almost unlimited forms of ornament, as statuary, wood carving, painted glass, etc., but frescos and gilding seem out of place. Sainte Chapelle, as previously described, is a gem, and one of the most perfect examples of Gothic extant. It is enclosed in the courtyard of the Palais de Justice, like a precious stone in a casket, but only the graceful spire can be seen from the street. The Madeleine, in imitation of a Grecian temple, is lighted by four domes, and the

NOTRE DAME, PARIS.

interior comprises a space two hundred and sixty-one feet in length, decorated with colored glass, marbles, statues, and paintings. It has a tragical interest, connected with the Communistic war, when, in May, 1871, three hundred rioters, driven from their barricades in the Rue Royal, having taken refuge in this church, were attacked by troops from Versailles, and every one perished. St. Germaine l'Auxerrais, one of the historical churches of Paris, is associated with some of the fearful scenes enacted here, while Notre Dame de Lorette is a modern structure built in the form of a Roman basilica. It suffered from the violence of the Communists in 1871.

May 4 we made our first visit to the Exposition, which we expect to repeat many times. Fountains and plots of flowers were scattered about the grounds, but many weeks must elapse before all the arrangements will be complete, though there is much to be seen and studied at this stage. The French department is, of course, the most nearly complete, if, perhaps, we except the English. The next day, in company with some of the guests at our pension, we went to Versailles, in order to escape from the crowd of a great city. The palace seemed larger, and the park more beautiful, than on our first visit. We had seen a great number of similar places in different countries, but for beauty and finish none surpassed Versailles. It is specially notable for its fountains, which attract the attention of the numerous visitors, including both sexes and all classes, who collect about them, some standing, others seated on the banks, to witness the play of these fountains all together, which occurs on a particular day or occasion. The crowds were cheerful, well behaved, and neatly dressed, even the peasants and servants; no disputing, loud talking, or disorder of any kind. It is necessary for the safety of large cities that the public should be entertained, and an attractive park offers, perhaps, the most harmless amusement.

The palaces of France must have been, during the monarchy, very magnificent and, judging from what remains of them, it must have required immense wealth to build and support them, for which the people were taxed, being one of the causes of the great Revolution. The Church of the Sorbonne contains the tomb of Cardinal Richelieu, who suffered death by the guillotine. It becomes wearisome to finite minds, to pursue the same subject for days in succession without change, therefore we formed the plan of visiting different places and objects of interest alternately and repeatedly. Following up this method, we went again to the Exposition, and gave some time to the examination of French marbles and other ornamental stones, though they have not the interest of the Roman antiques. The display of Bohemian glass was large, and much superior to that of Philadelphia, in 1876. The Japanese exhibits were also of a different character, there being fewer bronzes and porcelains, and more of some other articles. England had a remarkably fine display, next to that of France in size, while the United States was behind most other countries in the number of exhibits, and in the promptness of arrangement, though the cottage connected with this department was quite attractive. As the grounds and buildings of the Exposition will probably not be fully completed for some time to come, the later visitors will have the advantage of earlier ones.

The churches of Europe, like museums, need many visits and much careful study, if one wishes to become tolerably well acquainted with their character; therefore we comprised in our list several of those seen during our first visit, including the Pantheon, previously described. Near this famous building is the Church of St. Étienne du Mont, a large Gothic structure with a very high nave. The pillars supporting the roof are separated by arches, which carry galleries with balustrades. These are reached by spiral staircases on each side of the choir, while the numerous chapels are arranged along the sides of the nave and around the apse. The tomb of St. Geneviève occupies a large chapel decorated with gilt, and the shrine, at which tapers are usually burning, is also gilt. The screen across the nave connecting the spiral staircases consists of open carved wood-work. Like most of the French churches this one contains beautiful painted glass. St. Germaine des

Près is a very old church, and the burial-place of the French monarchs of the sixth and seventh centuries. The prison connected with the Abbey of this church became famous for the massacre of the prisoners in the Revolution of 1792. The building is Gothic, and first erected by Childebert, 550 A. D., but has been nearly all rebuilt. The columns of the interior are painted in various colors, the capitals are gilt, the stalls are carved, and the choir walls are ornamented with painting on gilt ground. It contains the remains of two Scottish earls of Angus, those of Boileau, John Casimir V., King of Poland, and several other distinguished persons.

Another visit to the Exposition introduced us to the Department of Beaux Arts, which contained some good, some mediocre, and some inferior pictures, and quite a collection of statues. Some of the latter were fine, but a good deal of modern sculpture, it seems to us, is wanting in nobility of subjects. They are too commonplace, and lose dignity and power by many accessories or ornaments. An excess of drapery, with ruffles, embroidery, lace, and flowers, detracts from the beauty and simplicity of sculpture. To delineate the grace and symmetry of the human form is the object of the plastic art, and not to adorn it by excessive ornaments. The modern French school of painting is below a high standard of morality. The number of nude figures, for which there is no excuse, is large. People in civilized countries do not go naked; but here are represented women perfectly nude in the presence of the other sex, without the least sign of shame or delicacy. Nude figures in painting are more objectionable than such in marble, since the former not only represents form but also flesh; in fact, all that constitute life and motion, hence it has the greater power to excite the imagination.

Some beautiful landscapes from Denmark are on exhibition which represent scenes in early summer. The bright, fresh verdure is charming, and gives one a pleasing impression of that country, while Switzerland represents her incomparable mountain scenery. One of the paintings delineated a glacier, which we had seen at Chamounix. The Dutch masters are represented by exquisite little flower pieces of charming hues. From the Exposition we went to Cluny and the Luxemburg Museums. Cluny reminds one of the antiquities of Rome. Portions of the palace are crumbling into ruins, but in its decay there lingers some of the magnificence of earlier days. It is now a great "curiosity shop," where all sorts of antique objects are collected. The most abundant and richest of these specimens consist of wood carving and inlaid wood. The Church of St. Sulpice is a magnificent building. The front is supported by fluted Doric columns, and its two towers are two hundred and thirty-one feet in height, surpassing those of Notre Dame by nine feet; the interior is four hundred and sixty feet in length, and the nave is one hundred and nine in height. The altars and chapels extending around the building are decorated with frescos, and a figure of the Madonna, standing on a globe, occupies a niche in the apse. The high Corinthian columns inside the main entrance give a majesty to the interior harmonizing with its immense elevation. In the place opposite is a fountain with the sitting statues of Fénélon, Bossuet, Fléchier, and Massillon.

May 10 we made another visit to the Exposition, and examined collections of ornamental marbles and the Indian Department of the English exhibits. There is no country except France so well represented as Great Britain. The gifts presented to the Prince of Wales during his visit to India, on exhibition, are very rich and numerous, and attract visitors; England has also a fine display of home manufactures. The next day we went to L'École des Mines, which has a large collection of minerals not much inferior to that at the Jardin des Plants.

May 12, being Sabbath, we started for the Greek Church in a distant part of the city; but as we were delayed by change of transit, the church was closed on our arrival, when we entered Park Monceau, for a short rest. Its streets and avenues were crowded with people, both native and foreign, so that it seemed as if all the nations of the world were represented here.

The Bibliothèque Nationale is considered the rarest, richest, and most extensive collection of its kind in the world. It is said to contain two million five hundred thousand printed volumes, one hundred and fifty thousand manuscripts, one million three hundred thousand engravings, and three hundred thousand maps and charts; the Hall of Engravings holds ninety thousand portraits. May 15 and 16 were given to the Exposition and desultory sight-seeing, including a visit to an artisan's shop to view some work in marbles, porphyries, serpentines, alabasters, and granites. We purchased a specimen of Orbicular diorite from Corsica, to add to our collection of antique marbles, mostly obtained in Rome. The Church of St. Clotilde is a fine Gothic structure, profuse in painted glass; the interior, though much smaller, resembles the Cologne Cathedral. The grand columns are not broken by galleries, and it has little ornament compared with some other churches.

The Hotel de Ville is in process of building, having been burned by the Communists May, 1871. It was then the scene of a terrible tragedy, when six hundred of the insurgents perished in the flames. A fierce conflict, lasting twelve hours, had been going on between the troops and the mutineers, when the latter set fire to the buildings held by them, which they had saturated with petroleum, thus lighting the fire of their own funeral pile.

The Hotel de Ville, built in 1628, has been one of the most celebrated buildings of Paris, on account of its connection with historical events. During the various revolutions and insurrections in the city, it was the place of bloody struggles and the scene of many political transactions. Its complete destruction was an irreparable loss as an interesting historical monument. The cost of rebuilding has been estimated at twelve million francs, or two million four hundred thousand dollars. It is remarkable that the Church of St. Gervais, near the Hotel de Ville, should have escaped destruction in the conflagration. It was erected in 1420, and is Grecian in the exterior but Gothic in the interior: it is too small for so massive columns. A bridge leads to the Isle of St. Louis, which contains a church of the same name and the Hotel Lambert, a building once occupied by Voltaire, and the place of Napoleon's conference in 1815.

Progress is made at the Exposition. The grounds about the Trocadéro are lovely; flowers, herbage, fountains, grottos, and other attractions render this part of the Exposition very interesting. On this side of the Seine, articles from Tunis, Morocco, and other African states are sold by natives dressed in national costumes. They were very importunate in soliciting custom, and thoroughly understood the tricks of trade. It is not fair to apply the epithet "sharp" exclusively to Americans, for we never knew or heard of such shrewdness and cunning at home as we have found in every foreign country yet visited.

The Museum of the Louvre maintains its high rank, even after having seen those of other countries, and it should be classed among the first in the world, as it combines so many departments. Its statuary falls behind that of the Vatican; but its pictures, perhaps, rank with those of Florence. Its gems and works of vertu are probably inferior to those of Dresden, and its Etruscan specimens are less than those of some other collections; but the amount and variety of its objects justify the high position it holds. Each gallery in Europe has its distinctive features, which need to be studied in order to obtain an idea of art in general.

May 20 we went to Rue de Provence to make arrangements for our voyage to America, after an absence of nearly one year. The thought of seeing our native land and friends again is cheering to our spirits, though we do not forget there is a wide ocean between us; but we hope the hand of our kind, heavenly Father, who has guided us on our journey thus far, will lead us safely over this bridgeless expanse, and restore us to our homes. We made our last visit to the Exposition, and spent considerable time among the landscapes of Denmark. So charming are they that we longed to see this little kingdom, for it must be delightful, unless its artists have highly idealized its natural scenery. We obtained our tickets for Boston, U. S. A., by way of London.

## CHAPTER XVI.

*From Paris to Boston.*

MAY 21. We left Paris this morning for the United States by way of England, over the Boulogne and Folkestone route, and on arriving at the Channel embarked on board the steamer Albert Edward. Taking a position on the upper deck, the better to enjoy the sea view that, to us, has its fascinations, we were exposed to a strong, cold breeze which caused the boat to move up and down, producing an effect similar to a swing. We enjoyed this peculiar motion, but most of our fellow-passengers did not, apparently; for judging from their looks, they seemed ready to plunge beneath the wave and end their misery, while the stewardess had more patients than one could attend. As we could afford no relief, we became interested in contemplating our surroundings: the water with its gem-like green and exquisite white foam in the wake of the boat, the sails of the vessels on the Channel, resembling white tents in the distance, and the billowy waves in constant motion. The steamers were inferior in size and accommodations, which seemed rather strange, for a line so important as that between Paris and London. The route from Folkestone to London is through a beautiful and highly cultivated region, as most of England appears to be; and when we arrived at the railway station, we almost regretted that our journey was ended, and we must attend to the disagreeable task of "going through the Custom House," securing porters, engaging carriages, paying fees,— this does not mean regular fare,— getting settled at one's lodgings, etc., and then arranging the terms. Finally we reached our boarding-house near the Strand.

As we were to spend some time in London before embarking for America, we made arrangements for examining new places or revisiting those previously seen during last year. At St. Paul's Cathedral, a new monument to the Duke of Wellington had just been placed in one of the transepts. It is of white marble and bronze, with a bronze statue of the duke reclining under a canopy. The monument is adorned by other figures, and is separated from the aisle by a screen of the same metal; but as a whole, it did not seem as grand as the character of the celebrated warrior demanded. The size and style of St. Paul's seem to require paintings and statuary, in which it is deficient. The British Museum still maintains its preëminence among those of the continent; it surpasses all others in ancient Greek architectural remains, including the original marbles of the Parthenon and from Halicarnassus. The statuary bears no comparison with that of the Vatican Museum, but we imagine the Egyptian and Assyrian collections superior to those of other countries; the Library contains rare autographs, and the department of minerals is large and well arranged. In whatever other respects London may have changed, it is certain the weather is the same — dull, rainy, cloudy, foggy.

Notwithstanding the rain, we went to St. James' Park, to see the "Trooping of the Colors," whatever that may be. We stood on the damp ground for awhile, saw a great crowd of people, the heads of some of the infantry, the heads of some of the cavalry horses with their riders, and two mounted men whom the people said were the Prince of Wales and the Crown Prince of Prussia; and that was all. It is the Queen's birthday, May 25; therefore there is to be a military review, and an illumination in the evening. It is proper that the sovereign of the great British Empire should be honored, for her reign has been signally successful and beneficent, but the English people are enthusiastic worshippers of rank. Though nobles and princes may be seen almost every day, yet whenever any of these persons appear in public, they attract as much attention as a company of soldiers on parade. The reverence for the aristocracy, with the independence of English character, forms one of the inconsistencies often seen in human nature.

The paintings of the National Gallery fall below some of those on the continent; we tried to discover the beauties of Turner, so highly lauded by Ruskin, but failed to do so. A few of his earlier pieces have more merit than his later productions. He has vivid coloring, but lacks form; many of his paintings appear as if they might have been the work of a madman. Of native artists, Landseer is the most natural. There is a strange fascination about Westminster Abbey, which frequently drew us to this venerable building. It is a church, a place for the coronation and burial of English sovereigns, and an abbey where monks have assembled in earlier days, and where the Order of the Bath held its convocations. It has answered so many purposes, and contained so many relics of the past, that it seems an epitome of English history. How grand, beautiful, and solemn is the interior! As we pass from aisle to aisle, from chapel to chapel, we walk amid the illustrious dead, and are taught the lesson that the King of Terrors spares neither rank nor talent. Time, with his relentless power, is slowly crumbling away the exquisite carving, making constant repairs necessary to prevent it from becoming a ruin.

The Royal Architectural Museum comprises casts of ancient architecture in the form of capitals, friezes, etc., found in different places, and also statues. They are good studies for the architect and draughtsman. We repeated our visits to the Museum of Practical Geology for the purpose of examining ornamental stones, especially marbles, and to the British Museum, where we saw the Crown Prince and Princess of Germany, who were on a visit to England. This museum has a large collection of antique marbles collected from Greece and Asia, also from Africa. There are more and better Greek or Greco-Roman statues in Rome and Naples, but the architectural monuments of remote antiquity can best be studied in London. We were conducted over the museum by a custodian who has charge of the Greek and Roman marbles, and were shown a specimen called marble by the workmen; but though it admitted of a high polish, it did not appear like marble. We asked whether it had ever been analyzed, when he replied that each one in the museum had his special department to which he was exclusively devoted, implying it was not his business to know whether the stone had been analyzed or not.

The English masses have far less general information than those of America. Even policemen are not always acquainted with localities not on their "beat," and are unable to give information on subjects outside their special calling. The English seem to think it is indecorous to have any knowledge of their neighbors' affairs.

At the time of our visit, the three most eminent preachers in London were Dean Stanley, Mr. Spurgeon, and Dr. Parker, all of whom we heard. The first two have since died, but the last still survives. They all drew immense houses, even to overflowing, and it was our privilege to hear these distinguished clergymen in their own pulpits.

June 3 we left London for Liverpool, where we were to embark for America. Our route took us through the centre of England, which is literally a garden, if not Eden, where every square foot of land appears to be brought to the highest state of cultivation. Verdant fields, cosy farmhouses, trim hedges, and busy manufacturing towns scattered along the way, indicated the thrift and industry of the rural population. In town and country are seen evidences of the wealth and power of this great nation; but aside from these considerations, there is a poetical charm connected with its scenery, so often celebrated in romance and in verse. It is not grand except in few localities, but exquisitely beautiful, with the lively green fields, delightful groves, clusters of trees, well-tilled farms, interesting hedge rows, neat cottages, and the quietness that reigns everywhere. One can imagine how delightful a journey from London to Liverpool must have been at this season of the year. The traveller through this region is not only impressed with its natural aspects, but also by its ceaseless activity in the manufacturing towns, indicated by the dense columns of smoke perpetually ascending like those rising from a volcano. The London fogs, like a curtain of vapor, enfolding one in a very small circle, are found in other places. The city of Liverpool was enveloped in fog, so that objects a few rods off were indistinct, while the sun appeared to be struggling for recognition by the inhabitants of earth.

On arriving at our place of destination, we proceeded to the hotel opposite St. George's Hall, the Picture Gallery, and the Museum. The hall is one of the finest buildings in Liverpool, and is constructed in the Corinthian style, with sixteen fluted columns on the side opposite the hotel, while the south end has a double row of columns supporting a pediment decorated with reliefs. The Picture Gallery contains some good paintings, and has one room appropriated to the works of Turner, which we preferred to those by this artist in the National Gallery of London. One large painting in this collection represents the last moments of Charles II. in Whitehall. The great number of courtiers of both sexes betray in their looks, dress, and amusements the heartlessness of a dissolute court. One is holding a watch in his hand, as if impatient for the fatal moment to come. Another is lounging in a manner that indicates weariness, and a third is amusing himself with a lap-dog. Even the ladies of the court express no signs of genuine grief, although one is holding a handkerchief to her face as an expression of sorrow, but at the same time is slyly watching the movements of the others. The door of the monarch's apartment is partly open, disclosing the presence of an attendant. The painting is a commentary upon the frivolous, dissolute manners of the court of Charles II. Another painting represents Cromwell refusing the crown of Great Britain when offered to him. He is sitting alone in deep thought, while his countenance reveals the struggle in his mind whether to accept or reject the gift.

The Museum contains a very large and fine collection of stuffed birds, probably more extensive than the one in the British Museum, besides beetles, butterflies, corals, shells and marine animals, minerals, fossils, porcelains, etc., with marbles from Numidia, taken from the quarries lately rediscovered, and which resembled giallo antico.

June 4, a rainy, foggy, disagreeable day. "Nasty" the English would call it, yet we paid a visit to St. George's Hall. The highly polished columns of the interior, composed of red granite with bases of gray granite, are very beautiful, while green Galway serpentine and a stone resembling English alabaster are used in the decoration of the hall. The organ has eight thousand pipes and one hundred and eight stops.

June 5. Morning foggy and dark, but later in the day there were some indications that the sun was still in the heavens. We gave most of the time to the Museum, examining the lower order of animals, beginning with protozoans, and ending with ants and bees. The Museum includes a great variety of objects, but no department equals that of stuffed birds. There is a collection of the miniatures of the Bonaparte family, and remarkably fine looking people they are.

Marine animals and quadrupeds occupy considerable space; and among the visitors were many seamen, showing their interest in this department of natural history. Such collections are valuable schools of object teaching, while painting and sculpture refine the taste and promote a love of the beautiful.

The English have a remarkable facility of classifying and making everything plain, so that one hardly needs to consult a catalogue when examining their cabinets. The names of species, genera, character, and history of specimens are given for the benefit of the visitor, and in their art collections the names of the subject and the artist are nearly always attached to their works.

June 6 we bade adieu to England and embarked on the British steamer Marathon, of the Cunard Line, for the United States; and after getting settled in our stateroom, we had the time and inclination to review our year's travel in foreign lands. Our journey had been, on the whole, very pleasant and instructive, with no accidents of a serious character and few disagreeable experiences. A brief residence in any place affords only a partial acquaintance with the people, and first impressions are sometimes erroneous; but at the same time, some profitable lessons may be learned.

England is a great, powerful, and prosperous country, including her foreign territory, east and west; and though the natives have sterling qualities, they are often concealed under a cold, not to say repulsive, exterior; they maintain a haughty reserve, but the better classes are exceedingly well bred. They are grand in their virtues, and perhaps their faults are equally conspicuous; but civilization owes much to these aggressive people. The Germans, especially the men, are sometimes wanting in refinement, and offend by a lack of proper regard for the feelings of others, but they command respect for intelligence, thrift, and progressive tendencies. They are the best educated nation in Europe. The French are witty, vivacious, and talkative; but we do not think they are the most polite nation, as they have sometimes been called. They are good humored and obliging to strangers, patient in answering questions, as a rule, but there are Frenchmen who are sometimes rude in their treatment of foreigners. They have had a strange and, in some respects, a tragical history, which may or may not have won for themselves the name of being fickle; but in one attribute, that is in taste, they excel all other nations.

The Swiss deserve the respect and sympathy of the world, for their industry and perseverance in gaining a livelihood from their rocky mountains, hardships which they prefer to the trial of leaving their native land, as the people of many other countries do.

Italy, of all the countries visited, possesses the greatest interest, both for its ancient history and relics, and on account of the struggles and character of its native population. We found the Italians civil, patient, and good natured, even the lower classes, who always seemed grateful for any gift however small.

June 7 the Marathon reached Queenstown, where it took on board more passengers, largely Irish emigrants. The weather was not propitious; but a sea voyage was not a novelty to us. How, then, could we best improve our time until we should reach home? At first the weather was threatening, but in spite of the rain we persisted in remaining on deck most of the time. The ocean is a boundless expanse of a beautiful blue, while there was not a sail in sight. How solitary was our condition! Our world consisted of a few planks and some dozens of human beings; but what were we compared to the great globe, or our freight of human beings to the myriads of living creatures in the waters beneath us? There is so little variety at sea, that one must amuse himself by watching the weather prognostics, the parts of the ship, and the sailors, especially when "taking log." One would suppose it an arduous task, since it requires so many hands to take in the cable; but *our* seamen did not appear to have a very hard time. We saw one or more whales, or only a part of their tails and heads, which were so far apart that their owners must have been monsters indeed. There were several children on board who were beginning to feel the restraints of their situation, and were not in the best humor. The high waves caused our ship to toss and pitch a good deal, so that we were rocked in our berths, sometimes sideways, and sometimes lengthwise, while the act of dressing was a difficult and ridiculous feat. The time passed in sleeping, eating, and listlessly gazing over the water, with an occasional tête-à-tête with an idle passenger; every one seems occupied in doing nothing. An outward passage is far more interesting, not only for its novelty, but also for the glowing anticipations regarding new places and new objects; but on a homeward voyage, there is nothing new to expect, and the only pleasure is the hope of meeting friends from whom one has been long separated.

How monotonous must be a sailor's life! No papers, no telegraph, no lectures, no intercourse with the rest of the world for long periods. How narrow the sphere of thought and action during the voyage! but as a compensation, he is brought eventually in contact with other nations, and has an opportunity of seeing other lands.

On a glorious evening the departing rays of the sun from behind a cloud cast their shadow upon the waters, imparting to it a rich, bright-red, of lustrous hue, such as is rarely seen on land. We were now approaching the "Banks."

June 15, towards evening, we came into a fog so dense that we could hardly discern the bow or the stern of the ship. The captain set a double watch, and he himself had been on deck since one o'clock in the morning, so as to guard against danger. In the evening the sailors gave an entertainment to the passengers, the most interesting part being the singing and playing upon the violin. They sang several songs, and the sweet hymn "The Beautiful River." The next morning the engines of the Marathon suddenly stopped, when all on board were on the alert to learn the cause. The passengers rushed on deck and found several of the officers and sailors watching two buoys of whose existence they were ignorant. Various conjectures were offered; some thought we had run foul of a wreck; others, that we had lost our bearings and gone too far north. Soundings were made, and it was proved that we were in sixty fathoms of water. Then it was proposed to send a boat to examine the buoys; but as we were in deep waters, we must be all right and the buoys all wrong. Finally, it was ascertained that they had been placed there by the Submarine Telegraph Company, and floated since the Marathon made her last trip, hence were not known to the officers of the ship.

At two o'clock A. M., June 17, a pilot was taken on board, and early in the morning we went on deck to catch the first glimpse of land, when the experienced eye of an old sailor caught sight of the sandy beach of Cape Cod. We had been furnished with blank papers from the Custom House to fill out and sign, and were momentarily expecting the government officials on board to administer the oath. At the same time, a quarantine officer appeared to ascertain whether our ship had brought any dangerous diseases; but, fortunately, neither cholera nor any other dreaded epidemic was detected, and we were allowed to enter the port of Boston, where we met our friends waiting for us. The inspection of our baggage caused us less delay than we had expected, while the officer performing that duty was very considerate and gentlemanly, and we were s placed in a carriage, with all our baggage, for our home in an adjacent city, after a year's interesting and instructive travel. During that time we were taught many important lessons; namely, a deeper love for our own native land and its cherished institutions, a greater respect for other nations and admiration for their achievements in art, and, though a commonplace observation, that human nature, with its excellences and defects, is much the same the world over. In order to receive the greatest advantages by travel, the tourist should have at least some general knowledge of literature in all its departments, of art in its various branches, and of the history of the different nations, especially those whose country he intends to visit; neither must he imagine that everything can be seen during a short trip, perhaps of a few weeks, though a brief visit is better than none.

www.ingramcontent.com/pod-product-compliance
Lightning Source LLC
Chambersburg PA
CBHW022022240426
43667CB00042B/1052